THE HUMAN AGENT

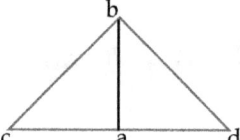

$(cb)^2=(ca)^2+(ab)^2$; or $x^2=y^2+z^2$, if $x=cb$, $y=ca$, and $z=ab$. If $y=3m$, $z=4m$, then $x=$square root of 3^2+4^2, $(=9+16, =25) =5m$. Therefore each of the metal sheets bc and bd should be 5meters long.
(see text on page 154)

THE HUMAN AGENT

Edward R W Makhene

Edward Makhene
2018

Copyright © 2012 by Edward R W Makhene
Revised edition 2018
All rights Reserved. This book or any portion thereof may not be reproduced or used in any manner whatsoever without the express written permission of the publisher except for the use of brief quotations in a book review or scholarly journal.

First Printing 2012

ISBN 978-0-9876970-1-1

Edward R W Makhene
Mississauga, Ontario.
Canada.
edmakhene@icloud.com

"What a piece of work is a man! how noble in reason! how infinite in faculty! in form and moving how express and admirable! in action how like an angel! in apprehension how like a God! the beauty of the world! the paragon of animals! And yet, to me, what is this quintessence of dust? man delights not me: no, nor woman neither. . . ." Shakespeare, *Hamlet,* 2. 2. 304.

Contents

Acknowledgements		ix
Chapter 1.	The Scope of Human Agency	1
Chapter 2.	What is a Person?	8
Chapter 3.	The Law of Persons and Persons' Rights	29
Chapter 4.	Ubuntu as Agency	47
Chapter 5.	Agent Action Analyzed	62
Chapter 6.	Is Agent Action Free or Determined?	78
Chapter 7.	Persons as Moral Agents	95
Chapter 8.	Unveiling Transcendence	111
Chapter 9.	The Challenge from Humanism	130
Chapter 10.	What's next?	146
Notes		149
Index		157

Acknowledgements

To the many unmentioned authors from whose ideas I have benefitted since the day I first took an interest in Philosophy.

I might even go further to acknowledge my indebtedness to everyone with whom I have shared ideas and everyone whose ideas I have read on any subject. Their ideas creep furtively and unacknowledged into the fabric of the ideas that I proclaim as my own. Who of us was born with any innate ideas at all? I certainly was not. All our ideas are acquired; mostly from other people.

To my wife Eileen who has had to live with my long addiction to my books and computer, and also with my insistence on linguistic precision as the only means of avoiding ambiguity, misunderstanding, and unintended results in communication.

Chapter 1

The Scope of Human Agency

The title of this book could easily have been *The Human Aznimal*, to convey the true nature of Homo sapiens and place him where he rightly belongs as just another animal with equally base instincts and habits. However, human animals have the purely fortuitous advantage of being endowed with a cognitive faculty that is superior to its equivalent in the other species of the animal kingdom that rank below him, besides also possessing an occasional moral sense that is apparently lacking in other species, and which, he boasts, sets him apart from them. On the other hand, the title could have been simply *Agency*, to highlight the fact that human persons are not the only agents, since many other animate and inanimate entities also exert agency in many ways. For instance, some predatory animals act as efficient agents of environmental control by hunting other animals that would otherwise ravage the environment by their exponential growth in numbers, e.g., the sap-sucking psyllid insect used to control the exuberant growth of Japanese knotweed, and wolves introduced into parks to control overgrazing elk populations that grow out of control for lack of predators and thereby upset the balance of regional fauna. Among inanimates, avalanches are agents of death for the unwary skier who triggers them with his careless style of skiing and for mountain climbers who have not done anything to trigger them; tornados and hurricanes are also agents of death and destruction in their own uncontrollable way. When we consider the behaviour of plants, we observe that they appear to exert their agency when they bend their stems towards illuminated areas where their leaves will be exposed to the sun, so that they can generate the energy required for their growth. The means by which all these and other entities produce their effects can be styled their agency actions.

In this discussion of agency, however, we will be concerned only with human agents, i.e., persons and their actions, since the moral consequences of their actions for humanity and for other living things are well within their control, which is hardly the case with animals and other entities that do not possess the moral sense to guide them in their various agent actions. (The reader will note that I am using the term "actions" loosely now, pending its detailed delineation in subsequent chapters, and that among living things, I include the living, self-regulating earth or Gaia with its many delicately balanced and interwoven components that humans are constantly trying to unravel and thoughtlessly throw into disarray). Besides, while animals are said to act instinctively in response to limited goals, and avalanches and plants follow mechanical forces and tropisms that govern them, humans act for reasons, with intention, selfishly or selflessly, and for short or long term goals in keeping with their capacity to conceptualize time and space; e.g., I am saving money today and over the next ten weeks so that I can fly to Florida for a break from the fettering cold weather of Iqaluit. Animals do what they have to do, and plants, winds, and avalanches bend to physical forces prevailing at that particular moment; they are not capable of planning for tomorrow and the days following, teleology notwithstanding, although it is conceivable that animals hunt instinctively to feed themselves, but also, I believe, purposefully to feed their young.

Despite these cognitive limitations to which animals are subject, however, some of them outdo many humans in the exercise of some of their limited faculties, including their concern and caring for those of their kind who deserve their compassion—a quality that is often sorely lacking in some human beings. For example, chimpanzees and elephants have often been seen to assume postures in relation to the lifeless members of the group that suggest that they are mourning the demise of their mates. The human agent, on the contrary, endowed as he is with qualities that he denies all non-human agents, viz., superior intellect, reason, discretion, choice, agency, morality, and responsibility, often deports himself in an ignoble manner that belies his self-assumed place far above most of these lowly creatures. He claims to be the only true agent who also enjoys the freedom to choose how to act with discretion in the best possible interests of his fellow humans to promote the common good[1] and flourishing of all people through caring; but he arrogantly neglects to perform common decencies that often make more difference in the lives of those people than all the verbal grandstanding that he vainly displays but does not have the graciousness to consolidate with commensurate deeds. He also chooses to remain precariously, but imperiously and self-assuredly perched on the topmost branches of the evolutionary tree from where he can aspire to vacuous transcendence and communication with the gods that he has invented for his comfort and from where he can tumble off at any moment, taking the rest of humanity and his world with him, if he does not clean up his selfish and reckless act. The threat of self-annihilation dogs him every day of his life, and it is only a matter of time before he incinerates himself with his own sophisticated weapons of self-defence from, or rather assault on, other humans who share the planet earth with him—the oxymoron of rational man (defined as one whose beliefs and bases for action are consistent and subject to logical justification) acting illogically and against reason (reason is characterized as the antecedent of all meaningful action) and also ironically acting meaninglessly against himself, but resorting to rationalizing his absurd actions with pseudo-reasons that do not add up.

The human animal, which is as naturally gregarious as other animals, from ants in their colonies, bees in their hives, birds in their migrations, to schools of whales and dolphins in their peregrinations, pretends that it has organized societies in which it lives under laws that govern interpersonal and international relations as proof of its emergence from the Hobbesian state of nature where a war of all against all prevails. But life in these societies is more perilous than that found in the companionship that exists among these lower forms that lack the kind of intellect by which human animals distinguish themselves from the rest of the animal kingdom. We still see primitive instincts of self-preservation that have been stretched to inhumane selfishness coupled with rampant and egregious violation of the rights of some by others who wield power, in spite of the existence of statutes that are supposed to set limits to how much liberty each person can accord herself (not at the expense of other persons). So what is the use of emerging from the state of nature, and of what use is the promulgation of laws that discriminate against some persons and those that can be brazenly ignored by other persons without the slightest fear of censure or punishment, because they have placed themselves or have been placed by those around them above those laws? We will examine the nature of the law of persons from so-called natural or universal law (not necessarily divine), which some people believe applies well in this state of nature where each one looks out for the other and where harm caused on others by abrogation of the law exacts fitting punishment without exception. We will compare it to the statutory or parochial laws of our societies that tend to favour certain classes of persons, and we will also examine the implications of those rights that each person holds regardless of her social or political ranking—an advantage that politicians, the rich, and the powerful appear to enjoy exclusively, judging by the amount of mischief that they get away with. Mendacious heads of state have become embodiments of crass lawlessness, besides vilifying the custodians of the laws of their states to cover up their egregious misdeeds or to subvert or obstruct justice in defiance of their solemn pledge to uphold, respect, and protect those laws, because they are terrified of having their muck exposed to the light of day.

We have so far been talking about the human agent even before we have delineated the characteristics of this complex entity whose actions are free but also determined by nature and by the laws by which he has chosen to govern his behaviour? One answer is that it is any human being; a person who happens to be the subject of conscious thought, a congeries of perceptual, cognitive and other experiences, and a wide variety of actions; a responsible entity with the power and ability to choose between alternative potential actions with a view to achieving or bringing about the results that she desires, intends, and considers to be consistent with her beliefs. And to the question what is a human being we can reply that it is a material object, a member of the species Homo sapiens, the species that has its genome embedded in 46 chromosomes—with variations. As with all other material objects, therefore, the bodily constitution of the human object can be reduced to the few chemical elements that make up to 99% of them, viz., only six elements: oxygen, hydrogen, nitrogen, calcium, phosphorus, and carbon. Of these elements, hydrogen and oxygen (in combination as H_2O or water) form 75% of body mass in the infant, with progressive reduction to

60% in the adult, and yet many of these barrels of water behave as if they are made of solid gold and all the other gems of this world.

Going further, since the person is the pivot around which all these concepts revolve, we must be clear who or what it is that bears the weight of the concepts in which we are dealing, if we are to avoid the mistake of assigning them to the wrong individuals. This latter sentiment is prompted by the fact that even though we may believe that we know the meaning of the word 'person' and how to use it in daily conversation, so much so that if anyone of us expressed ignorance about what we meant by it, we would not take her seriously or we would think that she was a bit wacky, yet we are justified in asking for clarity on the use of that word. This attitude takes into consideration the fact that in legal circles the designation 'person' has been extended to cover corporations and other non-human entities, and also that there are occasions when we call some humans, who consider themselves to be persons, animals for deliberately engaging in behaviour that we consider to be contrary to the accepted behavioural norms of human persons but fitting for wild animals, even though some animals are labelled as persons.

We will later select and give particular consideration to a concept of personhood styled *Ubuntu (botho)* to try to define what African culture considers to be the desirable attributes of personhood, especially personhood of the humane kind. Using Ubuntu as an example does not mean that other cultures fall short of these attributes of personhood that entail humaneness. It just happens to be the one on which most Africans like me were raised and one that they admire the most by virtue of having been steeped in it, unlike other cultures that they encountered later in life and which they still consider foreign (and sometimes unpalatable) to who they are.

In subsequent chapters of this book, we will consider wider questions that arise as a result of the short sketchy answers that we have already given to these pivotal questions about agency; e.g., what is a person, and what is choice, or action, or responsibility? How does attributive responsibility for an action differ from moral responsibility for it, since the latter is a value judgment on a physical process that can earn encomium or impute culpability to the agent to whom the action is attributed, because judging and evaluating the action is tantamount to judging the agent who is, after all, the architect of the action without whose agency the action would not occur?

To begin to answer these questions, however, we need criteria for assessing the effects of the agent's action rather than the acting agent herself about whom we are not likely to know much, and to whom we can only impute motives, unless we have walked in her shoes and can fully appreciate the prevailing circumstances under which she makes her choices. With this information in hand, we can evaluate the agent's action in terms of the manner in which it originated and why she chose action A instead of action B in the same circumstances in which someone else would have reversed the choice. Knowing what she now knows and with her improved capabilities at this time, could the agent have chosen and acted differently then, given the same problems in regard to which her action was taken? (many prosecutors and others who have contrived the proven wrongful convictions of the victims of their blind ambitions have said they would not change the wrong choices they made in the past, even with the damning evidence of DNA that has exposed their pernicious behaviour). Did she, in fact, have the liberty to make a choice, or was the action that she took the only one available to her by coercion or other limitation of free choice; did she know what she was doing or was she acting hastily, like our prosecutor friends, ignoring facts that would have prompted her to act differently, or was she insufficiently informed about all the facts surrounding her action (we can never know all the facts about anything and any situation, anyhow); did she command the intelligence to understand the nature and implications of her action, or was she mentally challenged and capable of acting only impulsively and irrationally; was she still relatively immature and lacking the insight that goes with the experience of the older person in evaluating situations before making what can be deemed to be the free and right choice and taking the right action?[2]

The wider concept of freedom is one under which both rational and irrational human agents operate from the many conceptions of freedom that they espouse without pretending to fully represent the entire extent of that concept. The concept of free agency, on the other hand, is the notion of one's actions being entirely up to one in such a way that one is basically responsible or accountable for them, while conceptions of freedom range from the notion that one could have chosen and acted otherwise than she has chosen and acted to the notion that how one acts is one's own business that need not be the concern of other people, unless it impinges adversely on them, which is more often the case than not. Freedom allows us the unhampered license to make fools of ourselves with our actions, if we choose to do so. It also turns the tables on us by restricting our ability to break from those same deleterious, habitual actions and some addictions that prompt us to make fools of ourselves. The freedom that persons enjoy obtains in spite of the determinism that rules their universe, because the behaviour of human bodies, which are also subject to this universal physical determinism, is powered by forces beyond those of other material bodies whose workings are governed by the all-encompassing deterministic laws and principles of Physics. According to determinism, antecedent events necessarily cause and determine the character of consequent events related to them, such that no other events could have followed them contingently; and yet we know that most of the time we choose the events that we intend to bring about, so that many that could have happened did not happen, because we did not choose to let them happen. It follows, therefore, that being able to supersede determinism, we don't need its complete absence to be able to act freely, even though we are an integral part of the determined world and universe by virtue of the material constitution that we share with the rest of determined animate and inanimate matter in our universe. We can still choose how to act, despite the universality of determinism, which does not impose any of its limiting causal conditions on our behaviour and actions.

We also do not need the imposition of restricting theistic religion on us to realize our humanity, because secular humanism can account adequately for every aspect of our moral life—no law says one must be religious to be moral, as evidenced by the multitudes of amoral and immoral religious human agents who populate our world and the crowds of non-religious but highly ethical human agents who share the same environment. Besides, even though some of us believe that the overwhelmingly intricate cellular and other functions of our bodies are divine gifts that make us special, the truth is that they are products of the evolutionary process whose tracks will remain with us for centuries to come, unless evolution brings about some wholly unforeseen changes. The deference to religion in the quest for the unravelling of human behaviour is the result of a superstition invoked to compensate for ignorance about natural processes that Science has not yet explained. The moon is now no longer that mysterious orb to which poets addressed their praises and pleas as if it was an oracle that was poised to perform miracles for humanity. Man has walked on its surface and not undergone transfiguration or returned to earth with a halo on his head or wings behind his back.

In analyzing human agency, we need to be clear about responsibility as referring to a situation that lacks moral connotations and implies only direct or indirect attribution for action but not blame, and culpability as entailing, directly or indirectly, the moral connotation of blame on the agent and/or those whose duty it was to advise her in the circumstances attending her chosen action. Also, having prefigured the extent of the territory to be traversed in the exploration of "choice" and "intention", we might go further and ask what we understand by "consciousness" in the context of conscious and unconscious actions. Are one's actions so causally determined that the freedom that one claims is nothing but a figment of the imagination? Does one have no control over what thoughts, desires, wishes, motives, and intentions one cherishes at any moment in one's life? If so, is pausing to make up one's mind about matters under consideration mere self-deception about one's abilities, and is calculated action only a sham? These are challenging questions that face anyone who intends to unravel human agency.

We have generated and assembled this litany of knotty philosophical issues and escalating conundrums with the concepts that we have chosen to employ to unravel the nature of the human agent. Ordinarily, all these questions might be regarded as superfluous, since everyone claims to know when she or someone else is making a choice of one thing in preference to another, what persons are, by virtue of the knowledge of herself as a person who makes choices, and what consciousness is from her knowledge of her own conscious states. Besides, we also recognize the agent as one who has the freedom, power, and ability to do things, to act rationally, and to carry the burden of responsibility of his actions, even to the extent of putting his life on the line for them. But the answers are not as clear-cut as we make them appear; there are problems related to all these answers, if we take the trouble to seek them out. In referring to the ability to do things as one of the qualifications of an agent, we have to take into consideration that only some doings can pass as actions, while others are disqualified from being actions, as we shall soon find out; i.e., not everything that someone does is an action. In anticipation, we might say that it is generally assumed that one of the features of these doings that makes them actions, or non-actions, is whether the agent does them consciously or unconsciously, actively or passively, inadvertently or by choice, voluntarily or under duress or physical restraint, intentionally or unintentionally, quite apart from the question of culpability or responsibility that we mentioned above. To illustrate these differences in action, we might ask what the difference is between raising my arm actively, consciously, deliberately, designedly or intentionally (by choice) to spill water on someone and my arm going up passively, unconsciously, or unintentionally when I do not choose to move it, but it is moved by someone else bumping into me, causing me to accidentally spill hot tea on the same person.

This book is intended for lay persons like me who are looking to vent their amateur philosophical ruminations without getting embroiled in the ivory tower jargon of the subject, and without pretending to be qualified to express authoritative opinions on any of the matters under discussion. So, if the ideas appear to be simplistic and outlandish, they should be placed in their proper context to infuse more sense into them, and to stimulate other non-professional philosophical thinkers to add their perspectives to this effort —every one of us is a philosophical animal, as I tried to indicate in my *What's That, Mummy? – a child's adventure with philosophy,* and we should delight in exercising and developing our innate philosophical tendencies in this fashion. The attitude that I suggest we embrace is contained in the opening sentence of a web article from Ohio Northern University which defines Philosophy as "a quest for a comprehensive understanding of human existence." That is precisely what we do every day of our lives, trying to understand our own actions and those of other people, as also the effects of all of them on all of us; in short, trying to understand human agency. We will attempt to tackle these complex philosophical issues, as many others have done before, without any guarantees of resolving them; but whatever the case, the intellectual exercise will ultimately have been well worth our while. Perhaps, then, we will begin to understand human existence in its multifarious presentations.

Chapter 2

What is a Person?

Since the person is justly believed to be the centre and origin of all the intentional activity of the human agent, we will begin with an analysis of the concept of *person* whose history is as old as humankind. To begin with, to be a member of the human species is not a necessary condition[1] for personhood, nor is it a sufficient condition, since it is logically possible that members of other species can also qualify as persons, depending on the definition of person that is being used or imposed on us, as indicated in the discussion of corporations below. Likewise, it is quite possible that some members of the human species fall short of the kind of demeanour that is required and expected of persons under a different definition, as we will discover later in our discussion. I will venture, at the outset, to state my concept of a person as that of a cognition and self-consciousness-endowed, autonomous human body, which consciously or unconsciously, voluntarily or involuntarily, displays all its integrated functions to varying degrees at different times and is capable of choosing and evaluating its actions against the backdrop of their effect on itself, others like or unlike itself, and the social milieu in which all of them exist.

Elsewhere, in my discussion of the concept of a person, I observed that

> Personhood cannot, however, be understood by dissecting human bodies and studying their constituents, but only by analyzing the actions of human agents who are steeped in a social milieu where each agent displays unique interaction with other agents consistent with his temperament, experiences, and personal history.... Included in these encounters [as indicated above] will be successes, failures, anticipations, disappointments, abilities, and disabilities that assume control of his life as the agent battles illness and adversarial relations with other agents, including an environment that can be hostile or conducive to the unfolding of his personhood.[2]

Looking at myself and being aware of my spontaneous bodily functions and my intentional actions by virtue of which I call myself a person, I can then extend the use of the same appellation to those bodies that I encounter in my world which resemble my body and its functions and actions—I see and hear them as much as they see and hear me, I am the subject of which they are the objects as much as they are the subjects of which I am now the object; I assume that they are thinking about what they see and hear in the same way as I am aware that those mental processes are occurring in me, and that when they eat it is because they feel hungry in the same way that I eat when I feel hungry, and so on with all other bodily functions and actions. How I interpret these functions and actions, what driving forces I attach to them will decide whether or not I believe that they and I have fictitious souls or other occult entities that make our bodies do what they do, without creating any solipsistic puzzles about the existence of other persons besides me. If I can assert my existence on the basis of all these experiences, then they also exist without being figments of my imagination.

Ordinarily, when we use the word "person" we apply it to the physical or material human being with or without consideration of her moral, social, metaphysical, religious or transcendent, and value aspects, which are mostly unknown to those who apply that term to persons that they may be meeting for the first time or the nth time. We do not withhold application of the term until we have been acquainted with all the psychic aspects of the bodies that we encounter; we are content with the presenting functions of these physical substances that match our own to apply the term "person" to them in the same way as we apply it to ourselves. From this encounter and from introspection, we formulate the concept *person*, regardless of whether we think that personhood entails more than the functioning material being of a human animal or that that material being must be complemented by a fictitious soul to constitute a person. This is the naïve perspective of personhood which does not present any problem to us as we go about our daily lives. That is how we talk, and it makes good sense to the unsophisticated mind. It is also strictly restricted to beings like oneself, and at no time do we ever entertain the thought of extending it to non-human entities like those that I will discuss in the ensuing pages.

Against that background, we will now consider briefly some the different categories of person with which we find ourselves compelled to deal everyday of our lives: corporate, legal, social, moral, and religious. Lately some people have added animals like dolphins to the list of (nonhuman) persons based on their ability to learn the basics of language and to communicate in their own "language" (which many other animal species do), besides being able to solve problems and to exhibit features of self-awareness. They display a type of intelligence that cannot be overlooked, in the same way that robots successfully engage champion chess players and even beat them at the game. Does this kind of artificial intelligence make them persons? What about other robots used in industry, robots that move goods in offices, or those that talk back at people and issue directions in response to enquiries? It seems that we have no choice but to accord them a person status of some kind.

Fortunately, however, we do not yet have to deal with genetically engineered persons, although that nightmare is always at the backs of our minds when we see what has been done to engineer living products of cloning. Such products are represented by animals like Dolly the sheep in Scotland, eight calves from a cow in Japan, two monkeys Zhongzhong and Huahua in China, a cow named Eve in Australia that has now produced a calf; but most chillingly by some unsubstantiated claims of successful cloning of a human embryo. The rate at which research is advancing in the field of cloning also raises ethical questions that we never had to deal with, as we fear the thought of what it will do to the human race—people choosing the sex, eye colour, physique, potential intellectual ability, and other features that will produce tailor-made offspring, in turn producing an artificial generation of persons while suppressing the natural generation that might have been. We will then have to add another class of persons to the above short list.

Our starting point in considering personhood dates back to the earliest use of the concept beyond its exclusively human connotations, to the sixth century CE when "person" was the term applied to members of the human species with legal standing, but also to corporations as entities with legal standing. It is evident from this particular usage of the concept of the corporate person that ethical considerations were excluded from consideration in the definition of persons, if corporations could satisfy the same description as human persons, simply because they were legal entities. Today the concept has been extended to include agencies, legal representatives, associations, labour organizations, estates, trustees, and partnerships. In fact, the concept covers any entity with legal rights that it enjoys separately from those of its members, as well as other entities, that lay claim to, and possess their own rights to be regarded as persons. This fact is made evident by the other fact that moral restrictions that apply to individual members of the corporation cannot be applied equally to the corporation that they constitute, although the being of the corporation is dependent on the being of its members, because without them there would not be any corporation, in the same way that without subjects there would not be a king. King of himself without subjects to exploit makes no sense; it amounts to a negation of the whole purpose for which the office has survived its rejection by politically awake citizens who are trying to reverse the universal practice of some persons living off other people.

However odd it may seem that non-living corporations should be called persons, such is still their legal status today, and that is why they can be sued like all other citizens, which they legally are, independently of the personnel in them, and they can exercise an indirect franchise to vote in elections and otherwise determine affairs of state by their direct influence on government personnel and other politicians. This concept of corporate personhood is clearly inconsistent with the basic fact that corporations, as abstract entities, don't have any relevance without the human elements that constitute them, nor do they have the human capacity to think and act; it is the human elements that constitute and manage those corporations who think and act and then hide behind the corporation to escape censure for wrong doing, because the law allows that this abstract but also personified entity, the corporation, can be sued independently of its personnel and summoned to appear before a judge to answer to any charges preferred against it! But who answers for the corporation in such cases? Does this abstract entity make a court appearance and plead, or do people appear and plead for it. Do lawyers take instructions from it and advise it how to plead? —strange exchange!

When the corporation is doing well, its human elements take all the credit and all the dividends away from it. It has no say in the matter. This peculiar tactic of the personification of corporations to which the rights of human persons have been assigned and by which they have been prostituted is just one of the many examples of the ways in which the powerful hold of money over human affairs can impel them to prostitute personhood by attributing it to an abstract entity that lacks a mind. Sadly, it is also the indirect imputation of moral responsibility to an amoral entity without imputing the same kind of responsibility to the sometimes immoral personnel of that entity, and it will never wash, because this abstract entity is incapable of taking concrete actions and committing transgressions by itself, besides not being the type of entity to which moral predicates can be attached. Unlike real, "rational" persons, it is not a moral being that is capable of making ethical decisions, although in the eyes of modern greedy man it has surpassed both its subordinate and its equality position with human persons to become the dominant person, thanks to the almighty dollar, yen, pound, euro, renminbi, rand all the other currencies of this world. The real persons are now mere minions of the corporate person, and as the saying goes and as politicians are proving every day, every one of them has a price; everyone can be bought. Individual and corporate transgressors against the dignity of some human persons have been known to buy their silence with money. The rich and powerful can swing any decision in their own favour in affairs of both state and church, as many of us can testify from our experiences; and the litany goes on.

The legal person, in his subordinate status to the corporation, is also the one whose civil rights are ostensibly protected by the secular laws of the land in which he lives as well as those of other lands in which he may find himself as a visitor. I do not include fetuses within this categorization nor do I intend to enter into the raging controversy about their personhood, which I have discussed elsewhere, with some people holding and trying to foist on others the view that fetuses, which are admittedly human beings and which are protected by laws that are specific to their status as potential persons, are actual persons to whom the rest of us should owe the same categories of moral and legal obligations that we owe to actual persons. Their stance, like that of Thomism which maintains that being human must entail being a person, would commit them to the absurdity of calling an acorn, which is only a potential oak tree, a real oak tree and also to the other absurdity of daring to go back to applying that designation to the product brought into being at the time of pollination to produce that acorn seed, like those who believe and maintain that fetuses became persons at the moment of their conception—let alone the date on which the theoretical "soul" that they claim for all persons took possession of the inner chambers of the body of this fetal "person" or its specific location within that body. They have no clue when and where that is supposed to take place, because it does not take place at any time and place, since it is non-existent, and no non-existent can be said to take place anytime or anywhere. However, it is important to attempt to demystify the person concept, if this controversy is ever to be resolved; but my suspicion is that no rational argument will ever convince or satisfy the dogmatists who argue for the personhood of fetuses, as time has proved. They will never compromise with rational thought at the expense of their solemnly held dogma — dogma does not require proof.

Similar concerns arise regarding anencephalics and severely cognitively impaired or brain damaged persons who are unaware of their surroundings and could be said to merely exist, instead of really living. Some people rightly maintain that they are human beings who are entitled to all the legal and moral rights that are entailed by that designation, but they are not persons, while others insist that they will always be persons and human beings with moral, legal, and other rights like the rest of the people who lay claim to those rights by virtue of being human persons. My own view is that they have moral and other rights that befit their status as members of the human race, even though their personhood is in dispute and probably unsustainable. In the same vein, we might consider the interests and legal rights of all future generations of persons on the basis of our own personhood and the fact that when these our remotely potential progeny of human beings have passed the precarious stage of being fetuses to become actual persons they will have the same legal and other entitlements that we enjoy as existing, actual persons. For the existing person these entitlements ensure that she is protected against assault, endangerment of life, unfair and unjust treatment, and exploitation, while she is ironically being subjected to the following indignities: indirectly deprived of her life by callous bureaucratic enforcement of inconsiderate civic laws that are framed to figuratively but also literally enslave her; exposed to pollution with devastating effects on her health, the health of her conceptus and the survival of both; unjustifiably discriminated against, because she is poor or she belongs to a different religion or racial group from those who are fortunate enough to belong to the racial or tribal group of those who hold the reins of power under the direction of their rich manipulators. Such is the case with indigenous peoples all over this world whose lands have been colonized by foreigners who now call these lands theirs and want to deny the owners and racial groups other than their own access to them — we don't want any more immigrants (which ones?); it is enough that we are here. These recent arrivals even go so far as to dare to promote their hateful attitude of advocating the expulsion of those "non-us" persons that they found in those lands — a forlorn dream. I have already discussed these odious attitudes in *Homan Inhomanity*.

The social person lives peacefully in a society where she should be free to associate with whomever she chooses, as long as that one accepts her readily, willingly, and without prejudice. She realizes and complements her personhood in the society to which she belongs and without which she cannot be a complete person. She enjoys recreational activities and amenities that are accessible to all members of the community; she does not go out of her way to be a nuisance to her neighbours in any one of the many ways that some persons do: playing their music loudly, racing up and down the street in their noise-making automobiles or motor cycles, littering on other people's property, leaving doggie poo on it instead of scooping it up, cutting across other people's lawns on foot or on their bicycles, etc. She participates in community watches, looking out for the welfare of her neighbours (against burglaries and other destruction to their properties) and especially for the safety of their children, and she cares about the preservation of a healthy environment in her neighbourhood and in her world at large. Her neighbourhood doesn't end at the circumference of the 100m diameter of her immediate environs or at the boundary of her plot of land, but it extends beyond those limits to reach into distant lands where people who are less fortunate than she are eking out a precariously marginal existence that can terminate in the blink of an eye under the stresses and direct lethal injuries of the deprivation that has been imposed on them by others. She extends her material and emotional generosity to where poor people are to be found, in the forgotten pits of misery into which they have been thrown by their rich brothers who deny any kinship with them while they are wringing the last sweat- and blood-smeared cent out of them.

When politicians sacrifice the survival of the living and posterity on the altar of money by giving a blind eye to polluting industries and the need to curb their deleterious emissions or by perpetrating other insults on the life-sustaining Gaia, she does not sit back in despair, but she rails against them to show them how idiotic their behaviour is. When the advocates of polluting industries hide behind the drivel that they spew about their products being clean compared to similar products that they imply are dirty ("dirtier" than theirs) simply because they are produced in countries that do not respect human rights and the rights of women, and when the same persons hypocritically bury their heads and their consciences in the sand and pretend that it is OK to pollute in countries with lower standards than theirs, or when they ignore as fictions the outcries against the gutter treatment that they are meting out to indigenous people of the lands on which they are squatting by depriving them of land, water, sanitation, and health rights, she daringly exposes their scurrilous hypocrisy and inhumanity for what it is. If only she could successfully knock sense into their thick skulls, she laments, before the money that they worship also assumes personhood in its own right, since money is now the tail that wags and corrupts the dog, even the largest of all dogs.

We see examples of this regrettable control that money wields on human affairs where elections to state office depend on how many votes some who pour millions of dollars into elections can buy and how much influence lobbyists and others also wield on elected representatives, getting them to ply the will of corporations and foreign states that they represent in response to the money and sometimes blackmail tactics that bought them the offices they hold. She shares and rejoices in the successes and joys of her neighbours, and she commiserates with them in their losses and sorrows; she is always ready to lend a helping hand where help is required, but she does not impose on her neighbours or become a bore to them. She cares about the poor people of the world and the universal exploitation and oppression to which they are subjected, and she never ceases to strive to better their lot and lighten the economic and political burdens that they are made to bear by politicians and their rich friends. When misguided ideologues claim that the only persons are those who belong to their tribe, thereby adumbrating the foundations for daring to treat everyone else as non-persons who do not deserve decent treatment as their social and moral equals, she goes to great lengths to dissuade them from their obsession with themselves and force them to treat others with due respect and not as their tools. She deals in spreading the carrot of love from which the respect that others want to impose with the stick flows of necessity; she is all love.

The moral person and her values will be discussed in chapter 7, but those values do not veer too far from those outlined above; and the religious person and his transcendent beliefs will be the subject of chapter 8. In all these aspects of personhood, action through agency constitutes an essential part of the definition of the word "person", since persons are always active in all the different states and phases of their lives, even when they claim to be doing nothing when asked what they are doing. Their minds are never at rest or just blank; they are always active whether they are awake, thinking about something, or asleep and dreaming about one thing or another. It is also noteworthy that the many categories of personhood themselves take their origin from the metaphysical concept of the person, which is logically prior to them. It is this concept that allows us to classify a certain existent as belonging to the category of beings who merit consideration as persons as understood in the many roles in which he actively participates as agent. That means we have to identify particular features or properties of these beings that set them apart from non-persons without being seen to promote a family of immutable, transcendent forms like those that were conceptualized by Plato in his theory of Forms[3] (Forms of love, virtue, justice, goodness, truth, etc.), because the person defines himself with time in many more ways than any closed concept of him allows. The closed concept of person that is based on limited parameters cannot hold for long, since these connotative characteristics cannot continue to define him during his extended period of change, as Jean-Paul Sartre so aptly stated it, "Man is nothing else but that which he makes of himself."[4] In contrast to persons, triangles, circles, electric bulbs, clocks, bells, pencils, and all other manufactured objects have defined boundaries or functions from which they do not deviate and from which new and multifarious boundaries or functions will never evolve, unlike the case of the person who is evolving all the time by adding to and subtracting from the totality of his defining characteristics. Unless the human person is understood as the product of a dynamic prototype that admits of variations that are consistent with its particular circumstances, controversies about who or what is or is not a person will always burden our thinking and our social and other relationships, because many of us lack the good sense to accommodate opinions other than the ones that we cling to, but about which we cannot claim absoluteness, as if our own opinions are gospel. We prefer to operate on the lower, ignoble plain of perpetual polarization and lethal confrontation (like the anti-abortionists), instead of rising to the higher plane of compromise. As I have indicated before in my other writings, the formula that we need in our lives can be depicted in the following diagram:

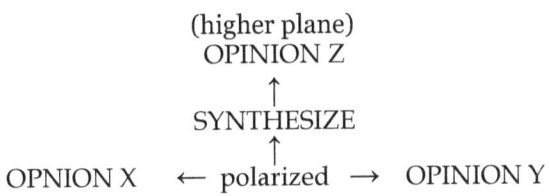

In formulating our varying concepts of a person, we tend to fall victim to the principle of composition; viz., attributing the properties of individuals to the whole that they compose, e.g., Hydrogen and Oxygen are gases that combine chemically in the ratio of 2:1 atoms, under specified conditions, to form a liquid, H_2O or water. Water, in turn, has properties that differ so drastically from the properties of the two gases, that its properties cannot be deduced or predicted from those of the gases. Similarly, we cannot reduce the person to his physical constituents (see pages 3- 4), like the hydrogen and oxygen that make up water, and hope to deduce his nature from studying those constituents. Persons are indivisible wholes, even though their physical aspects are subject to changes and slow disintegration with the flux of time. None of us is the same person as or qualitatively identical with the person that she was yesterday, last year, last decade, or in childhood. Old body cells have disintegrated and been replaced by new ones, and we have acquired new psychic characteristics, and yet we all claim to be the same persons through time, implying that our personhood persists indestructibly through the time in which our physical bodies are undergoing change. It is this same personhood that we immortalize when we memorialize the deceased whose works we continue to praise long after their material bodies have decayed and disintegrated. Unfortunately, we also have to continue to condemn some who brought misery into our world before they died, and others who are doing the same but are still with us; their turn to rot will come and we will continue to condemn them even as we are condemning them now but remain powerless to bring them to justice—the evil that they do will live after them.

John Locke, following the trend laid down by Cicero when he extolled reason or rationality as the faculty by which we surpass all other members of the animal kingdom (of which we are incontestably a part), defined his necessary and sufficient conditions for personhood as those of a "thinking, intelligent Being, that has reason and reflection, and can consider it self as it self, the same thinking thing in different times and places; which it does only by that consciousness, which is inseparable from thinking, and as it seems to me, essential to it: . . . "[5]. With these words Locke tossed out being human and substituted the memory possessed by his thinking thing (assume object or body, but not necessarily human body) as the essence or gist of personhood, simply by virtue of its action-directing consciousness. On his theory, persons are defined by consciousness, which, as we well know, drives the body into any kind of present or future purposive action; hence the body alone is not a person, nor is the mind, but the conscious, thinking, remembering mind in its living body is a person. So where does that leave fetuses, anencephalics, and vegetative state[11] individuals, all of whom cannot lay claim to these mental attributes, or people who suffer temporary loss of memory or consciousness or permanent loss of memory? In doing this, however, Locke did not answer the question: what is a person? He first assumed personhood, and then went on to define personal identity in terms of memory, which he then attributed to the person who manifests that personhood, without answering the crucial question: what is a person?

Warren Bourgeois points out another difficulty with Locke's memory theory: that several persons can share the same personhood simply by virtue of remembering the same events or sharing the same memories, while the same body can harbour different persons depending on what it remembers (e.g., in the split personalities of schizophrenic states where the patient can be one person at time t_1 and another person at time t_2 depending on his actual or imaginary memories), or no persons, if it is interrupted by sleep, or dulling or loss of consciousness and memories. In this latter scenario, moral responsibility for actions can easily have no subject, or else it will be randomly assigned, as unfortunately happens in some unjust justice systems of this world where people are concerned more with earning points from like-minded closed minds to further their disreputable careers by convicting more and more innocent victims for whom they are building more and more unnecessary institutions of incarceration for petty offences. Show them their mistake, and their stock answer, with apparently clear consciences, is: "If I had to do it all over again, I would not do it differently. I have no doubt that I put the right person in prison where he belongs". They are the ones who deserve to be put there, instead of being promoted to higher ranks for their despicable, status-driven, self-promoting conduct that does not respect the lives of other persons but is ready to waste them on the altar of their self-service. Those who promote them are, of course, no different; otherwise they would instead censure their unacceptable behaviour by demoting them.

The most famous treatment of personhood on which the heavenly abode of human souls (post-demise) is based is that enunciated by Renè Descartes. He postulated a body-mind dualism that defines the person as an association of these two wholly separate and distinct elements, ontological wholes that are capable of independent existence: one a tangible body governed by the laws of Physics, and the other an intangible mind capable of driving the tangible body in the manner of what Gilbert Ryle called the mythical ghost in the machine, determining all its choices and actions, but not subject to its influence and to the laws of Physics. Ryle contends that in this role mind does not cause behaviour but is manifested in behaviour; so we can conclude that the language of mind is simply a way of describing bodily actions and people's dispositions to behave automatically in certain ways in response to events in their environment. From this it follows that when we say of someone that he is angry, we are not describing his state of mind, but we are referring to his observable behavioural patterns from which we infer his state of mind—he is pacing up and down, cursing, waving his fists, threatening to strike someone, etc. But how many dispositions are enough to satisfy the application of the statement "Jim is angry", and why do we need mind when it does not seem to be performing any function? Also, he could be angry without displaying any overt behaviour or any disposition to act, like the brittle plate of glass that is not engaged in shattering, unless a stone hits it and simultaneously satisfies many more conditions (the type of glass, the force with which the stone was thrown, the distance of the glass from the point of origin of the stone, the size of the glass, the size of the stone etc.) before its brittleness can be realized in the shattering. Besides, any one of these conditions can fail to be realized, with the result that the glass does not break as expected, as much as all the necessary conditions can be realized without Jim acting angry. To say that glass is brittle is therefore not to say that it is breaking all the time; it is to state its propensity to break only if a certain concatenation of conditions is fulfilled, but to say that Jim is angry is not to state his propensity to behave in certain ways under certain conditions, since he is not a determined object; he has the free choice of altering his behaviour at will and defy expectations, which a plate of glass cannot do.

Discussing the same subject, however, Arthur Danto is of the opinion that Descartes' unity of mind and body is not one of a ghost occupying a machine and piloting it, but rather one of two constitutive states of the person regulating his actions jointly. He says, "his final conception appears to have been that the mind is one with the body, that mind and body form a certain unity . . . that when mind and body are together, they really are together, totally and almost indistinguishably"[6]. But Descartes clearly states his position on the essence of personhood as follows: "But what then am I? A thing which thinks. . . . What is a thing which thinks? It is a thing which doubts, understands, [conceives], affirms, denies, wills, refuses, which also imagines and feels."[7] The implication of this strictly mentalist description is to place the mind in the position of a pilot directing this mindless, rudderless thing whose attributes he does not even care to mention, and this would seem to contradict Danto's contention and to favour the possibility of the existence of disembodied minds that serve to retain and perpetuate the person's identity and are capable of inhabiting celestial abodes, from which follows the fiction of body-inhabiting imaginary entities called souls. The body, whose existence Descartes can doubt without committing a logical contradiction, thus becomes a mere vehicle for the all essential thinking mind and can be sacrificed for the purity and survival of the mind (soul) in its quest for transcendence. According to Descartes, he also cannot claim to exist when he is not thinking, as only a mind possessing thing can do, without committing a logical howler. Regrettably, his ruminations about body and soul were adopted and distorted by past and modern opportunists who promote neglect of the bodily existence of people in favour of the preservation of the sanctity of their souls, while they are taking extremely good care of their own bodies at the expense of their own souls. They urge unfortunate persons not to dwell on their grossly deficient material circumstances, but to expend their energy in ensuring that their souls remain undefiled by carnal yearnings and pursuits, so that spiritual ambitions can have room to flourish in the absence of restricting mundane concerns that can be readily sacrificed for the good of their souls. This way they can ensure their entry into paradise and eternal life!

In anticipation of the discussion of transcendence in chapter 8 below, let us take note that in Descartes' ontology, the indescribable and unidentifiable soul served the same essential function as it did in Aristotelian cosmology, viz., that of reasoning capacity without which the body that remained had lost the essence of personhood and was no longer a person, even though this erstwhile person still retained all his other known identification attributes: brown eyes, short stature, slim build, grey hair, etc., all of which are termed his accidental attributes as distinct from his lost essential attribute, the soul or the mind (the necessary and sufficient condition of being a person or the attribute that made him what he is), which was, in any case, unknown and indescribable to begin with. In contrast to this Cartesian concept of the possibility of the independent existence of disembodied minds, however, other people like St. Thomas Aquinas believed that if the identity of the whole person (body and soul) is to survive his death and persist in after-life (as far-fetched as it sounds for a disintegrated body to survive), the soul as "form" has to be an inseparable and determining part of its biological unity with matter to constitute the ensouled body. Such a union would then characterize the person under the direction of the soul ("form"). According to this design, therefore, matter as potential being + form as actuality or actualizing agent = actual being; i.e., form is always instantiated in matter, and matter, as the physical part of the human organism, is not able to attain its final reality without the participation of form, in the same way that without mind or soul the body alone cannot be a person (body +soul = person). The body thus derives its significance in personhood from the soul with which it is created contemporaneously to form the person and from which it cannot be separated and still retain its person status. This primordial relationship automatically eliminates the daunting problem of the interaction between body and mind that plagues Cartesian dualism of substances—mental and physical, and it mandates the divesting of personhood from a body that does not have a soul. (We will have more to say about the soul in chapter 8.)

The above Thomistic approach to personhood also has relics of Plato's Forms and Aristotle's matter and form[8] in addition to having the seeds of the perspectives espoused by Benedict De Spinoza and Peter Strawson as outlined below. In another respect, Aquinas foreshadows Jean-Paul Sartre's utterance that human existence or being precedes its essence or character, because the person first exists before she determines what she will become; hence she is always trying to shape her character to conform with her ideal self. For Aquinas, however, it is essence that precedes existence logically, though not temporally or ontologically, since all things are combinations of form and matter, or essence and existence; i.e., matter always exists in some form or other. Matter also acquires its final being in the actualization of the potentiality that it is: "matter . . . is not created without form; for though everything created is actual, still it is not pure act. Hence it is necessary that even what is potential in it should be created . . . ."[9] For him also, essence does not imply existence, in the same way that the essence "unicornness" does not imply the sure existence of unicorns; i.e., the concept *unicorn* may lack instantiation, and it does, in spite of the fact that we can use the word "unicorn" meaningfully in discourse from knowing the necessary and sufficient conditions for something to be included within the concept *unicorn*. Only God has existence as part of his essence. For everything else that already exists as potentiality, God has to add existence to those essences to convert their potentiality into actuality as certain kinds of things with a definitive way of being; i.e., instantiate form in matter.

Spinoza circumvents the problem of the interface of body and mind in the same person that was created by Descartes' dichotomy by denying the separateness of body and mind and declaring them to be the two different ways in which the person (or what he calls substance, which depends on God for its existence) is expressed. He recognizes an unchanging soul whose attributes are thinking and knowing, and which imparts identity to the person, and a body that changes over time but remains united with the soul. Similarly, Strawson postulates material and psychic (M and P) predicates as primordially joint and inseparable aspects of a single foundational or irreducible ontological whole that do not allow the concept of a person to be dichotomized into body and mind without destroying the indivisible entity that it is. He draws a distinction between persons and things by referring to persons as bearers of both M (material) and P (psychic) predicates, and things as bearers of only M predicates, while P predicates cannot possibly exist alone apart from any being or thing. He says, "states of consciousness... are ascribed *to the very same thing* to which these physical characteristics, this physical situation, is ascribed."[10] Thus, in Strawson's ontology, the person as basic particular negates the teasing apart of the mental and physical attributes of this person to bestow ascendancy of the psychic over the material as Descartes did with his person, reducing him to separate and separable, distinct and non-interacting mental and physical components with opposite properties: body, occupying position in space, capable of being measured, (weight, height) and sensed (touched, seen), and mind, having no position and measurements, and incapable of being sensed, but still the dominant partner in this relationship. Strawson's person can thus be described as short or weighing 40Kg, but simultaneously as being ill or angry or happy without subjecting his material attributes to the whim of his psychic ones as in the "thinking thing" of Descartes in which the material body has no respectable status. The material description deals with space-occupying matter, whose attributes can be readily and directly observed from both first and third person perspectives, whereas the psychic description does not admit of similar manipulation; its characteristics can be delineated directly from first person self-knowledge, but only indirectly from third person observation of the other person's behaviour, and from comparing it with first person experiences of our own feelings and behaviour in similar circumstances, as indicated on pages 8-9. In so doing, however, we must assume that the behaviour that we are witnessing is genuine and not put on, because we have no other way yet of telling what is in the other person's mind or what he is feeling; e.g., pain is what someone feels, not how he behaves, regardless of how accurately he portrays pain behaviour, genuinely or fictitiously, or satisfies the behavioural criteria for the experience of pain. No one else can feel or share another's pain, so that he can depict it precisely, and no pain can occur without an owner so that it can be analyzed independently. By recognizing two kinds of properties in the world: psychological and material predicates, Strawson's concept of a person makes possible the ascription of psychological predicates to this specialized lump of matter in a dualism of properties (M&P), whereas Descartes recognizes two kinds of substances in the world: mind, a thinking, non-extended thing, and matter, an extended, non-thinking thing. The person is, therefore, not to be characterized as the sum of his predicates, although they can be applied in unified terms as aspects that belong to the indefinable and irreducible person who is by his nature the unity of his parts but also more than the sum of those parts. As to the interface between the mental and the material or physical on these theories, that still remains an enigma; i.e., how does a physically inflicted pinprick convert into a psychic sensation of pain?

In the end, however, persons are pragmatically identified by their bodies, with particular psychic characteristics of rationality, intentions, wishes, and desires completing the picture. In daily life the same body=the same person, even after sleep, a long lapse of memory, or unconsciousness. The actions of this person are guided largely by reason in the choices that she makes in the circumstances that prevail around her, although raw and irrational desire, impulse, and beliefs sometimes play a significant role in determining some of her actions. Without these features as features of that particular body, there cannot be a person, because the features cannot exist *in vacuo* but must be tied to a body; and even if the behaviour and bodily characteristics change over time, this change is rarely so drastic that the body cannot be accurately identified, in spite of changes that might have occurred in a person's psychic characteristics and that can be so drastic as to merit the description: he is not the same person, uttered on the basis of recognizing him by his corporeal features but not his now unrecognizable behavioural characteristics. So, those features that identify a human being with an active mind also identify a person, ruling out dead bodies, but raising controversy about fetuses, and brain damaged human beings in a vegetative state.

On the other hand, David Hume says of persons, "I may venture to affirm of the rest of mankind, that they are nothing but a bundle or collection of different perceptions, which succeed each other with an inconceivable rapidity, and are in a perpetual flux and movement."[12] What he forgot to add is that these individual perceptions of the world combine into a cohesive stream of consciousnesses that succeed one another in a cause and effect relationship (consciousness$_1$ being sufficient to cause its effect, consciousness$_2$, which, in turn causes its effect, consciousness$_3$, which in turn causes its effect, consciousness$_4$, and so on) that characterizes the rational person or self whose experiences, memories, thoughts, and mental states they are, and without whom there cannot be a persisting, freely acting agent to whom responsibility, culpability, or credit for happenings can be ascribed over time—in the sense of happenings versus actions. But this is not to suggest that a kind of metaphysical unifying mental substance around which they congregate underlies these perceptions, because no one has so far been able to demonstrate the existence of such a substance, and no one will likely ever demonstrate it at any time, but only to say that there must be a unifying and systematizing factor that imparts rationality to this agglomeration of properties and perceptions, even if it is no more than the person's brain, which cannot be passed off as a collection of different perceptions even as we are handling it, weighing it, and cutting it—feats that we cannot achieve with perceptions. Without such a nidus, perceptions would lack a point of origin and float freely, ready to attach to anything and producing a chaotic world.

The source of our confusion happens to be the syntax of language that is structured to have a subject about which qualities are predicated, and which we then legitimately transpose to the structure of reality as the only sensible way that we can talk about it, forgetting that grammar does not entail ontology; i.e., a syntactical subject does not entail an ontological reality. For instance, x does not exist does not mean that an entity styled x whose property is non-existence exists (which is nonsense); it means the universe does not contain any x that satisfies the predicate "exists", i.e. no one of existing things in this universe is an x. Nevertheless, eliminating subjects from subject-predicate sentences is like eliminating objects from the world and making concepts the sole referents of our talk; e.g., we would have to talk about white, spherical, solidity measuring 44mm in diameter and weighting 42 grams, etc., to refer to a golf ball, on the assumption that no other conglomeration of those specific qualities answers to the use that we have in mind for what we are describing; but mere mention of the juxtaposed words "golf" and "ball" is enough to convey to the hearer what we are talking about without having to enter into descriptive contortions. Everyone will admit that this would be a cumbersome way to communicate, besides being open to misrepresentations. Similarly, trying to eliminate use of the various forms of the verb "to be", would leave us with a cumbersome way of expressing ourselves; e.g., John is the king = John had a crown placed on his head as a symbol of his authority over his people, so we refer to him as the king. The long phrase "had a crown…we refer to him as" can be conveniently replaced by the word "is", making it quite clear that we cannot dispense with the use of the various modes of the verb "to be" and still communicate easily, plainly, and conveniently. On the other hand, what does sound more plausible and practical is the elimination of "there is", a form of the verb "to be", in statements like "there is a knock on the door" and substituting "someone (or something) is knocking at the door", since anything can knock against the door and sound like the knock of someone asking to be admitted, and animals are known to scratch at doors when they want people to open them, but only persons can knock in the standard way that is intended to move those on the other side to open the door. Many other examples can be cited to illustrate the ease with which use of forms of the verb "to be" can be conveniently eliminated while retaining the sense of expressions from which they have been eliminated and further elucidating the precise circumstances in which the substituted verb is functioning; e.g., if a car happens to be on the driveway, one can report the scenario more meaningfully in a variety of appropriate ways without the use of a form of the verb "to be" as in "there is a car on the driveway" by stating that a car is parked on the driveway, or a car has stopped on the driveway, or a car has stalled on the driveway, or a car has been abandoned on the driveway, or a car has crashed on the driveway, etc., and thereby convey the most fitting impression of the situation under description to one's listeners.

The quandary created by this set-up is similar to the one generated by Locke's postulation of primary and secondary qualities of material substances, where primary qualities (solidity, extension, figure, motion, rest, number) are supposed to be inherent in and inseparable from material objects, while secondary qualities (colour, taste, smell, feel, sound) are those that are added on by different observers under the power of existing primary qualities to produce different sensations in the observer — a clear adaptation of Descartes' theory of knowledge derived from his concept of substance and attributes as reflected in a piece of wax that undergoes elusive to knowledge changes of state (changes in attributes or qualities) from solid to liquid when it is subjected to heat over a period of time, while it remains essentially the same substance that the intellect can grasp and know in its different modes of being. He does not say anything about the ultimate change of state into vapour as a result of continued heating, after which there will be no more primary qualities left. The snag with Locke's attribution of primary and secondary qualities to objects is that both qualities are assigned to the object by the observer who has no other way of claiming that the primary qualities are the only ones that remain with the object when he is not sensing them, like George Berkeley's claim that the being of objects resides in their sensing—their *esse est percipi*—as that is the only means of affirming their presence. We can't vouch for their existence if we have not perceived them and formulated some referential facts about them to give them meaning in our particular domain of discourse, a meaning that might be different from that given by persons in other domains in accordance with the referential facts that they have formulated about the same objects. Besides, since Locke's primary qualities can vary with the assessments of different observers, they are not immutable; e.g., the weight and linear dimensions of any object are judged by established subjectively derived objective parameters, since the same piece of heavy matter can feel heavy to someone who is of slight build (weighing 72Kg) or light to another person who is of sturdy, muscular build (weighing 114Kg), in the same way that "standardly" white objects wear a yellow tinge to the jaundiced eye and a clear white one to the "normal" eye. I have used quotation marks to indicate that white objects and normal eyes do not come labelled as such, but are called such by virtue of the parameters that have been agreed upon and laid down in conformity with the physics of light (also subjectively derived objective parameters). For instance, red light is visible light with a wave length of 650nm (nanometers), green light 510nm, blue light 475nm, while the entire range of visible light is limited to only 400-700nm. The rest of the vast light spectrum from 10^{-6} nm to 10km is covered in order by gamma rays, x rays, ultraviolet rays, infrared rays, microwaves, and radio waves. White light is the light that is produced by a combination the primary colours red, green, and blue, which can in turn be broken down into the entire visible light spectrum, violet, indigo, blue, green, yellow, orange, and red by passing the white light through a prism.

No single subject can ever be the standard of either primary and secondary qualities, because his appreciation of them is different from that of other subjects, in much the same way as value tags on of all reality vary with individual observers. So it is only through a consensus of subjective impressions that these now objective parameters referred to above have been established. Likewise, the concept of normality is always fixed by the statistical stipulations used in different disciplines to determine acceptable ranges of operation; e.g., normal is the designation given to a quantity that lies between 5th and 95th percentiles, or within two standard deviations of the mean. In human behaviour, the use of this concept depends on what the majority of any particular community accepts as normal. Putting frail old people out to die so that their spirits can ascend directly to heaven is normal and accepted practice in some old cultures, but taboo in others; torture and humiliation, including waterboarding to extract information out of people, is immoral practice in the eyes of many rational people who respect the rule of law against such inhumane behaviour, but ranked as perfectly acceptable by some perverted, civilized minds, as long as they are not subjected to it, regardless of how much they may deserve it for this and other crimes against humanity that they commit because they have the power to do so.

In African philosophy the comparable concept to that of personhood is that of *Ubu-ntu*. Ubuntu has been depicted as composed of two ontologically inseparable and indivisible components, *ubu* and *ntu*, in whose reciprocal relationship *ubu* is always incomplete, and hence meaningless, without *ntu*, in the same way as the philosophies of Aquinas, Spinoza, and Strawson do not permit separation of the components of a person, so that any description of the person in terms of only one of his aspects is incomplete and meaningless, because one aspect always entails the presence of the other aspect in combination with it. This concept of person is strictly at variance with Descartes', and yet Africans believe in the survival and extraterrestrial existence of spirits, the spirits of their ancestors that still hover around them, waiting to exert their influence on the events of their daily lives, if and when they are called upon to do so. How they reconcile the two concepts is the question, since the wholeness of Ubuntu should not allow for the separation of *ubu* and *ntu* to make possible the existence of the spiritual component of *umuntu* (person) solely by itself, in a disembodied state. It is pertinent that they do not speak of bodily survival of death and its resurrection as some religions maintain. They have probably chosen to perpetuate the spirit because it is inaccessible to all alike and they can posit any fictions about it that they cannot do in the case of the body whose fate everyone can readily apprehend, making it impossible for them and other believers in bodily resurrection to claim and prove that $body_1$ is the same body at time t_1 as $body_2$ at time t_2 after the universally recognizable decay of $body_1$ in death. Even the trick of re-creation (of at least one renewed body that is identical to, or a replica of, that of the dead person) in which others have sought refuge will not help their case, because it will still not be the original body, and there is always a possibility that re-creation can result in more than one body, causing the abiding problem of confusing multiple physical (rather than mental) personalities.

In the second paragraph of the introduction to this book, I asked the question, what is a human being? The short answer was that it is a member of the species Homo sapiens, designated sapiens sapiens, because it is presumed to be wise in the extreme. (sapientia = Latin for wisdom; homo = Latin for man or human being). "Human" thus refers to the animal species at the top of the tree of evolution (or creation) distinguished by possession of a mind and other features, such as a 46XX/XY chromosomal constitution (with variations like 46XXY, 46XYY, etc.), perception via various modalities, consciousness, desires for food and satisfaction of other natural needs, thinking (which they possibly share with the lower species), language (to which they cannot claim a monopoly, since they do not understand animal language), intention, and, most importantly, moral sensibility—the ability to add value and meaning to their actions, which is lacking in lower species. The question of value in human life presents its own problems in the sense of the questionable morality of some individuals of the sapiens species as judged by their disreputable actions; for instance, if Homo sapiens sapiens is extra wise, why is it homophobic and averse to promotion of peaceful co-existence, why does it always display a lack of virtue, altruism, sound and lofty judgment etc., why is it so prone to displaying base values? Some of their base actions directed at members of their own species stand in stark contrast to the "lofty" actions of lower species toward their own members, and they convey the impression that those are the only actions that their perpetrators know, and the only ones that they live for. Their callous attitude does not end with other persons; it extends to self-destruction through neglect of the environment and sacrifice of natural habitats for the vanities of modern life, short-sightedness as in living only for today, lying, greed and selfishness which impel them to display inhumanity towards their kind—discussed in another context, in my *Homan Inhomanity*—and many other unbecoming attitudes toward their fellow beings. If all these attitudes and actions are what wisdom consists in, then Homo sapiens is still evolving as Homo ignārum at a lower level than sapiens.

Their civilizations are decaying and self-consuming oligarchies where human rights are constantly abused, even if selectively so, to the detriment of only certain tribal groups. They have become rogue states that engage in endless wars that have been glamorized unduly for the self-aggrandizement of nations and their leaders in the guise of self-defence—against phantoms—proffered as protection of the nation's sovereignty and its "freedoms". They are driven to these despicable pursuits by a variety of motives, most of which have no bearing on the welfare of the citizens who are dragged into these conflicts by their self-serving leaders, e.g., vain displays of power, expansionism, imperialism, and acquisition of resources. They fashion and utilize biological weapons, as if enough threat from naturally occurring biological afflictions in the form of microbial toxins does not already threaten human survival; they are embroiled in a perpetual nuclear arms race that constitutes an ongoing threat to the survival of their species, because of their mistrust of one another, their desire to dominate, and hence their reluctance to finally destroy all nuclear arsenals. The result is that other non-nuclear nations are perpetuating the race, because they realize that the only way to have clout in a nuclear world is to have your own weapon with which you can dare the bully to try to victimize you. They have seen nuclear powers tread carefully when they confront those who have the same weapons as they, while they walk all over those who don't have them. Meanwhile they are exploiting the patriotism of their citizens who naïvely look upon these senseless ventures as making the ultimate sacrifice for their countries, not for the glory of their self-serving leaders! This self-destructive intelligence of Homo sapiens sapiens (alias Homo sapiens et ignārum) is certainly not the one to tout as exceeding that of all living creatures, as indicated in one of my other writings:

> The primacy of the human being is not lost; it is rather being forced to recognize and accommodate other existents with less intellect and sentience

than humans. We may have intellect and sentience, and be adept at many skills, but we still lack the sophistication shown by some animals. For example, we lack the keen vision of the hawk, the sonic sensitivity of the bat, the strength and majestic poise of the lion, and the graceful flight of the bird. All we can do is mimic these wonderful qualities with our telescopes, sonar equipment, heavy machinery, and airplanes. The animals have taught us, and are still teaching us many useful lessons. Even bacteria like the ones that produce the deadly toxin of botulism have taught us how to relieve our disabling muscle contractures, and how to smoothen our unwanted wrinkles with their toxin. Still, we lack the humility and the grace to respect animals.[13]

Homo sapiens has learnt the value of sonar location for the use of blind persons who learn to navigate their environment by emitting sounds that bounce back to them and inform them of the relative locations of objects in space and their textures—softer and porous objects absorb much of the sound waves, while harder and smooth surfaces reflect sound better, preparing the blind person for his encounter with his unseen world. But Homo sapiens has also used his intelligence to spell his own doom. Having discovered antibiotics to treat infectious diseases against which his only defence was his efficient immune system, which is often overwhelmed by micro-organisms, culminating in his demise, he has gone overboard and overused them, ignoring the fact that the bugs have means of developing resistance to these drugs. Today we speak of super bugs that are threatening our existence, and we seem to be helpless to prevent the Armageddon that awaits us as more and more bugs resist or circumvent our efforts to destroy them; they are destroying us instead. The fact that some of these superbugs originate in and are initially confined to specific areas of our world is cold comfort, because rapid intercontinental travel has shrunk the world and made it possible for them to be transported over long distances in a few hours; e.g., drug resistant tuberculosis. We have been smart enough to realize that an unchecked nuclear arms race is a certain death sentence for our species, but we have lacked the foresight to prevent or deal with the threat of super bugs even while we can see them encroaching on us and beginning to wreak their havoc. Much of the blame for this problem rests with the indiscriminate and senseless use of antibiotics for treating colds and coughs, and for treating fevers without regard to their origin and their role in disease as nature's way of disarming the bugs that cause us distress, especially the less harmful ones like cold viruses. No defence can be mounted for the use of antibiotics to treat fever whose cause is unknown, and hence administering needless treatment, which only encourages bacteria to develop resistance to a whole family of antibiotics, putting human lives at risk well into the foreseeable future, and no defence can be mounted against the branding of Homo sapiens as nothing but ignārum.

These difficulties that are threatening the survival of humanity are due to the fact that positive behaviour and morality cannot be legislated, like telling people that they will love their neighbours or face the wrath of the law; that they will refrain from prescribing antibiotics to treat colds or lose their licenses to practice medicine. People have to rely on their moral judgment to make such decisions, especially when it comes to treating others fairly and with respect, and in so doing they set the tone of their society: liberal, apartheid, neoconservative, etc., hence the need for all legal systems to rest on a moral foundation, because the reverse situation carries with it the propensity to disregard the moral rights of people and sacrifice them on the altar of the expediency of statutory laws, some of which are power trips of governments to intimidate and control the people and deserve to be defied rather than observed. These unwritten laws of conduct go a longer way towards preserving the integrity of the species than the negative, promulgated laws by which we live that tell us that it is not our duty to help those in need, such as the many who are injured or assaulted in our presence while we legally stand idly by and watch, or else look away, because we do not want to be involved or to have to answer questions. Sometimes, even the injured who are being helped and whose lives are saved by that help will turn around and sue their helpers for having contributed to any complications that might arise from their injuries, even if these would have occurred without the intervention of their helpers. That is the kind of world in which we live; one that is bereft of gratitude, but also one that is also defiled by depraved adults who cannot be trusted to help children in need without exploiting them (with lethal consequences), and who have become so inhuman that they will kidnap these children from their bedrooms, while their parents are sleeping, and subject them to the basest of indignities before ending their lives. Unfortunately, the (punitive) laws of the land can deal with these beasts only after, but not before, the fact: "we cannot intervene on the basis of suspicion"; and yet they intervene on the same basis when they are racially profiling some persons: "he looks as if he is up to no good; these types have a high risk of offending; etc."

The upshot of the above short tour of the nature of persons and their incomprehensible attributes should convince us that persons remain perennial enigmas that defy precise and comprehensive definition. Ultimately, the person is what every one of us sees when he or she looks squarely in a mirror and has the guts to pass honest judgment, positively or negatively, on the one whose image appears in it. Some persons will see their images in their mirrors and think that they are the only persons in this world. These are reckless and garrulous narcissists who live in a fantasy world where anything that they fancy happens, a world populated by alternative facts where truth is not truth, where lies are the norm, where they project their miserably amoral and despicable characters on to other persons to make themselves appear like the principled persons that they are not, where worthless ignoramuses pat their own backs for nothing besides their abject failures; where the actions of one idiot can put the whole world at risk or even ignite an all-consuming conflagration that no one can stop. These creatures are a curse on the world, but also a test of the tolerance of the rest of their world. The only problem is that some insincere, mealy-mouthed characters who should be curbing the kind of gong show that goes on within the territory of these fantasizers have either become immune to it after first submitting to it or they are capitalizing on the problem by obfuscating it for their own advantage, getting what they want from these ignoramuses while the going is good—it is true that it takes all kinds to make this world.

Chapter 3

The Law of Persons and Persons' Rights

Through the ages, philosophers and others have often referred to "natural law" as the standard by which humankind should govern itself. But what are we to understand by natural law as opposed to statutory or positive laws, both of which should rightly be based on the moral law, which we will discuss in chapter 7. We know that many states have formulated and promulgated laws to govern the conduct and actions of their citizens and to help sustain the moral tone of their societies, laws for the infringement of which they can be punished in any one of many ways, including the extreme situation of being put to death for the unlawful killing of other persons; but the nature of natural law (and its close companion, natural rights) still evades many of those who have not taken the time to ponder over it. In The People's Law Dictionary, law is defined as "any system of regulations to govern the conduct of the people of a community, society or nation, in response to the need for regularity, consistency and justice based upon collective human experience."[1] Natural law, on the other hand is a "common law" or "higher law" that is "founded on reason . . . [and] . . . can be rationally recognized everywhere . . . it is not enforced through mechanisms in nature. We can choose to act in accordance with it or not."[2] One is essentially regulatory and conduct limiting; the other is essentially rational and optional. Now because we are free agents who have the ability and prerogative to choose how to act in any situation—each one of us does that every day of our lives when we are presented with several possible actions to choose from in response to the demands of living—some of us use the opportunity to deliberate wisely and make rational choices that carry the maximum possible utility for everyone, while others make irrational choices that are inimical to their own welfare and, unfortunately, to the welfare of others on whom their resultant actions will impinge adversely. In doing all of these things, we are constantly trying to abide by statutory laws for fear of punishment, if we should contravene them, and also because we are law-abiding citizens who recognize that these laws were framed for our protection and the protection of our rights and liberties in most instances, if they are just and non-discriminatory. But we also often take advantage of natural laws, sometimes slighting them with impunity, because no one will punish us for disregarding them, but forgetting that the order that exists in the universe derives from the strict regularity of those laws. Without them, chaos would reign supreme in the universe, and we would be uncharitable brutes who live like wild beasts (as we sometimes or often do).

Nature dictates the character of reality and the functions of every organism from the human to the lowest form and in the process lays down the laws by which these processes will be regulated and how the subjects of those processes will be treated, in accordance with the different roles and behavioural characteristics of all the living forms of the earth. The latter are in turn determined by the genetic codes of these individuals and the influence of their natural environments well before the intervention of humans with their contrived laws that are structured to maximize their fondest parochial wishes and desires, which often conflict with the dictates of natural law at the risk of compromising the welfare and lives of many innocent persons, as we have observed. As can be readily deduced from their terms, the moral implications of natural law are universal, transcending time, race, culture, nationality, and government. They are not the prerogative of some persons only, and they are not limited by state boundaries or by statutes of limitation like many secular laws. With these characteristics, these universal moral standards should therefore form the basis of our individual and collective relationships, if we intend to establish just societies in which all persons will flourish without hindrance. And so, to ensure the just application of these laws, every living person should be endowed first with universal rights, and then with parochial rights, both of which should be seen as entitlements that will ensure that she lives her life to the full, beyond the whim of those who have given themselves the power to control the lives of everyone else in this world for their own benefit; e.g. self-serving governments and the corporations that own and control them. The possession of these rights should dictate that all immoral and unjust laws be subject to deliberate contravention, because they do not deserve any one's respect by their very nature.

Each rational person is expected, therefore, to readily recognize his moral duty toward others of his kind intuitively[3], such as knowing that it is of necessity wrong to kill another person without the reason of genuine self-defence, or to deprive another person of the food, water, and air that sustain his life; knowing that we do to others what good we would want done to us and that we not do to them the evil or harm that we would not want done to us. Therefore, everywhere in our world unforced benevolence is demanded of every person, unlike in the case of binding conventional demands such as driving on the right hand side of the road, which is the law in some states but not in those where people drive on the left hand side of the road. People are aware of the potential chaos and life endangerment that can result from transgressing this and other secular laws, for which punishment is exacted, but they are mostly oblivious to, and uncaring about, the incalculable harm that can result from their disregard of those natural laws that can seriously and adversely affect the lives of many of their fellow beings and for which they may be subjected to blame but not punishment. Who of the rich people has ever been punished for ignoring the suffering of the poor around him, even if they are dropping dead like flies as is the case in the famine-stricken areas of the world, or perishing from the lethal effects of recurrent natural disasters, both of which are not his fault, but both of which are a challenge to his moral obligation to come to the aid of his fellow beings. He shirks this moral responsibility by rightly claiming that he did not intentionally set out to cause the calamities that have devastated the lives of the poor, forgetting that his economic policies kill them directly and also indirectly by creating conditions in which their chances of surviving the onslaught of natural disasters are greatly diminished by those policies, besides also making it impossible for them to meet the lowly demands of daily living and thus exposing them to the temptation of acquiring what they need by illegal and anti-social means. And then he turns around and pins unsavoury labels on them and incarcerates them by the thousands for breaking his laws. I have discussed these policies at length in chapter 6 of *Our World and its Values* and in chapter 13 of *Homan Inhomanity*.

Aristotle (BC 384–322) is considered by many to be the father of "natural law" by drawing attention to the rational, universal, intuitive truths mentioned above as distinct from the sometimes irrational, parochial half-truths of particular laws that people have adopted to suit conditions that they have created in their various communities; hence the saying: the law is an ass. His list of virtues, which includes modesty, magnanimity, pride (proper ambition), courage, temperance, patience, magnificence, liberality, truthfulness, friendliness, wittiness, and righteous indignation does not need to be legislated; it is a necessary intuitive code of conduct that every rational person should acquire by living the kind of life that is consistent with them, without any prodding from an external constraining source. Therefore, if any state intends to impose just laws on the people, it should ensure that they are consistent with the promotion of these virtues. To live with deficiencies or excesses of these virtues, is to live irrationally and, in some cases, immorally; e.g., the fearful coward who lacks courage will allow other people to take advantage of him and situations to take control of him when he should be asserting his right forcefully, while the rash and overconfident individual will endanger his own life and welfare, as well as the lives and welfare of other people, by rushing into action without stopping to plan carefully. Only the man of courage will exercise the balanced discretion required to face all situations in their multifariousness. Similarly the state that is hard on its citizens, like some modern autocracies and dictatorships will only succeed in stirring them to the kind of rebellion that we are witnessing in our world, while those states that are literally lawless in their liberality will encourage some of the carnage that characterizes other areas of our world. Only those states that have achieved a stable mean will prosper, if they can steer clear of the greed that is shrouding our world. The Stoics, on the other hand, held that what constituted natural law was the rational and purposeful order to the universe in accordance with which rational (human) beings also lived as part of this cosmic order. At no time, however, did they pretend to recognize a transcendent divine source of origin of this order; their god was material and immanent in the universe that he directed meticulously. Besides, they embraced and pursued virtue for the happiness that it bestows, not for rewards from or fear of the wrath of a transcendent being. It is regrettable that modern humans have elected not to learn anything from the wisdom of the past.

Natural laws also have a physical dimension that is as basic as that of moral laws. In this physical sense, they are not some mysterious injunctions that have been issued from on high to direct events in our world or handed to humanity on a platter under the cover of thunder and lightning to dictate and guide human actions; they are statistical averages resulting from the human compilation of observations of how events over which we have little or no control happen in our world and universe, and they would have been otherwise if the universe had been different. That metals expand when they are heated and contract when they are cooled is an observation that prompted a law relating to these phenomena and explaining why railway tracks must have spaces along their lengths to prevent warping from expansion of the metal when it is exposed to sources of heat like that from the sun on a hot day. Similarly, the property of water to expand when it freezes explains why pipes containing water burst when they are exposed to temperatures well below the freezing point of water. These causal relationships, which are descriptive rather than prescriptive, do not, like prescriptive laws purport to govern the world as much as they reflect the recognizable order and regularity that spontaneously exist in the universe, and violation of them, although not easily accomplished, does not exact the censure that goes with transgressing positive prescriptive laws, but it can spell disaster as in warped bridges under the influence of the hot sun where allowance has not been made for the expansion of the metal framework, or burst pipes that have not been adequately conditioned for freezing weather.

In African society the ruling principle is that of the protection of all life by supernatural forces of good that constitute the basis of their natural law. Ubuntu law, as their supreme governance is styled, based as it is on natural law, is tied to a morality of brotherly love and truthfulness, and is therefore as irreproachable and timeless as truth itself; hence its lack of confinement by such devices as statutes of limitation, which would otherwise render it stale and unenforceable and which are a convenient ploy for schemers in some ecclesiastical circles to invoke for protecting some of their "honourable" transgressors from the clutches of justice. This link to morality also clearly discredits any attempt by some persons to deny certain racial groups personhood and the right to humane treatment by a stunt devised by Immanuel Kant that I have described in *Homan Inhomanity*:

> Kantono . . . first lays down the requirement for anything to be a moral being as the possession of rationality, then he goes on to extol the homanity that exists in its greatest perfection in his favoured race. From these unfounded premises, he concludes, by a vicious logic, that the other tribes do not possess rationality, and hence do not also qualify as moral agents worthy of respect. He opens the way for them to be used as means to the ends of the perfect tribe and to be treated worse than

animals . . . Indeed, to confirm his deviant, colour-coded reasoning, Kantono further goes on to say (like the other two brown bashers, Humono and Lacka) that their cognitive deficiency barred browns from acquiring the moral status of ends in themselves, and so moral laws did not apply to them and they could, therefore, be used as means to any end that pleased the whims of pinks, thereby exonerating pinks from responsibility for the heinous crimes that they are committing against browns. So his postulated universal imperative of duty is a mere colour-coded sham that has limited and bigoted application to pinks, based on the wider assumption that browns do not (on purely moral grounds) have the rights to justify recognition of their tacit claim of duty toward them from pinks, and that they will remain eternally inferior to pinks, simply because they are of a darker hue.[4]

The dictum "no one is above the law" has proved to be empty rhetoric and an adulteration of a meaningful concept by abusers of the law of persons and their rights; it is a mere collection of words that don't represent what they purport, and should therefore have no place in the vocabularies of the nations. Far too many select persons who wield power of some kind are above the law in many of this world's jurisdictions—the rich, the famous, the police, and corrupt politicians. The ordinary citizen who either has no clout or is poor, and the head of state who does not kowtow to the wishes of the those who wield power in this world are hauled before the different categories of courts of these types, while their own offenders against the humanity of other persons roam freely with loads of misdeeds on their backs and shoulders but are not hunted down like rabbits and do not have warrants of arrest issued against them for their share of crimes against humanity. These are the same people who intentionally deceive the citizens into believing that they possess the power to determine the direction in which their states will evolve by virtue of the democracies that govern them, and that if they have any grievances about these matters they still have the means to seek redress for them; but they know that they are pulling a hoax, and that the concerns of the citizens will slide by their deaf ears as water slides over a duck's back. Poor creatures, even they don't have the power that they pretend to possess; real power belongs exclusively to the cliques and unelected backroom boys who control them, the ones in whom the people have unwittingly vested it when they thought that they were electing their representatives and to whom they have abdicated it with their votes that put their proxies in office. The only response they get to their protests at the hijacking of their rights is, "we won't yield to mob rule"—mob rule?

The so-called leaders, including the dull-witted despots and opportunists who were elected and the unelected who imposed themselves on the people, all of whom have no semblance of statesmanship to their credit, have assumed what power the backroom boys have allowed them to wield so that they can cater to their own political and economic ends, and not to the welfare of the people that they ostensibly represent. Their self-serving (striving to win nomination for the Nobel Peace Prize), biased (oppressing racial groups other than their own), venomously short-sighted (always thinking only of the next election and how to rig it to their advantage while demonizing their competitors), and self-aggrandizing agendas are always at variance with what is good for the people and with the will of the same people who have placed themselves under their direction for their common good. That is the price the people have to pay for their naïveté and misplaced trust in political establishments where these prevaricators have proved their lack of respect for the people who put them in office and for the same trust that they have vested in them to execute their most cherished hopes and aspirations for themselves as autonomous agents and for their progeny, not to manipulate and deceive them so that they can cater to their own selfish interests at the expense of the public good. But people never seem to learn that they get the governments that they deserve, which are the ones that they elect, because they promise them the moon, even when it is quite clear that the promises are empty; e.g., in the midst of a recession when jobs are evaporating like dew before the rising sun either because the market is at an ebb, or because those who can provide the jobs are holding them back so that certain sections of the citizenry can blame the leader that they want to discredit and replace him with one who blends in better with them, these people believe (or so they pretend) that the latter can pull millions of jobs out of a hat like a magician — how naïve! They vote with their hearts or biases, instead of with their heads, or else the content of their heads leaves much to be desired, as I have often heard others say, and that is why they don't use them. No one can use what he does not have.

These characters brazenly defy the people's laws as laid down in the statutes of their states, and they arrogantly thumb their noses at international laws like International Criminal Court that govern the relationships among nation states and prohibit unjustified belligerence and wanton murder of civilians, trespassing in and occupying other people's territories by force, and torturing their victims to subdue and humiliate them and to gratify their morbid dispositions, not to extract authentic information out of them. That illegal technique has repeatedly been proved to be unreliable for this purpose but ideal for getting victims to confess to what their torturers and their superiors want to incriminate them with, since their victims are in such agony that they will comply with any order that will ensure their freedom from the hell in which they are forced to live. To everyone's chagrin also, it is always the more powerful states victimizing the weak ones, which they label as threats to democracy and to the security of the whole world — ridiculous nonsense which really amounts to: you have what we want and we will use any means to take it from you, even if it means making the lame peace of the world more insecure. In their opinion might is right, even if what they are doing is dead wrong. The weak ones are easy victims, because they do not have the matching means to defend themselves or strike back. As I have indicated in another context, the bullies only bark loudly at those who likely have the capacity to defend themselves with similar dreaded weaponry without daring to accost them. Regrettably for citizens, this practice is universal in all ranks of law enforcement, local and international. Escape from it is as impossible as escape from the practices of wrongful incarceration and the ever disgusting and barbarous practice of executing people, because those concerned with these particular aspects of law enforcement have to make amends for their own deficiencies and failings, or else enhance their status and thus qualify for promotion to higher ranks by registering more and more prosecutions. They pursue this course regardless of the innocence and violated civil rights of the victimized people who are being sacrificed on the altars of their selfish ambitions.

Societies that are governed by principles of justice and fairness do not engage in such demeaning behaviour; they show respect, not only for a select few, but also for all the persons who constitute any community as moral equals, even though some other societies may be in the ingrained habit of arbitrarily relegating them to an inferior position by means of the economic, political, and other criteria that they, as their self-appointed superiors, have imposed on some of them and are sworn to maintaining. The perennial and proverbial gap between rich and poor, which gapes wider with the passage of time, imposes more and more hardship and suffering on poor people, keeping them in the bondage out of which the rich have no intention of lifting them, because it works to their advantage to have cheap labour that is eternally grateful for the pittance in wages that is tossed their way for running their economies. Only societies that recognize the rights of other peoples to freedom and justice always make it their duty to ensure that they live under the protection of the same non-discriminating civic and natural laws that govern their own lives. They do not just pay lip service to their laws, but they live by them, and they will go out of their way to facilitate the achievement of those goals of freedom and justice pronounced in them for all their citizens, with no strings attached. They do not harbour any ulterior motives of using the less fortunate members of society to advance their own agendas as is unfortunately so often the case with the big boys and some big girls who promote proxy wars and are always looking for situations in which they can intervene and which they can exploit to further their own interests and ambitions; they have said it often enough that it is no secret now.

Shamefully, their poor pawns and accomplices, who are the so-called leaders and rulers of some of those states, succumb to the lure of the money that they stand to receive if they slaughter their own people to facilitate the exploitative ventures of their benefactors, and they oblige without hesitation. The slaughter that occurs in different parts of the world among peoples who can least afford to engage in such low down behaviour is as pathetic as it is sickening; but the role of those outsiders who settle their scores in these lands is even more nauseating. It is quite clear from the conduct of these absurdities that the worship of money, which underlies them, has taken over people's reason and left empty shells in which electronic devices can be installed to make them do anything that any manipulator of puppets wants.

However, the deconstruction of money, which is the only hope of reversing these trends and saving humanity from itself, looks like a forlorn hope, especially in view of the fact that replacing hard currency with plastic money in the form of credit, debit, and other cards has not done anything to quench the insatiable thirst of humanity for this infernal commodity. Each time a new substitute for money looms on the horizon, fond but ephemeral anticipation replaces the despair that has plagued generations and now seems to be a roaring inferno of iniquity, but the infernal dollar and its compatriots continue to rear their ugly heads and corrupt people even more. Today there is cryptocurrency, e.g., Bitcoin, and there is use of smart phones to conduct small daily transactions that would otherwise require the use of the preceding modalities of purchase; but however much one would hope that the concept of money and its worth for purchasing human life and worth will gradually sink into oblivion as an offspring of these many innovations, one is still left with the lingering sense of despondency that human greed will ever be ameliorated, or better still, eliminated by them. So what should the law of persons demand of all people? Following the example of John Rawls I will list those demands as

(a). Creating conditions in which not only locals whose governments have the ability to provide them with opportunities for a sound basic and higher education to uplift the cognitive functioning of the nation but also the less fortunate in poor countries can drink deep from the fountain of knowledge created by the same conditions, for the sake of improving their own lot and survival in this world where the race is to the swift and the battle to the strong, because these qualities of swiftness and strength will place them in the right places at the right times. Chance alone will not help the person to shape her world to satisfy her needs; she needs the tools to compete successfully in a world of equals. Therefore her training and preparedness for the competition of survival should not be trammelled by unjustifiably designed discriminatory disadvantaging.

(b). Spreading the wealth around (however repugnant that concept might sound to the super rich), so that those who lack the necessities of life as a result of the policies and practices of those who alone enjoy the luxuries of life can keep their heads above water and begin to endure less hardship and live above the level of their present bare existence. It is no exaggeration to say that millions of deprived people can be helped to survive on the astronomical excesses of the few who control the riches of this world that they have accumulated on the backs of the same deprived millions in most cases. One only has to think of the scourge of colonialism, clothed in the garb of Christianity, that has denuded Africa and other continents of their mineral and other resources without doing anything much for the majority of the people of those lands who are now burdened with debts that they have incurred with the lending institutions of the same colonialists to improve the lot of their people. But even here, they are trapped in the vicious circle of sacrificing the health, education, and total welfare of their citizens to pay off the mounting interest on their debt without making a dent on the principal—

an ignominious arrangement that has committed them to perpetual serfdom. The perpetrators of these injustices may pretend and relish the lie that they are not doing anything directly and actively to multiply the burdens and miseries that are bound to end the lives of poor people and should not, therefore, be held responsible for their sorry plight, but they are deliberately omitting acts of benevolence that would otherwise save those lives, and that alone renders them culpable.

Rawls has very aptly defined the concept of equalizing (to a limited degree) the playing field of survival to extend a generously lifting hand to the many disadvantaged of our world in his two principles of justice (and fairness):

(i). whatever basic liberties there are in a society, they should be equally accessible to everyone as a matter of right. Right now, equal opportunity, even though it does not guarantee equal outcome, is a utopian dream for those who have been unjustly discriminated against for centuries, because it still does not exist anywhere in many cases, and when the empty gesture is made to offer it to them, they cannot avail themselves of it for lack of basic preparation or funds. The law of the land can prescribe that requirement, but the practice still favours persons who have been handed a better head start by the traditionally biased socio-economic circumstances of their society, and hence better chances at availing themselves preferentially of those enviable opportunities, besides being favoured for other obvious reasons which will be vehemently denied by them. Regrettably also, even the dispensation of justice is lopsided in favour of the rich and famous, some of whom suffer from the disease "affluenza", and of those with the right tribal affiliations as determined by the distribution of epidermal melanin.

(ii). In the face of these prejudicially and selfishly arranged inequalities, disarrangement should be undertaken, so that the underdog now receives preferential treatment—affirmative action—to which the heretofore selectively privileged are now objecting loudly as discriminating against them. For them, it is OK when the other people are the victims of crippling and unjustified discrimination that has been imposed on them by those with privilege who continue to place a decent, basic livelihood beyond their reach, but not when the privilege is extended to them even without changing the status quo; that is just too much for the dogs in the manger to accommodate. It's as if they have been asked to give up their entire bodies, when only their useless nail clippings are being offered to the other people, let alone their hands or arms. These are the people who lack a sense of justice, and of whom Rawls says that they lack "certain fundamental attitudes and capacities included under the notion of humanity."[5] They refuse to recognize that the basic needs of the other people are the same as their own that they have exceeded with their loads of money; the merchants do not charge the poor less for the same goods that both of them purchase; both must pay ±$1.80 for that litre of milk that the poor can barely afford; hence their susceptibility to undernutrition and ill health for whose treatment they also cannot pay, even as their rich brothers deny them insurance for the health services that they enjoy, and which are paid for by the same poor people with their taxes. Provide every family with the means to afford nourishing food, and they will not fall victim to ill health, and the well-fed will not have to smother their consciences (if they have any) when they encounter hunger and deprivation, if they ever venture into surroundings where the intruding presence of this scourge will force itself into the cognitive field of only those situations that they selectively choose to recognize.

c). Health care should be universal and managed by a responsible authority, other than insurance companies or private companies that are in it to make money while sacrificing the lives and welfare of patients for profit. Health care systems that are privately operated have been known to deny patients costly special investigations of their ailments meant to elucidate obscurities in their clinical presentations, and to deny them treatments that are considered to be expensive, even if they are the only proven and ideal ones for restoring them to good health. They prefer to use old, inadequate, cheaper tests and treatments, because that enables them to reap greater profits from the health systems that they are operating. This is a regrettable, inhumane, and uncaring attitude that also denigrates the efforts of physicians and of the time they spend unraveling patients' complaints and illnesses instead of glossing over everything and seeing more patients so that the total cash flow from those consultations can be greater, since remunerations for services rendered are calculated per patient rather than per duration of consultation. We are not talking here about the political kind of consultation where the bilkers are paid large sums of money by their friends in government for consulting with themselves, if that makes any sense at all—imagine a consultant holding a telephone over each of her ears, feeding herself questions or problems through the consulter telephone and answering them through the consultant telephone, until she becomes so confused that she directs questions and answers into the wrong telephones and ends up talking nonsense into both phones at the same time. That is how some government consultants operate, as one and the same consulter and consultant at the same time. The obvious result is that physicians who follow this selfish directive end up with inadequate knowledge about the besetting problems of their patients. They treat the presenting problems which are the tips of the proverbial iceberg and leave the patient with a burden of unresolved problems that will eventually take their premature toll on her long term health and life. Unfortunately, again, it is the people who lack the means to afford cadillac health services who suffer this injustice, while the rich enjoy the best available health care, which they deny the poor. The obvious effect is to stunt the physical and intellectual development of poor people and to relegate them forever to the lowest rungs of the ladder of socio-economic upward mobility where they cannot afford to develop the qualities required for emergence from their pit of misery in which these qualities are further stunted and eventually effaced—a self-fulfilling prophesy.

These kinds of attitudes are not surprising, considering that most governments are more concerned with promoting the success of capitalist corporations than with guarding the rights and welfare of the citizens. In fact, to say that governments are traditional violators of people's rights is to state a truism. Misusing the power given to them by the citizens, they cut social programs while pouring money into corporations that have mishandled their finances knowing that they will be rescued by governments with the money of people who have no one to rescue them from their own financial woes and from their daily lack of the means to stay fed and alive. How many lives of sick and hungry families, especially children, could not have been saved with all the monies that have been given to failed corporations and to their executives to reward their failures with obscene bonuses? Comparatively speaking, how many others would have benefitted from the absurd astronomical amounts of money spent in running for public office and ensuring that the donors of the largest sums will reap the economic benefits of their contributions from the policies of their beneficiaries (who are beholden to them) once they are in office? Clearly, such governments have no regard or respect for the people's fundamental right to life that they are abusing; let alone their other rights that they also abuse on a daily basis. As far as they are concerned, these people and their labour are the necessary tools required for enriching the corporations, which are bound to reward them in many shady ways for channeling the people's money to them. That is why they can so glibly coin legislation to force them back to work when they should be respecting their bargaining rights with their employers who still have the temerity ask them to take a pay cut while they siphon off large bonuses from the companies that they claim to be trying to save from bankruptcy. In the end, the selfishly guarded rights of the corporations and their cheerleaders (government) triumph over the rights of the people, because the government wields the ultimate power in all matters. But this absurd set up will soon have to give way to the will of the people; they cannot swallow the bitter pills of abuse dished up by their dictatorial and uncaring governments any longer. They have seen the chasm between their miserable economic status and the super comfort of their rich oppressors widen exponentially with time, and they realize that the status quo cannot be allowed to continue without placing their survival in worse jeopardy, allowing the greed that surrounds them to gobble them up.

So, what are these rights that governments that are supposedly elected to represent the people and guard their interests are failing to respect and protect but are instead violating, and of which the rich camaraderie of executives of corporations and politicians, from whom all citizens ironically have to be protected, has stripped the poor and the powerless? They have been defined in many terms, but I will use the one that defines them as "moral principle(s) defining and sanctioning a man's freedom of action [and autonomy] in a social context".[6] They are claims on other people to respect the person of another and not interfere with her. Many of them are regulated by our socio-political and legal systems and are therefore subject to the tenor of those systems, practically eclipsing those of our basic human "right(s) to life, liberty, and security of person" that originate in natural law, which applies to all persons alike by virtue of their humanity. Their origin from within a social context renders them amenable to manipulation and distortion by persons who do not respect their moral foundations and regard them as structured for their own convenience, to bestow or withhold as they see fit. On the other hand, they empower the holder to take any reasonable deterrent or retributive action against those who are planning to or who willingly violate her human rights.

These rights are defined as universal, inalienable, irrevocable, non-negotiable, non-transferable, and duty-imposing on those against whom they are held; but they can become alienable, negotiable, and transferrable by the holder's choice. In that case he allows actions on or against him that would not otherwise be permissible, e.g., consent to medical treatment, power of attorney granted to someone else to exercise the subject's rights, and they can be rendered revocable by his breaking of statutory law or a contract into which he has entered voluntarily. By and large, rights bestow an unfair advantage on those who hold them and are passively waiting for them to be delivered without doing anything useful to merit them, except that in most cases the holders are victims of circumstances brought about by those against whom they hold these rights, and from whom they should be protected. That is why negative rights that don't require any actions from those against whom they are held, because they are upheld preferentially by liberal societies against positive rights, which require action from those against whom they are held. So, while it is feasible that a so-called positive right can be claimed against the government to promote conditions that favour the creation of jobs to enable citizens to support their livelihoods, it is also not possible to force anyone to provide those jobs if resources do not permit such action—the excuse of racists when they want to exclude other people from jobs that they would rather give to those of their own race.

But there are, nevertheless, challenging and genuinely weighty situations in which some rights can be justly overridden and the bearer's freedom curtailed. For instance, the absolute right to life can be trumped by the need to sacrifice one life for the sake of saving a good many others that are being harmed or terminated by that one, or where some other kind of choice has to be made between saving one life at the cost of many others. In this latter respect, philosophers have formulated thought experiments like the one in which an engineer who is controlling a railway track is faced with the moral dilemma of letting a runaway train engine take track A and kill one child on the track, or letting it take track B and kill three children.[7] Most people would, *ceteris paribus* (all other things being equal), favour sacrificing the life of one child for the sake of saving the lives of more than one, basing their decision on the questionable assumption that human lives can be evaluated in numbers. Nevertheless, as we all know, many factors, some known and others unknown, determine the worth of each human life, and what is initially a simple mathematical solution to the problem at hand (3>1) becomes complex and difficult to resolve with numbers. On the other hand, practical, perennial problems of the right to life of fetuses, which I referred to on pages 11-12, as well as the right of terminally ill and suffering persons to terminate their own lives or have them terminated when they are unable to do so themselves, as happens in most cases, constantly have to be faced and resolved. Controversies relating to both these situations are commonplace, and I have already discussed them in chapters 18, 19, and 20 of *Philosophy for Medical Students and Practitioners*.

At this point, we will take a brief look at the categories of rights that individuals and peoples can lay claim to with the backing of the laws of their lands, unlike moral rights, which can be upheld without the need for legal enforcement but depend for their universal validity entirely on the sharing of a common humanity by all people. For instance, no moral law gives the one child or the three or more children the right to preferred treatment in the example quoted above; they all have equal moral worth; and yet, civilized communities that dare to contradict this basic tenet of decency by claiming moral superiority over others for themselves and their children by their own warped criteria are not in short supply. They insouciantly and callously sacrifice the lives of aboriginal and other underprivileged children (and those of their parents) all the time with amazingly base callousness, never stopping to ask themselves how they would feel if they or their children had to endure the discrimination and mistreatment that they are doling out to other parents and their children. They are content that these things will never happen to them, because they are secure in their position of superiority, forgetting that nothing lasts forever. The sun will set in their lives as it has set in the dominance of the great empires of our time.

According to the categorization laid out by Wesley N. Hohfeld, we can recognize rights as:

(a). Claim rights—where Bob has a claim against Jim to carry out a certain function demanded of him by his duty or obligation to Bob, or not to discriminate against him in any way for anything, because state law forbids discrimination. In this and similar situations, Jim has a legal duty towards Bob to carry out the function deservedly requested or demanded of him by Bob, even if it involves a third party who has no right claim on Jim and to whom Jim is only indirectly bound by duty to Bob as a result of his promise to him to do something to/with the third party. In all cases, Jim has the liberty to disregard his duty to Bob, if Bob's right over him demands illegal (and immoral) action from him. These are essentially controlling rights that serve the interests of the holder of the right, such as the right not to be interfered with in any way, and for the infringement or violation of which persons who are obligated to observe them can be punished. Some so-called democratic governments flagrantly infringe these rights that citizens hold over them by agreement most of the time. Unfortunately, the citizens let them get away with it after they have broken many of the promises they made when they asked to be elected into office to represent them and carry out their rational wishes. Suddenly they think that they know it all and they have the power and the audacity to do as they please with the trust that has been placed with them.

(b). Privileges (liberties) — where Bob has a privilege against Jim to give him a job if he asks for it, because no law forbids Bob from assuming that job; but no law compels Jim to give it to him either. Since Jim is not bound by law and duty to Bob to give him that job, he is free to give or withhold the job at his pleasure, and Bob has no recourse against him, since he has no claim over him. Jim now has a privilege over Bob. A student who has the privilege to use the school van for running errands, unlike other students who do not have that privilege and can be punished for unilaterally availing themselves of it, is free to do so without prohibition, even if he never gets around to exercising the privilege and using the van. His privilege right applies without regard to his ability to perform the action for which he is privileged, and although it might not be possible for him to exercise that privilege when the van is in use, that situation does not remove his privilege when the van is not in use.

(c). Powers (authority rights) — where Jim has the power to refuse Bob a job, because he controls the rules that allow Bob access to the job; i.e., he can override all of Bob's rights pertaining to the awarding of jobs under his control. These rights prevent Jim from being tied down by Bob's claim rights, and they may be rights that no other persons are qualified to exercise. On the other hand, if he has underlings who arbitrarily deny Bob the job for which he is eminently qualified and which he deserves, he has the right to overrule them and offer him that job. The problem arises when rights and powers are in conflict, and none of them trumps the others, as is often the case with the suppression of the civil rights of citizens by governments that claim to be exercising the powers bestowed on them exclusively by the citizens to protect the state from destructive external and internal forces and to protect the very rights that they are infringing and often violating outright with impunity, but also taking advantage of this maneuver to entrench themselves and consolidate their control of the same citizens. Citizens lose out, because governments can silence them with laws and even throw them in jail for protesting violation of their rights. These guys ensure that they always have the last word, even if it conflicts with citizens' rights — they will get away with anything, if the citizens are not awake to their shenanigans.

(d). Immunities — where someone does not have the powers stated above to override the special rights of another person; e.g., Silvio (foreign country diplomat) has immunity against arrest by Mike (law enforcement officer of local state) for any alleged crime, because Mike has no rights of arrest over Silvio in the state where Silvio is a representative of a foreign country. In this instance, Silvio's immunity rights trump Mike's power rights. Meanwhile, Silvio's rights can be trumped by the power rights of his supervisor whose own rights can be trumped by the powers of his superiors, and so on up to the highest level. How often have presidents not been granted immunity from prosecution by virtue of their offices while they continue to engage in forbidden activities and misdemeanours, and by their successors after they have left office and are now eligible for prosecution for the misdeeds that they committed while they were in office and virtually untouchable?

In addition to the fundamental right of persons to the ownership of their bodies, to do with them as they please and to forbid other persons from interfering with them in any way, even if that entails instituting medical measures meant to save their lives, there are also rights to liberty or freedom of action, restricted only by the rights of other persons; the right to freely (within the bounds set by the rights of other persons) pursue one's happiness wherever it is to be found, at whatever cost to oneself, including making a fool of oneself; the right to self-defence—protecting one's own life, even if that entails taking the life of the one who is threatening to take it (controversy has arisen over when this right can be exercised, depending on who initiates the aggression that triggers the need to "stand your ground". The aggressor really has no ground to stand on, since he accosted someone who had nothing to do with him, was not a threat to him, and was going his own way far away from him and oblivious of his presence, and yet his plea has been known to receive sympathetic hearing!); the right to speak freely on any subjects, without fear of prosecution or persecution (by presidents), even on those subjects that are highly critical of governments and their personnel in their official capacities, as long as the speeches do not advocate violence, maliciously defame the characters of other persons, or encroach on their legal rights; There are also children's rights, which are necessitated by the inability of children to fend for themselves, and there are rights of other persons who also cannot speak for themselves due to cognitive incompetence; and then there are animal rights, which are not part of our discussion but are also necessitated by limitations similar to those suffered by children. All these are the rights about which John Stuart Mill said, "If all mankind minus one were of one opinion, mankind would be no more justified in silencing that one person than he, if he had the power, would be in silencing mankind."[8] Political "bosses" of the people should have this statement brilliantly printed and prominently displayed everywhere they go in the chambers, offices, and hallways of the power that so often goes to their heads and heavily clouds their thinking (did I say thinking?).

It should be evident from daily experience that rights can be asserted in singles and in combination, with one or more rights buttressing others; e.g., freedom of action can present as a complex of any or all of the above: acting via the medium of free speech to seek one's happiness, or doing so by exercising one's claim to privileges and immunities that can shield one from the illegal and deleterious exercise of power over one's legal rights by unprincipled government personnel. Also, the right to fair, just, and equal treatment supports the aboriginal child's rights of access to the clean water that he is denied, but which generations of immigrants' children enjoy alone. Legal rights restrict other persons' actions toward one within the limits set by state laws—they cannot infringe one's civil rights (of free speech, freedom of religion, freedom of association, sexual orientation, etc.), political rights (free exercise of franchise, freedom to offer oneself and to run for political office, etc.), or economic rights (freedom to pursue legitimate business enterprises of one's choice, access to financial benefits that are open to all citizens, equal pay for equal work, etc.), as well as the right to make a fool of oneself.

It is unfortunate that positive rights, like the ones referred to above, lack the power of negative rights, which absolutely forbid anyone from interfering with the individual's right to do as he pleases with his body, as already mentioned. Nevertheless they do not excuse the rest of the people from the obligation of heeding the natural law of persons that imposes on them the moral responsibility of ensuring that those of their fellow citizens of the world who do not have the means to institute and maintain a decent lifestyle, which provides the bare essentials of survival and progress, receive enough to live on from the excesses that they enjoy at their expense. Who can deny the exploitation of the have-nots by the haves who have arranged their trade and other relations with other nations so that they can benefit at the expense of those who have willy-nilly had to make trade deals with them to fend off lurking economic and social catastrophes to their countries? No one advocates a situation where people just hang around doing nothing but just waiting to exercise their right to be housed, clothed, fed and carted around; we are only asking that the millions of dollars that the people with political power waste on costly self-serving and irresponsible projects be put to better use, looking after the dire needs of those without the entitlements of those who are living on the gravy train at their enormous expense.

Regrettably, no government seems to be willing to coerce the haves into a contract that would see them assuming, also willy-nilly, their fair and proportionate share of the tax burden to help relieve the universal problem of want. Instead, people have to resort to their human and statutory rights to protect themselves against government terrorism and victimization to which they are subjected all the time as governments carry out the selfish will of corporations. That is why governments have no appetite for such a contract, because it would paradoxically impose a duty on them to do what they are determined to obstruct, i.e., afford relief from the ills of poverty to the have-nots on the backs of the haves who keep them in power and also keep their bellies filled with good cheer. The only contractual rights that they are willing to impose on the people are those that would see the flow of capital from where it is desperately needed into their already overflowing barrels. In this kind of situation, moral rights as rights that respect the humanity of persons and will not brook seeing them reduced to subhuman levels, have been relegated to the lowest rungs of the ladder of consideration where they will be the last to be elevated, if ever, to the pedestals close to those on which all inward looking rights and entitlements of those in power occupy a respectable place.

Although moral rights are supposed to be unassailably and respectably placed, their mortal sin in the eyes of the egoists of this world is that they entail the imposition of imperative, categorical, and unqualified responsibility and duty on those who are thus bound to exercise them without exceptions when they would rather settle for what is expedient. But they are also unpopular, because they demand the moral equality of all persons, where some morally bankrupt ones would rather espouse differential ranking of persons on the basis of selfish criteria that favour their own privilege, autonomy, and supremacy, while they preach *de jure* equality at the same time as they practice *de facto* inequality. This kind of ranking allows them to sacrifice other persons for promoting their own ends as a group without compunction and on the pretext of promoting the happiness of the many (their kind who are the privileged few with excessive means) as against that of a few (the multitudes who are underprivileged, deprived or destitute, and have no status beyond that of property – the property of the rich – which they exploit freely and wantonly) in concordance with the terms of utilitarian principles (the ends-justify-the-means principle), but making a mockery of the benevolent attitude expressed in the saying: "Happiest are the people who give most happiness [*eudaemonism,* flourishing, or well-being] to others".[9]

The truth of this noble statement is borne out by the fact that the greatest contributor to anyone's happiness is her character, rather than her possessions, as well by the observation that individuals who altruistically pursue rational activities that benefit other people besides themselves derive pleasure from such pursuits while they bring happiness to those who are affected by their benevolent actions; thus all get to be happy. It is doubtful if the same can be said of someone who believes and lives by the discipline of egotism, which is self-centred and exclusive of the good that should also be directed at persons other than her own self. In today's world, we are besieged by national leaders who make no bones about their self-centredness as they blatantly manipulate the power that the people have bestowed on them by virtue of the offices into which they have cheated their way. They flagrantly violate the laws, statutes, and established practices relating to matters of state, and they have no hesitation in proclaiming themselves to be above the laws of their states and unbound by its traditions in government that they are incessantly attacking and vilifying against their oath of office: to respect and protect the constitutions of their nation states.

It is regrettable that the branches of government that could check this outlandish behaviour of their so-called leaders are also wrapped up in themselves and looking at how they can also use their positions to amass the fortunes that their "leaders" are shamelessly acquiring from the world-wide contacts that they are able to establish by virtue of their positions. Leaders and moneymen from other countries patronize these corrupt leaders' "arms-length" properties, pouring in millions of dollars, pounds, euros, or other currencies into their "arms-length" businesses in contravention of the statutes of the land and the oath of office to which these con artists owe solemn allegiance.

In this kind of environment, the rights of the people become secondary to the hubris and greed of the leader who victimizes in any one of many ways, including the use of gutter language, anyone who crosses his path. A sad state of affairs prevails that reflects the level of decay to which modern states have sunk, where morals have lost their clout; where leaders no longer set the moral tone of the country; where corruption and disrespect for public funds are the order of the day; and where the good that was done by predecessors is dismantled and destroyed out of sheer spite and smallness of mind. Men of courage and rectitude have become spineless cowards and charlatans when they should be standing up to the other men who have subverted democracy and are reducing their states to the level of banana republics (the epithet that they reserve for other states that they consider inferior to their own), exercising longed for dictatorial powers to which their offices do not entitle them. Instead they have become bootlickers and nocturnal snoops who connive with "leaders" who are not fit to hold the offices that they are using to to fling mud at other people. No one else is left to protect the state and its laws and citizens from what I will name "recklessness unleashed".

Our world is in dire need of saviours from ignorant narcissists and fortune hunters who are itching for dictatorial powers and the freedom to give vent to the racist sentiments on which they have been nurtured. We need leadership that respects everyone's personhood and promotes cordial, beneficent, cooperative, non-combative relationships. There is still time for redemption if we are prepared to learn from those who live these virtues.

Chapter 4
Ubuntu as Agency

Ubuntu (humaneness) is an African humanist and existentialist concept based on the affirmation of one's humanity by acknowledging the humanity of other persons and cultivating cordial relations, mutual respect, and trust with them, irrespective of their colour, ethnicity, creed, or sexual orientation. Within the Ubuntu culture, any person's status in the community is sustained by his mutual relationship of caring, sharing, and harmonious living with others, without which his public persona is a worthless empty shell. The concept of Ubuntu entails the realization of one's being in the being of others with whom one shares these relationships, without losing her individual moral and legal rights to the primacy and dominance of the group to which she belongs. Ubuntu acknowledges that "there can be no self apart from others. I have no identity without a social setting in which that identity is initially forged and recognized."[1] It also subscribes to the opinion expressed in the statements that follow: "I owe to others my life, my language, my family, my locality, my nation, my culture, my education, my horizons and aspirations. I begin my life wholly dependent on others and on the possibilities they afford me. . . . Others may come to depend on me, but I also come to depend on them and on others."[2] Further, under the umbrella of Ubuntu, no single person or racial group is denied its human rights and recognition for its contribution to our world's goodwill and prosperity. Its basic message, expressed in different terms, is the same as that stated in the preceding quotations: "I am because you are". In affirming his own humanity, the subject also acknowledges and affirms the humanity of other persons in his shared world; and, as it has been said "the be-ing of an African person is not only imbedded in the community, but in the universe as a whole."[3] In another context, it has been said of Ubuntu, in words that are reminiscent of Strawson's concept of a person who cannot be fragmented into body and soul in typical Cartesian fashion, "*Ubuntu* is a wellspring that flows within African existence and epistemology in which the two aspects *Ubu* and *ntu* constitute a wholeness and oneness. Thus *Ubuntu* expresses the generality and oneness of being human. *Ubuntu* cannot be fragmented because it is continuous and always in motion."[4]

Ubuntu serves as a reminder to those who are sitting comfortably on the results of the labour and sweat of the less privileged and engage in empty boasting about how they have transformed natural habitats into flourishing metropolises. They forget the havoc that they have wrought in the process, and their stepping stones who are the poor that are suffering from the end results of inhaling asbestos fibres and other ill effects of their transforming but harmful civilization and its industrialization of their lives. Those who claim to have brought enlightenment to their world while trying to minimize or totally deny the contribution of other racial groups to world knowledge and harm-free civilization can also retract a little and look more closely and honestly at the history of knowledge, while also calculating the often irreparable harm that they have caused to their world's inhabitants with their sophisticated weapons of wars that they provoke readily so that they can put those weapons to use. They did not make them so that they could keep them idle in storage for admiration; they made them to kill other people with—remember, this is a "kill" society; every minute of the day, someone is killing someone else in more ways than one at both state and individual citizen levels for some flimsy reason or other. If they had any semblance of Ubuntu philosophy to replace their arsenal of lethal toys, they would use it as a means of reconciliation and settling petty personal disputes and potential conflicts among themselves instead of resorting to their lethal weapons and involving whole nations in their insane escapades of self-aggrandizement. To say the least, change is overdue in prevailing attitudes and practices of belligerence that blatantly defy the desperately needed "respect for human values and the recognition of the human worth that is based on a philosophy of humanism"[5] and Ubuntu.

Ubuntu denotes a concept whose object is *umuntu* (person), a maker of her world, a world that is continually emerging and constantly changing with its maker, as asserted by Sartre when he stated that any person's existence precedes his essence; he is continually making himself into what he wishes to become, guided by the worthwhile ideals that he has set for himself to make his world a better place for all to live in. Unlike inanimate objects whose makers have predetermined their essence before they come into existence— knives for cutting, pens for writing, ladders for climbing, etc., although some items in this category may be adapted for other uses. He comes into being with unlimited potential for shaping himself and his life in any one or more of the many ways that his intellectual (and physical) abilities will permit him to do, as long as he is not thwarted by others who wish to use him like the tools that are listed above. Their functions as tools do not evolve with time, and the listed effects that are occasioned by their use are not free but determined. The person, on the other hand, has the freedom to create his society and the practices and rules by which he will live peacefully in it by the actions that he chooses to perform. Whether he chooses to be a warmonger and strife-loving monster or a lover of peaceful and harmonious coexistence, the choice is his to make.

With that background, and with comments on Ubuntu reflected in my *Homan Inhomanity* pages 14-16, we can now enumerate, following Johann Broodryk, some of the features that distinguish Ubuntu from other humanities and contrast it with some well-known inhumanities of our world. Community is essential to the being of Ubuntu, because without the spirit of belonging to a community (not passively, but actively) *umuntu* cannot realize her Ubuntu. In African culture big tasks are commonly carried out with the help of neighbours and others in what is styled "letsema", an assembly of persons with a purpose where everyone participates with willingness and commitment. Noble purpose permeates their actions and the prevailing spirit of communalism extends to all walks of life in the community, constituting a society where mutual help is an integral part of social life and contrasting very sharply with the capitalistic selfishness, greed, one-upmanship, and cutthroat competition found in other societies where dog eats dog. Here, everyone participates for the common good and for the better living of all citizens in all aspects of community life, and everyone's rational input into the conduct of affairs and culture of the community is regarded as relevant to the ongoing dialogue to achieve the negotiated consensus that is essential to democratic governance, since absolute consensus is not always possible, nor does it necessarily facilitate harmonious living among persons whose opinions are as many as the heads (brains, minds) in which those opinions are formulated.

Compassion and empathy are inseparable from Ubuntu, again in sharp distinction with the mere sympathy that is difficult to extract from members of other notable communities where your problem is yours to shoulder alone. Ubuntu communities are not allowed to disintegrate, and their people are not pushed into situations where they become the victims of nervous breakdowns and other mental disorders caused by the stresses that accompany so-called highly civilized lives. People's concern for others is not polluted by the air of detachment that is found in other communities where it is not unusual for neighbours not to know one another or even talk to one another. In these other communities, a death can occur one or two doors away from one's home without one knowing about it, and even if one does know about it, one is forced to stay out of other people's business and not offer condolences, as one would do in Ubuntu society where everyone who can stops by to comfort the bereaved family and make them feel that they are not carrying their burden of loss alone. Everyone offers her shoulder for the family to cry on in the genial spirit of the saying "a sorrow shared is a sorrow halved". Such compassion is also a part of the preparation for the inevitable —death—when a neighbour (every member of the community is a neighbour) is facing that prospect in her family; it lightens the dreadful anticipation of the event and imparts strength and courage to those who have to face it. In Ubuntu the ruling philosophy is that of sharing; no one should ever face the onerous existential burden of adversity alone when there are other people in her community who can lighten the burden for her. This attitude applies to any and every situation in life: no one should be left to go hungry, families will share their last morsel with a stranger who is hungry; no one should be left to the mercy of the elements without a roof over her head or a garment over her back; even complete strangers are welcomed into the household and given protection and body covering, as did the many who came into my home. Of course, in the present perverted state of our world, one never knows if one is letting a killer into the home— the curse of modern civilization with its idolization of money on which everyone wants to lay his hands at any cost wherever it is to be found, including taking the lives of other persons who have extended kindness to him in any one of many ways: a ride, shelter, a refusal to a panhandler who will not take no for an answer, etc.

The attitude of involvement with others and concern for their welfare stands in stark contrast against the modern-day detachment from other persons, which is evident when people ask: how are you today? They don't really want to know how you are, what is bothering you, how they can help to ease your burden or remove it altogether, if they can do so. The truth is they don't want to be bothered with your problems, and that is why they will not even wait for an answer before they move on to the next thing they want to do or say, leaving you to wonder what was the point of asking the question. In Ubuntu society such a question serves as an invitation to share one's joys or sorrows with the questioner who is always ready to rejoice or commiserate with one and add to one's jubilation or lighten one's burden, as the case may be. The questioner will in turn become the one who has to answer the same question, so that both parties can eventually and genuinely share their joys and sorrows in a sincere spirit of fellowship. From this encounter word will be disseminated in the community, if need be, for others to visit the rejoicing or grieving family, demonstrating the concern of the entire tribe for the welfare of every one of its members and thus retaining the ties that bind them. Everyone in the community takes delight in expressing a greeting (*dumelang, molweni*, or *sanibonani* = hello) to anyone that she meets, including complete strangers, to acknowledge their presence, their being, their personhood. Striking up a conversation with a stranger to the community is not an offence, like the one where a visitor to a civilized society from another civilized society is reported to have felt so threatened and offended by an innocent engaging greeting from a local that he said he would have used his gun if he had had it with him—a sad state of affairs when one can be shot for displaying verbal goodwill to a stranger.

Generosity in Ubuntu culture is not limited only to the categories mentioned above, but it manifests itself in the reciprocity that eschews selfishness or claiming credit for oneself alone, deservedly and sometimes undeservedly. No *umuntu* (person) wants to shine alone or monopolize all the accolades, even those earned by other persons without any help from him but which he usurps by virtue of his superior rank as some senior partners and executives commonly do and some narcissistic national leaders do, claiming credit for thriving economies that were structured and stimulated by their predecessors but also blaming them for the messes that they perpetrate. Ubuntu provides each participant in a common project an opportunity to feel proud about her contributions to it by allowing enough scope for all to contribute positively and share in the glory that crowns their efforts, as a professor expressed it to his ex-student when he was congratulating him on the meritorious achievement that won him distinction and a medal in his Science degree Zoology examination, "I, as your professor, bask in your reflected glory". Hence these communities do not engage in the fierce wrangling that we often see in other communities where people fervidly vilify one another for self-aggrandizement and personal credit, proving that where generosity is lacking, constant effort to bring down the one who is ahead or in a leadership role as determined by the community's laws is the norm, especially if this one happens to be from a less favoured tribal group. At the same time, the leaders in all fields do not go out of their way to belittle their subordinates in order to look big. Furthermore, they do not engage in the repulsive practices of squatters on aboriginal land who claim to be the owners of the country and who think that other squatters like them, or even the original owners of the land do not have a right to be leaders, even if they have been elected by some of their ilk, because they belong to the wrong tribe. These unsavoury characters bicker about everything, including problems that arose long before her time, but about which they were quiet, because they were caused or they arose during the stewardship of one or more of their ilk. Their naked racism is clear for all to see, but they will deny it fervidly and turn the tables on their accusers by accusing them of carrying chips on their shoulders; never mind the fact that only certain tribal groups are profiled and carded or that they are more often the subjects of police brutality, that for every aboriginal girl who is sterilized without her (or her proxy's) consent, or an underprivileged male who is experimentally infected with syphilis without his (or his proxy's) consent no settler girls or males are similarly assaulted and dehumanized. Examples of these and other antipathetic attitudes and behaviour are legion; they are not fictions; e.g., the more subtle racists will cry foul when images that resemble those of persons of other tribes are depicted on the currency notes of their state, but remain mum when images that resemble those of persons from their own tribe replace the former. (I discuss racism fully in *Homan Inhomanity – the oxymoron of racism*.)

In all cultures the children's demeanour reflects largely on parental teaching. In Ubuntu culture all adults have authority over minors, which is equal to that of their own parents. Minors dare not respond to correction by any adult for their deviant behaviour by saying "you are not my mother and you can't tell me what to do and what not to do", and parents will not tell other parents who bring to their attention their children's misdemeanours, "you have no right to correct my child, I will correct him if he does wrong." But this stupid parent is not always with her child to see the wrongs that he is committing out there. Instead of being grateful to the other parent for acting as her eyes and ears in what should be a joint effort to shape the characters of their children, some parents assume a superior attitude and will actually claim, "I know my son, he would never do anything like what you are accusing him of" (what I call the not-my-Johnny syndrome), until her son rudely surprises her by admitting to the misdemeanour when he cannot take the heat any longer. But these parents never learn their lesson; they remain as vain, arrogant, and foolish as before; and that is why modern societies are decaying so fast—parents and their children don't get along, siblings are at war, close relatives are enemies, the entire family structure is in tatters.

There should be no problem about mutual respect among all sections of the community, adults respecting adults and children, children respecting children and adults. The readiness to show respect to all alike should come naturally to everyone. But lack of respect among individual persons and peoples as a group, contrary to what Ubuntu philosophy preaches and what only some Ubuntu communities practice, has gripped society to the extent that some persons don't hesitate to cause harm to other persons and groups for no good reason. If they don't like how you are looking at them, or how you are driving or reacting to their offensive driving, or the slight nudge from you on a crowded street, they knife you or they gun you down. The decency of saying "I'm sorry" to those who have been offended has been replaced by a dose of bullets or knife blades. If they dislike your life style they will cause you grievous bodily harm or kill you, even if you have not done anything to offend them directly. If they disapprove of your assisting those who wish to exercise their rights over what they do with and to their bodies, they will sneak up on you and kill you. If their tribal groups feel threatened by the mere existence of your tribal group in their midst (where they found you living your peaceful life for centuries, anyway), they will concoct reasons to violate your rights to existence and eliminate you with violence—a kind of ethnic cleansing that is perpetrated by some people who should know better from their own tribal experience of this kind of mistreatment. The list goes on and on.

In some cultures parents do not only neglect to correct the deviant or inhumane behaviour of their children, they actually teach them how to disrespect others (including adults) whom they regard as inferior to them. Of late hatred-inspiring camps are being organized in certain societies where the misguided youth of privileged tribes are taught to abandon their ideas of the dignity of all persons and embrace the nefarious prejudices and hatred of their elders toward other persons who have been driven by oppression into situations where they are forced to live desperate lives by the circumstances that have been cast upon them by the same people who are denigrating them. It is unconscionable to force people into poverty where they are more likely to engage in deviant behaviour to make ends meet and then chastise them verbally and physically for their induced misbehaviour, whilst committing the so-called fundamental attribution error of blaming their characters instead of the circumstances in which they have been placed by events beyond their control by your doing. Moral condemnation in such untenable circumstances is itself immoral. In Ubuntu homes, by contrast, children are taught to respect the personhood of everyone and to call adults "*ntate* x = father x, *mme* y = mother y, *rangoane* z = uncle z" etc., not boy or girl, Jim or Annie (all used derogatorily), as they do in some "civilized" societies where they are taught that that is the way to address adult persons from "inferior" races to belittle and deride them, and to "keep them in their place" — wherever that is.

The indigenous culture of mutual respect and especially respect for the wisdom of tribal elders prevails in all Ubuntu societies. Among them, arrogant self-assertion of young executives who are enchanted by fanciful phantoms of delight that adorn their superficial achievements and who have no qualms about deprecating the experience and expertise of their elders is unknown. Deferring to the experience of these elders is never a problem for Ubuntu youth in all matters affecting the welfare of their community. No one has the audacity to tell the elders that they are over the hill at 50 years of age and have to be retrenched to make way for ambitious upstarts (some of whom tout forged, useless pieces of paper that they pass off as academic and professional documents of their achievements) who are so full of themselves, thinking that they know it all, and then going on to mess up left, right, and centre only to reward themselves by siphoning large bonuses and severance packages for failing in their tasks and leaving the people who depended on their expertise in deep water. In the traditional setting, elders have a moderating influence over these aggressive, yet desultory, tendencies of sprightly youth who, in their turn, are unreservedly content to acquire their expertise and proficiency under the careful guidance and mentorship of the elders. They do not persist in immodest, ostentatious blabber about their "abilities" that we hear so often, while having nothing to show for all that big talk. They also do not regard respect of persons in authority as subservience, self-deprecation, or suppression of their "talents" that are itching for vain, erratic display when they should be smugly and disrespectfully showing themselves off to their world so that they can clinch that enviable executive position and start raking in the dollars. In Ubuntu culture, primitive as it may be discredited to be, children and youth learn the just laws and cultural practices of the community from their parents and other elders—respect, diligence, and all other virtues rolled into one bundle that will mold them into honourable citizens, not the blight of their society as happens in advanced civilizations where lack of guidance and permissiveness prevails and children are left to find out things for themselves and formulate their own (deviant) behaviour patterns with the tacit consent of their parents. Furthermore, they do not claim to know everything and end up messing up everything like the many experts in other communities who will not defer to those who know more than they do about matters under consideration, often because they are jealous of their achievements, which exceed theirs, or they belong to "inferior" tribes. A father learnt the most expensive lesson of his life when he lost his child to a devastating illness, because he would not let one from these despised tribes who commanded the necessary expertise and had saved the lives of all the children who came under his care with this rapidly lethal illness attend to his child, and this in spite of assurances from the nursing staff that his child would be in good hands. By the time the preferred expert from his tribe came around to trying to save this child's life, the child had passed the point where she could be treated successfully and rescued. What a pity, what an avoidable tragedy, what an expensive lesson! I often wonder if this tragedy ever changed his self- and other-destructive attitude.

Ubuntu respect for culture, tradition, customs, and religion is demonstrated by the spirit of mutual tolerance and cooperation and the harmony that exists among different tribes and religious sects. Under the guidance of those who are skilled in its practice, novices learn the proper approach to a comprehensive understanding of the process of cultivating cohesion and positive human interaction with one another and with the rest of humanity. No one group derides the others' culture and religion as inferior or provokes them by denigrating their prophets and then crying foul when the other people react violently to the deliberate insults, as they are wont to do after such events—"these are all unprovoked attacks that we don't deserve, because we didn't do anything except demean these 'savages'"; no one coerces others to abandon their inferior cultures and religions to become subservient to his corrupt superior culture and religion as some other cultural groups do; instead, they come together from their respective backgrounds to form cultural and religious associations to promote their common good, which includes technics for casting off the cursed burdens of oppression and unjustified discrimination for doing which their oppressors punish them severely. No one group feels superior to others, and no group descends so low as to inculcate the attitude of superiority and disrespect for others in its children so that they grow up with this venom as the basis of their relations with them, as we noted above. Such attitudes are not part of the connotation of Ubuntu.

Ubuntu is a philosophy of love and peace, virtues that are lacking in our highly civilized and sophisticated nuclear world that is always tittering on the brink of self-annihilation, because pacifists are regarded as "sissies" (not my chauvinistic terminology). In Ubuntu society peaceful co-existence and flourishing of different nationalities, cultures, and "races" under an umbrella of mutual appreciation and forbearance is the norm. The stresses that characterize highly civilized societies, resulting in regional skirmishes (religious and secular) and world wars are unknown in Ubuntu culture where stress-free life imparts health that is not plagued by modern diseases of the heart, blood pressure and sugar control, and disorders of the mind culminating in suicide of all age groups caused by the hardships imposed on dispossessed persons by people with money and power. (The rich and powerful also take their own lives, and they demise from stress related illnesses caused by their constant concern about the safety of their money in offshore havens and by their never-ending scheming how to make more money, by hook or crook). Post-traumatic stress disorder with all its regrettable consequences is unknown in Ubuntu communities, because the atrocities of unnecessary wars of domination do not constitute part of the daily experience of people who live in peace with their neighbours. So they are not afflicted by the sorry plight of young people who are the victims of those who don't realize that their warmongering ruins the lives of the young men and women that they send out to perpetrate acts that leave indelible traumatic impressions on their minds. These young lives are committed to premature termination or to the doom of the perpetual misery that dogs them every day in the form of memories of their role in decimating the lives of men, women, and children of other nationalities, human beings and persons like themselves who love life as much as they do, even if it is not on the same enviable, affluent scale as theirs.

If these reckless warmongers could only stop to think about the damage that they are causing to young lives (and others not so young), they would desist from ordering them to go on these inhumane escapades from behind their desks where they nurse their spurious pedal orthopaedic infirmities, and where they are not exposed to the mental trauma that they are inflicting on these young people, ruining their lives without the slightest prick of conscience. If they claim to suffer pricks of conscience for their inhumane orders, then let them refrain from issuing them, instead of mouthing meaningless regrets at being compelled by circumstances to ruin the lives and futures of young people who are not doing anything to mess up their lives of comfort; and for those whose lives they have already damaged, let them show some concern and help them to return to a semblance of normal existence. But they don't care a hoot, because those who are suffering are not their children—their children are sheltered from these ravages of war by being diverted to harmless paramilitary pursuits where they will never be called upon to put their lives and welfare on the line, or their parents (who are legislators or have close ties with legislators) avoid the imposition of a military draft, which will obligate them to join the dispensable others in perilous escapades. Some superciliously retort that they are not making the "ultimate sacrifice" that others are making or they are not showcasing their esteemed and extreme patriotism, because they are helping with the political campaigns of their parents. The warmongers deny the afflicted veterans the full care that they deserve for the mental and physical trauma that they sustained in their sacrifices while they continue to enjoy their elite status and pursue their ruinous escapades with the same determination, because they have to feed their benefactors in the industries that produce war machinery. Perhaps the world would be a more peaceful place if more emphasis were placed instead on teaching humility, respect, decency, and tolerance with opinions and practices other than one's own without implying that they are at fault and one's opinions are the only right ones; in short, teaching Ubuntu.

If the concept of Ubuntu could indeed be consciously applied in any society, even in the whole world, then perhaps humans could easily prevent or avoid cultural and other conflicts; but lack of inclusiveness of others in what should be a universal bond of love that binds humanity in its search for its common destiny, whether it is oblivion or transcendent survival, and self-regard of the highest order serve only to promote eternal strife and division among the nations of the world. Nevertheless, Ubuntu urges every reason-endowed individual or group of individuals with any sense of values to allow even a semblance of humaneness to govern their actions toward other persons and help them to live respectable lives. For Ubuntu, the motive for any kind of action, its overall consequences, and its effects on other *muntus* (persons) determine whether such actions will be lauded or condemned, and hence, whether the agent will be respected or shunned by his society for being their architect. But as things stand in our world, lack of Ubuntu and greed for possessions, even those belonging to others, happens to be one of the major motives behind this bellicosity and the separation that obtains among peoples and nations, replacing the necessary bonds that should knit us into one peaceful family. In the prevailing atmosphere, every group that considers itself superior to the others believes that these others are dispensable elements in its existence. Each one of these groups, like many individual vaunters in them, believes that it is an island sufficient unto itself, contrary to the admonition of John Donne against that kind of selfish attitude. His words, quoted below, will ring true for ages to come in this and any possible world[6]:

> No man is an island,
> Entire of itself.
> Each is a piece of the continent,
> A part of the main.
> …
> Each man's death diminishes me,
> For I am involved in mankind.
> Therefore, send not to know
> For whom the bell tolls,
> It tolls for thee.[7]

Ubuntu recognizes interdependence among persons in all walks of life. The bell that tolls for James today will be tolling for Mike or Juliet or Sarah tomorrow, until it has tolled enough times to bid farewell to all the members of their generation. None is exempt from the destiny that faces the others, and each one needs to cultivate the necessary kinship that can make the transient stay of all persons in this world worthwhile. In this kinship, relationships assume characteristics of the all-important extended family, which functions like a spider's web. Contact with one section of the web spreads to every corner of it and summons the entire kinship to be on the alert and ready to spring into action for the good of the whole. No one is ever alone, even if one does not have an extended family; the community becomes her family and they adopt her and look after her needs. If parents have been wiped out by modern infectious epidemics like AIDS, their children are happily cared for by grannies and the community, rather than being placed in orphanages where mass caring, which is sometimes heartless, replaces the round-the-clock individual caring and attention that they can receive at home. Regrettably, such enterprises do not attract the monetary attention and support of those with the funds as much as other pursuits of lesser consequence do. One does not have to guess the difference that would result from the diversion of millions of dollars to such causes from practices like the freezing of pets after their demise, just so that people can still continue to dote on them, and from entertainment of all kinds, including the sometimes lavish prizes that go with it, as well as from other dispensable pleasures that we all enjoy and find it extremely difficult to forgo for the sake of saving lives other than our own or of our close family and friends, if not simply for these vanities of life. But who has the right to tell others how they should spend their money, or even how they should live their lives, for that matter? No one has the right to control the lives of other persons who, in turn, should not yield to degrading treatment by others and believe that they have no worth as persons, as these others would have them believe. However, in this world of haves and have-nots where the latter are kicked around because they are powerless, the best that can be done is to draw the reluctant attention of those who have everything to these problems while asking them for their help, and hope that they harbour enough benevolence to respond positively to requests for their exclusive liberal assistance in the humble efforts of concerned others to conquer these scourges of humanity.

When Ubuntu societies have been reluctantly forced to take up arms to defend their honour and their property against marauders and enslavers who came to disturb and disrupt their peaceful existence, they have been reported to have undergone, at the behest of their traditional leaders, a process of "soul cleansing" to restore peace to their troubled minds for some of the gross misdeeds that they have been forced to commit in war. But they go even further and undertake reparations to the victims of these misdeeds or make amends by rendering other kinds of service, if they do not have the means to meet that first undertaking, to convey their sincere contrition and to reconcile with the victims of their misguided violence. From this kind of behaviour they all learn the need to live in peace and harmony with other tribes and to avoid unnecessary combat when they can settle conflicts humanely through negotiation. No tribe is forced into adopting the ways of living of the other tribe; each tribe believes in living and letting live, thus avoiding friction between them, because no one wants to be the victim of greed and dispossession by others, and no one will willingly agree to live under subservience to other tribes. And so, even in matters of catering to the needs and wants of their own communities, they do not misappropriate the possessions of others by the illegitimate use of force, they bargain for them and trade what they have (which the other tribe needs) for what they need. It makes so much more sense to live this way than to live under constant threat of assault by greedy rogue states that are always looking for excuses to attack others so that they can deprive them of what they have—oil, diamonds, etc.

In our world, however, the appeal of money in all its many currencies has made such peaceful co-existence impossible among individuals and nations. People maim and murder for it as much as nations do, and, to all intents and purposes, it appears that the preaching of Ubuntu to them does not persuade them to change their covetous ways. Even some of those from whom this philosophy of Ubuntu originated are now sadly the culprits who violate it without compunction in their quest for power and riches. That is why when others want to cheat them into agreements that tie their hands to sign contracts that give them the upper hand economically and the leeway to continue to exploit them, while allowing them to amuse themselves with the toys of purported government and access to limited amounts of money for themselves only, they beat them with the stick of Ubuntu by appealing to their Ubuntu nature to escape the wrath that they should be facing for many centuries of brutal oppression and murder to which they subjected the people over whom they wielded their self-assumed, cruel, and beastly authority. They even dupe them into forgiving them for centuries of savage oppression while they still persist in the practice on the sly, but sometimes also blatantly, as when someone is thrown into a lions' den for insignificant transgressions, or beaten to death for harnessing a black mule and a white mule to pull a cart—apparently an affront to the ideology of apartheid, which advocates strict separation of "black" and "white" races, a sad reflection of the level of moral development of some specimens of humanity.

So, when the chickens came home to roost, as in such cases and others in some contemporary situations of transition where the oppressor saw the tide turning against him, appeal to the *Ubuntu* nature of those who were poised to pay him back with his own coin, invoking their humanity to save his hide, paid handsome dividends. Giving them a taste of what they have hitherto lacked in their lives by enriching them with a minute fraction of his enormous heaps of money to make them feel big and important and to alienate them from the poor masses of people that they promised to lift out of the pits of misery where they all used to wallow together but which they have now left for better quarters in which they are so comfortable and prosperous that they never bother to think of those they left behind proved to be the best sop to buy him protection from his just deserts. Suddenly, inane Ubuntu had meaning for the oppressor; equally suddenly, he realized to his chagrin that humanity will have to be shared with the underdog if he is to retain his heretofore over-inflated, but now deflated, humanity that didn't want to recognize the humanity of others as constitutive of his selfishly cherished super-humanness; suddenly, he became aware that brazen refusal to affirm their humanity and establish respectful human relations with them was no longer economically viable for him both locally and internationally; suddenly and miraculously, he was born again, if we are to defy Hume and believe in miracles by believing that he is now a new person, in spite of continuing evidence to the contrary, as in the cases quoted above and also the case of the rich forked-tongue politician who derides people who do not have the means that he and his rich audience have by claiming callously that they, forty-seven per cent (47%) of his country's population, do not pay any taxes or take responsibility for their lives—all of which is untrue—suddenly realizing that he has pulled the rug from under his own feet and somersaulting to now claim that that he was mistaken in his utterance that was a true reflection about how he felt about hose people that he despises. Some people pin the unpalatable label of "hypocrisy" on that kind of behaviour. Others pin other labels like deceitfulness, dishonesty, duplicity, all of which amount to saying that the person involved cannot be trusted to tell the truth, as I stated in *Our World and its Values*:

> people engage in diverse methods of deception by pretending to be what they are not—the hypocrites who act like saints; dissimulation by pretending not to be what they are—the empty tins that make the most noise; and disinformation—deliberate spreading of twisted and untrue information. All of these maneuvers are meant to subvert the truth and give them an unfair advantage over others. They think nothing of misrepresenting themselves, ... deliberately disseminating deceptive fabrications about them to create negative impressions that they know will not endear them to the rest.[8]

In other respects, and every so often as we have noted, we encounter situations where the lack of Ubuntu shows itself unmistakably and most regrettably when people smear others with crimes that they know they did not commit, while they have all the evidence to that effect that they are suppressing, and can even go so far as to manufacture other evidence to make their lies stick on their victim. This kind of low down behaviour is a clear sign of inhumanity on the part of the Christians that they claim to be—bearing false witness against their neighbours in blatant contravention of the ninth commandment of their faith, all in the name of seeking promotion and gaining more power and money. Ubuntu philosophy does not subscribe to that kind of morality; it believes in relationships based on truthfulness, sincerity, and helping others overcome adversity, rather than making it up for them to fall into; dealing fairly with them, instead of dealing underhandedly; using positions of power to protect others, instead of misusing power to victimize them in their helplessness and lack of power, which renders them incapable of combating the lies of their powerful framers that somehow always trump the truth of the victims. Unfortunately for the victims, lack of Ubuntu in these societies always propels these insincere liars to positions of leadership, instead of punishing them for their inhumanity. Should we conclude that might is right and nice guys always finish last in a prevailing culture of base values, dishonesty, and inhumanity where people are insensitive to the evil that they perpetrate and perpetuate on others and thereby fail to provide inspiration and respect for themselves and their public offices and positions? These same infallible and incorrigible persons will stubbornly insist that they would misbehave in the same manner if they had to do it all over again after their deliberate mistakes and failings have been exposed. They even lack the common decency to apologize to anyone for the hurt that they have caused, because they are obsessed with their false infallibility and blind ambition. They just want to climb that ladder of "success" (if we may prostitute the meaning of that word) on the shoulders and backs of everyone else, and they will not hesitate to do so as dishonestly as it is necessary for them to be on top. Ubuntu has no meaning for them, placing it before them is like the proverbial casting pearls before swine.

In conclusion, Ubuntu does not subscribe to any of the beliefs listed below, which are lifted from an article by Les Whittington in the Toronto

Star of April 22, 2012: ending national welfare advisory councils, closing national health organizations that promote the health of native people (that breed of fourth class citizens!), trimming the budgets of broadcasting corporations that freely criticize government, cutting funding for agencies that regulate food inspection and air safety (resulting in illnesses and death from food contaminants like E. coli bacteria), scrapping environmental panels, trimming the foreign aid budget, eliminating professionals and scientists most of whom protect the safety of citizens in food and product testing and environmental monitoring, making it harder for future seniors to collect pension benefits and clamping down on recipients of employment insurance to make sure they don't turn down job offers, but never cutting the padded earnings and pensions of "law makers". In addition, an Ubuntu government of the people, by the people, for the people (not the kinds of plutocracies and semi-totalitarian states that engulf us) will not embark on the wholesale axing of useful programs that were instituted by previous governments, simply because they did not subscribe to their mean-spirited ideological attitudes, since such behaviour is inconsistent with Ubuntu philosophy and praxis. Besides, governments that subscribe to Ubuntu will not dare deprive refugees of access to health care when they can't afford it and then have the audacity to fish for compliments from the citizens for saving them money with their callous action, nor will they jeopardize women's health by axing programs that advise on how their policies and regulations affect women's health while they hypocritically make the world believe that the health issues of women and children have priority status on their agenda. They will also not spend tax payers' money in legal fees shamelessly fighting, from the safe comfort of their offices, disabled veterans' opposition to unfair claw back of the pensions that they earned at great risk to their lives on the unforgiving battle fields to which they were sent by the same ungrateful bums who do not now have the decency to show appreciation for their services, while their own juicy pensions and monies that they waste on themselves and their pet projects remain untouched; nor will they deny that many of their citizens, including the same veterans, are victims of avoidable hunger or live on the streets for lack of housing in the developed, rich countries that they boast of being when they indulge in their usual vacuous self-characterization. Furthermore, they will not undertake inflexible planning to boost polluting oil mines by routing oil pipe-lines through environmentally sensitive aboriginal territory and other parts of the land, in spite of all the known perils of oil spills and other calamities that accompany pollution of people's habitats; nor will they plan for the mass incarceration of citizens whose unfortunate circumstances sometimes force them to break laws and whose social programs for keeping them out of jail they have slashed, instead of expanding them and embarking on liberal education programs to make better citizens of them, rather than the more hardened law-breakers and recidivists who come out of these jails to nothing, only to be forced right back into jail by the same conditions that sent them there in the first place.

It appears, therefore, that Ubuntu is destined to fight a never ending battle with human greed and selfishness, but in spite of the morally polluted atmosphere in which it exists, its sublimity and lustre are so highly polished that it will resist any chances of being tarnished by contact with such corrosive influences. It will still remain as the outstanding example of how decent human relations should be conducted, if humanity seriously intends to make this world a better place for all to live and die in.

Chapter 5

Agent Action Analyzed

Having defined what it means to be a person, we now have to define in broad terms what an agent is before we consider some of the implications of the concept *agency* and what it means for a person to be an agent, as opposed to the other agents referred to on page 1 above. Within this context, therefore, we will use as our working definition one that describes the agent as a person who has the power to cause events to happen and who exercises this power directly or indirectly, intentionally or fortuitously, in his ever changing social milieu. Depending on how the agent's causal power is related to it, the same caused event can be described as an action or a non-action.

Action, on the other hand, has been defined as "the bringing about of something"[1], somehow causing something to happen, and also as a "goal-directed event. . . . An event is an action if it has an object, and if its rationality depends both on that object being desirable and on the object's being sufficiently likely to be attained through the event's occurrence."[2] Other definitions refer to bodily movement as one of the essential constituents of action in conjunction with people's desires, beliefs, and goals or purposes or intentions. The first definition does not require bodily movements of persons only to be a critical component of action if something can be brought about without them; e.g., the bodily movements of animals can bring about something. In the second definition, we have to assume that the event that constitutes an action is caused only by persons with bodies, rationality, and desires, since rationality is the sole property of embodied persons; i.e., the participation of the bodies of persons in causing actions is implied. This definition, together with others that state explicitly that action is not possible without bodily movement, seems to be out of sync with the first one and with such actions as tasting, listening, smelling, and seeing, which can be accomplished without moving the body, unless we assume that the bringing about of something is the genus under which all other definitions fall as its species, as depicted in the diagram below,

$$
\begin{array}{c}
\text{action} \\
\downarrow \\
\text{bringing about something} \\
\swarrow \qquad \searrow \\
\text{rationally causing an event} \qquad \text{body movement with intention}
\end{array}
$$

from which we also conclude that we cannot count every bodily movement that brings about something as an action if intention is lacking. But even this broad definition does not encompass the passive sensing of something, which is itself a form of action or doing something, albeit passively. Of note in this regard is that we don't say smelling or hearing or seeing or tasting is happening to us as passive agents, but we state emphatically that we are smelling, hearing, seeing, or tasting something; i.e., we are doing something. Similarly, when we are meditating we do not perform any physical action, but we are still doing something. In keeping with these definitions, the central role of bodily movement in causing anything to happen outside of our bodies is rendered evident by the fact that no one of us has the ability to initiate physical motion with mental power or cause anything to happen merely by thinking about it or by desiring it. Mental acts (desiring, wishing, hoping, and fearing) that do not culminate in the relevant bodily movements are, therefore, not considered to be actions, nor are purposeless bodily motions that are not directed at the achievement of particular goals. They are only mental or physical events that fall short of being actions within the ambit of these definitions of action.

So it is pertinent to ask why wild animals engaged in their daily activities of hunting, tending to their young, running away from danger, or attacking adversaries cannot be said to perform actions; and why a series of falling dominoes that eventually trigger a light switch and thereby illuminate an arena can also not be said to perform an action. On the first definition both activities count as actions, but the second definition disqualifies them from being so designated, because they do not involve purposive bodily movements of persons, but rather reflect mere causal relations among pieces of wood that do not possess the capability to exercise intentionality; and yet one can argue that the purpose of the hunting animal is to provide food for itself and its young, and that it is also driven by purpose to protect them from the danger posed by other animals to their valued lives. We cannot justify calling this behaviour instinctive while calling the same behaviour on our part purposive or intentional when it rightly also qualifies for the same designation as animal behaviour, which we choose to call instinctive—we share the same evolutionary instincts. In the same breath, we can't justify classifying human infanticide as somehow more evolved or civilized than animal infanticide. Insects, rodents, birds, other mammals kill their young for practically the same reasons as human do, including stress among some species of squirrels in captivity, in the same way that some stressed or mentally unbalanced persons will kill their children. So, which species is engaged in action and which one is not?

In keeping with this imposition of non-purposive character to non-human activities, "act" is defined in Webster's dictionary as "the doing of a thing: deed", like the closing of a door or the deed of killing; also as "the process of doing: action", like engaging in the process of shutting doors or action associated with killing. (Act=deed=doing of a thing. Act=process of doing=action. Therefore act=action). "<u>Act</u>" is further defined as "something done voluntarily", like killing someone out of choice, although not necessarily intentionally or purposely, but rather without coercion or other conditions that would render the action involuntary as in insanity, accident, or sleep-walking. <u>Action</u>, on the other hand, is defined as "an act of the will" = a (voluntary doing of something) of the will: the (deed) of the will = (the process of doing: <u>action</u>) of the will, all of which amounts to circularity in definition. The term to be defined, viz., <u>action</u>, appears in both the definiens (defining words) and the definiendum (word to be defined). The definition also elevates "will" to the status of an entity that is as nondescript as "soul", a process known as hypostatization. From this definition, it follows that any entity that does not possess this thing called human "will" is incapable of action; e.g., animals and dominoes. At this point, we might as well be clear about the nature of the will, since it is not an existent, but has rather been defined as the "capacity for rational desire"[3] and the "capacity for rational decision-making"[4], a capacity that is lacking in animals and dominoes.

Action is further defined as "a thing done", like a killing done by an animal that is hunting for food, or a domino tipping the next one in line after the first one in the sequence has been given the initiating push by a human or other agent mentioned on page 1, causing it to trigger the rest of them to fall in succession up to the last one. The confusing outcome of these definitions is that act = doing = action = thing done + choice = overt behaviour + motive. In these definitions, the equating of act with action is a conceptual conflation of the two terms that does not advance the unraveling of the use meanings of these terms and hence their roles in defining the respective concepts that they are meant to define. On the other hand, we know that some states of mind directed intentionally at certain objects of thought and styled mental acts can exist as believing (that my soccer team will win the game, because it is better trained and more skilled and experienced than the opposing team) or desiring (it should win, simply because it is my home team and I favour it) or doubting (that it will win, because it has been on a losing streak). These states of mind are directed at a particular goal—winning in this case—without being actions in the sense of being bodily movements or processes of doing as demanded by one of the definitions of action. So, within the context of our many definitions of action, it is quite possible that mental acts *per se* do not exist, since their existence would imply the existence of an acting entity or thing called mind, which we have already concluded does not exist as an entity. In any case, it would be difficult to envisage what a mental movement would look like, without conflating the thought with the action in which it is intended to culminate. The thought of doing something can never be the same as the doing of the thing, because in all situations where the action or doing of that thing does not happen spontaneously, it must occur after the subject's deliberation has reached its endpoint in the decision as to whether or not it should be done, and that is not the action as defined above.

Goal directed actions and physical events or doings are intentionally produced, freely chosen events, rather than accidental occurrences; e.g., the raising of my arm involuntarily caused by a human agent, even though it may be an action on his part, if he moved my arm purposely to achieve something, is still not an action on my part, since I did not initiate the movement voluntarily and intentionally, as the definition demands. The definition also demands that if something other than a human agent moved my arm, both this causal agent and I did not perform an action. My arm movement becomes an action only when I raise my arm voluntarily and intentionally, for the purpose of doing something; i.e., the raising of my arm has to be unforced and solely under my direct control, and it should be done intentionally or with a purpose in mind (intention anticipates action); it should not be just "a thing done" randomly, without motivation and purpose like a quantum jump. Here we have another circularity in definition where bodily movement (bm) + motive (m) = action (x), while action (x) = bodily movement (bm)+ motive (m) for doing x (the action); i.e., (bm) + (m) = (x), and (x) = (bm) + (m); from which it follows that (bm) or (m) alone = ~(x) or non-action. Motive for action, which is here loosely used to represent intention, should not be confused with the cause of the action, since the cause precedes the motive for action in many situations; e.g., Jill's jealousy of Kate's popularity provided the motive for her despicable deed of lacing her juice with a hallucinogenic drug to cause her to behave unseemly and thus lose her esteem, rather than lace it with arsenic, which might have killed her. Her desire, and hence her subsequent motive, was to disgrace her, not kill her, and she believed that the drug would do the job that she intended and thus gratify her jealousy, which in turn was the cause of her action and without which she would not have had the desire and the motive in this instance. Since actions are the results of our prior intentions arrived at by deliberation over our desires and beliefs and not simply the direct result of merely harbouring those dormant sentiments, and since our beliefs are caused by those states of affairs that make them true (Jill believes that she will disgrace Kate if she makes it true that Kate should act like a drunk), unintentional doings that are not directed at those states of affairs but accidentally bring about desired goals are not actions in this sense; they are mere happenings whose results happen to coincide with what we would have intended to cause to happen in order to fulfill our desires in conformity with our beliefs; e.g., when Jill accidentally and unwittingly spills the drug into Kate's Juice causing Kate's unseemly behaviour that disgraces her and gratifying Jill's cherished wish before she had time to plan how she was going to do it without exposing herself.

There is, however, a sense of happening that can pass easily as, and hence imply that it is the result of agent action when it is only the mechanical effect of mechanical causes; e.g., in one scenario, the agent intentionally uses his muscular movements to flex his forearm to achieve the end that he desires, which is to wave a fly off his face; but the same muscles can be stimulated into action by a tap on his biceps tendon or the passage of an electric current through the group of muscles that he uses for flexing his forearm without his effort and regardless of the fact that he might not desire to carry out that movement. Both the casual and the keen observers of the movements alone will not be able to perceive any difference between the two movements, so that if both his movements result in him patting his face and waving off the fly, neither will be able to tell which movement was intentional and which one was the necessary result of the mechanical chain reaction that was triggered by the tap on his biceps tendon or the passage of an electric current, unless he happened to see the tapping or the application of the current, and they will label both movements as actions, as defined.

So, in all categories of action, it is difficult to prove intention when all that we can see is a happening without verbalized intent, and when intention can be dissembled by a distracting stimuli. Besides, we cannot guess at the intention of the agent if we do not know the reasons for his actions, but we can guess at what the agent hopes to achieve by his action if we know why he is undertaking it, and that will tell us his intention in acting as he is doing. When Jim says my reason for breaking down this old shed is to deprive wild animals of a place to make their home, we can guess that his intention is to keep them away from his environment for the safety of his family and his neighbours by depriving them of a place to make their home. His reason is not the cause of his action, because the cause is his fear that his family and neighbours may be harmed by the wild animals; and depriving the animals of a home does not cause him to break the shed, it only tells us the reason why he is doing it. So, while it is right to say that "the agent [Jim] performed the action *because* he had the reason"[5], viz., depriving wild animals of a place, it seems to me that it cannot be right to say that "the primary reason for an action is its cause"[6]; i.e., depriving wild animals of a place is the cause of breaking down the shed, because the reason only explains why the action was taken without explaining or being the cause, as I indicated above. It might refer to the cause, but it is not the cause.

Most of the time we think first about what we want to do, and then we act; or else we act at the same time as we are thinking about what to do. When I am thinking about buying a car, I consider its purchase and operational costs, the fluctuating cost of gasoline, the savings that I would be sacrificing in using it for commuting to my place of employment instead of using public transportation, the convenience of driving the car straight out of my garage versus walking to the train station or bus stop in inclement weather, and many other factors. At other times we act before we think or think thoroughly through, i.e., we act impulsively and then we mostly create difficulties for ourselves and for others who are affected by our actions. I might have been annoyed by fellow passengers on the train or bus on several occasions but tolerated the annoyance; but one day I might reach the end of my tether after someone has annoyed me, and then I impulsively go out to purchase a car so that I don't have to be bothered with other people and their annoying habits or actions. In this situation, this may turn out to be the correct move by a fluke, taking all of the above considerations into account; but sometimes I might discover later that I acted wrongly in light of the same considerations. In both cases, however, the cause of my action is the same, viz., annoyance with my fellow travellers, and the intention is the same as the reason for my action, viz., to rid myself of this nuisance. At no time can I bring it about that the cause should serve as the primary reason for my action, because the cause is the annoyance with other people and the reason is to rid myself of the annoyance or the cause of my distress; but I could just as well have done something different to remove the annoyance.

Similarly, reasons cannot be causes, because my reason for raising my arm, which is my wish to strike Jim, underlies my formed intention to raise my arm, which in turn causes my act of approaching him with my arms flinging. I flung my arms with the intention or objective of striking him; the result of striking him was my goal, but it was not the cause of my flinging my arms. Striking him could not be the cause of my action by any stretch of the imagination, but my desire to strike might, because of what he said about me or what he did to me. My reasons for flinging my arms are the causal explanation for my action (of flinging my arms), while the reason and goal of flinging my arms was to satisfy the desire to strike him—the desire triggered the goal. That means reasons, good or bad, are not causes; the two concepts belong to logically different categories. My desire to cause λ may be the reason for doing δ, (my desire to cause myself to strike Jim may be the reason for flinging my arms) without being the reason for the occurrence of λ (without being the reason for my striking him; the reason being that he annoyed me). In this case, δ is the cause of λ, but the reason for the occurrence of λ is β (my annoyance is the cause of flinging my arms and striking him, but the reason for my striking him is to satisfy my desire to be even with him).

In a different scenario, I could be trying to swat a pesky fly when Jim unwittingly walks into the path of my swinging arm and suffers a strike. In this case I am the agent who carried out the intentional action of swatting the fly, and also the unintentional proximate cause of his ordeal, but the ultimate cause was the pesky fly that kept sitting on my nose and at which my action was intentionally but unsuccessfully directed: "a man is the agent of an act if what he does can be described under an aspect that makes it intentional"[7]. In this case, I did not strike him intentionally, but mistakenly; but that does not nullify what I did as my action and me as the responsible agent or doer of the deed, although I can argue that my responsibility for the action does not entail my culpability in its outcome, because it lacks the element of choice and intent. The question of culpability may arise when we consider that the agent did not take enough care to ensure that his action does not produce unintended effects. In this particular case, that consists of misjudging my unintended victim's proximity or swatting without first looking to see who is nearby. Similar argument applies when I set up apparatus so that touching one end of the set up produces a domino effect that results in positive or negative effects on someone else. I cannot possibly deny responsibility for the ultimate effect of the ensuing series of events, provided that no other agent endowed with the free choice that I also claim to have has intervened in the series of mechanical events that followed my triggering action. To deny responsibility for the ultimate happening as not being the equivalent of an action that I brought about seems to imply that the intervening series of events were individually or severally responsible for causing the ultimate happening on their own, independently of my triggering action as the ultimate cause, and it will not wash.

Nevertheless, people often blur the line of demarcation between the sequelae of an action and the action itself to shift responsibility for their actions on to other persons in an effort to escape blame, in contrast to others in charge who recognize the continuity of this line of action and admit that the buck ends with them as the stewards who must assume ultimate responsibility for directing the actions of their underlings. In any world, ours included, responsibility for actions rests with their architects and directors as the ones who actually chose to initiate the deeds for which others are taking undeserved blame, but very often, the "stewards" are too much of cowards to own up to their responsibilities. We can thus understand why some people rightly blame the persons who pull the triggers for causing the gunshot carnage that is plaguing our societies, arguing that "guns don't kill people; people kill people", but then turning around and fighting to keep those same guns in loosely regulated circulation where killers can easily lay their hands on them so that they can kill other people — strange logic. This is the same logic that says children can play with toy guns because violence is an innate propensity that they act out in play, instead of sparing no effort to suppress this particular aspect of violence that they encourage with their movies that depict violence, and with their endless production of assault weapons. When children live with these negative influences on their lives they learn to adopt them as their own way of life. What is so difficult in exposing them to the positive things in life? Is it the difference in the amount of money that the unsavoury pursuits can generate?

In a different scenario where actions end in unintended consequences, raising doubts, not about my responsibility for them as the initiator of the movement that brought them about but about my culpability in the end result of my initiating action, the question arises whether doing something and having something(s) else follow from it may be a part of the act or a consequence of the act without being the whole act. In such situations the line of demarcation between events that are the consequences of an act and those that are a part of the act is often difficult to draw, and its position depends mainly on the circumstances surrounding the action. I may be responsible for the action that brought about the event of crashing the car that I am driving without being responsible for the event, because in the first scenario I was driving the car and I did the crashing, while in the second scenario I was driving the car, but someone else crashed into me or cut me off and forced me to steer into a ditch, causing the crash. In both scenarios, I am identified as the one who crashed the car in a strictly descriptive way of a car crashing with this driver in it, but not in the ascriptive way of the agent who crashed it, without the implication of moral blame in the occurrence of the crash by acting in certain unacceptable ways. What is lacking from these actions is the intent to crash the car, or the carelessness with which I might have been driving it, both of which would immediately render my action culpable. I smashed the car = fact, only because I and no one else was driving it at the time. I am responsible for smashing it = arguable fact, because the event occurred while I was driving it and I may be construed to be the indirect cause of the crash; but the car was hit by another car driven by another driver or it was swept off the road by a minor tornado, causing me to lose control of it and allow it to crash, so I can disclaim responsibility for the crash. I am culpable for smashing it = not fact, because I was driving carefully, but third parties intervened: someone else drove into me, or a minor tornado swept the car off the road. I did not cause the crash (willfully or otherwise), although I was driving the car at the time that the crash occurred; I wasn't the active agent in the event of the crashing of the car. Thus, responsibility and culpability for, and exculpation from culpability for this and other actions can be justified by a variety of circumstances, including duress, intention, or accident, instead of being attributed to the incidental juxtaposition of two or more processes, events, or objects like car and driver.

An agent who is trying to demonstrate the formation of ripples in a pond may succeed in achieving his goals, or his hoped for success may be thwarted by extraneous physical impediments and restraints or by the intervention of unintended events like being pushed, so that the stone that he was going to toss into the pond ends up in the face of one of his spectators; or internal restrictions like a sudden seizure may misdirect his aim and produce the same end result, i.e., injury of a spectator. Still, these outcomes are attributable to him as the originator of the action that brought them about. But is he culpable after these events have derailed and distorted his intended actions? In other situations, an action might produce the best possible results that the agent intends, but then go on to produce other unintended results; e.g., a bullet that ricochets from its practice target to cause unintended damage to a passing automobile. This is the kind of action that does not stop with the agent's goals, but extends to the unintended consequences of the achievement of those goals, and the agent as the only one whose action caused that state of affairs must rightly bear responsibility for it. If that is not the case, the consequences of any action cannot be rightly attributed to the agent who brought it about, even if indirectly so, because they formed no part of his intended and "willed" goals. But is he culpable? Similarly, if the agent committed a mistake in the execution of a task, like pouring oil into the gasoline tank of a small engine, the unintended action for which he is responsible does not render him culpable, since it was not his intended and willed goal.

This brings us to the case of the challenging and debatable aspect of culpability presented by the moral significance of seriously adverse, unintended, unavoidable, and unwilled but foreseen bad effects supervening on the good effects that an agent genuinely intends in specific situations where his actions neither violate accepted moral practices and the rights and autonomy of other persons nor use other persons as means to his and other people's ends. This dilemma is subsumed under the Doctrine of

Double Effect, which appears to essentially exempt him from culpability for deliberately allowing inevitable and foreseen harm to happen as a consequence of the well-meaning actions that he undertook. Hence it is that palliative treatment with known lethal effects can be administered to a terminally ill patient to allay her suffering, as long as it is done cautiously, judiciously, and solely for the purpose stated, and not as a disguised means of terminating her life. If the patient dies in the process, no blame attaches to the agent who performed the action strictly under those circumstances and not with the intention of easing the patient out of her suffering by killing her, regardless of the fact that the same end result is precipitated in both cases. I will not discuss the issue further, as I have already dealt with it and the related problem of acts and omissions in chapters 19 and 20 of *Philosophy for Medical Students and Practitioners*. This is probably the gravest and most extreme example of exculpation of the agent from actions for which he is responsible for performing by choice — a kind of Hobson's choice. Of course, even without the protection offered by this doctrine, one can always argue that most of the time we do not know which one of the possible actions that we can take in any situation will produce the best or the worst results in spite of our best calculations to avoid accidents that will mar our good intentions. Sometimes, also, even after we have chosen what we think is the best of all the possible actions that we can take in the circumstances, "chaos effect" where we can never know all the initial conditions of a complex system like the human mind in sufficient detail and can therefore not predict its behaviour, which may surprise us. or error creeps in unbeknownst to us, and catastrophe befalls our best laid plans. Such are the accidents that regrettably befell two recent flights into space and back from there even after the careful training of their crews and the meticulous planning that went into the preparation for those flights to ensure that nothing went wrong and that only the best possible results would follow from them; nothing else could have been done, if the planners had so chosen, that would have produced better results, barring the unforeseen.

So, in answer to the question of culpability, let us agree that if I chose (freely) to do x, I am responsible for x. The act may be described as simply the doing of x (killing), or we may choose to attach a value tag to it, extending my responsibility to culpability and converting the x (killing) into a case of x_1 (murder), depending on the presence of intent and discoverable motives on my part, or on motives imputed to me by mischievous others with an agenda or an axe to grind, e.g., anti-abortionists who call the simple killing of fetuses in utero murder with all the connotations that are involved in the use of that word; viz., culpability, liability to punishment, which can result in cold-blooded execution in their kangaroo courts, or a jail sentence in the civic courts of some states. Choice plays a crucial role in determining whether an agent's action as described will be classified as involuntary and unintentional and therefore exculpable, or voluntary and intentional and therefore culpable. Since choice is governed by reason without which it is irrational and self-defeating, those who do not have the capacity to exercise choice, as we have already noted, cannot bear culpability; and so, other than those who perform acts unintentionally, under duress, or accidentally, some of the only exculpable persons are those who are cognitively challenged and unwittingly choose to undertake actions whose telling effects they do not always have the intellectual ability to anticipate or even recognize. However much they may be the responsible agents for the performance of those actions, they still escape culpability for them by virtue of their limited understanding of the import of their actions. And that is why even in legal circles, we do not punish such persons (and others mentioned above) for actions that merit retribution when they are done by "normal" persons who are supposed to know what they are doing at all times. We cannot claim that these people always know what they are doing. We therefore take into consideration the fact that even though we operate with the general principle of "ought implies can", in this case the "can" part of this implication relationship has been disabled by the person's incompetent state of mind, which is not of his own doing and cannot, therefore, qualify her as freely capable of the intention and choice that would render her behaviour culpable, reckless, negligent, or unethical, if not immoral; and so the "ought" ceases to have legitimate application in this case. A person who cannot do what capable people can do ought not to be judged by the same standards as the others, since it would be unfair to expect him to do what is beyond her capabilities.

In the opening paragraph of this chapter I tried to reconcile two definitions of action that, if taken on par, would have left us with a situation where the same occurrence could be defined as an intentional action under one description and a mere bringing about of something or an unintentional occurrence under another description. For instance, one can suffer a muscular twitch that produces a movement exactly like nodding to acquiesce in a request by someone else for permission to perform an unpalatable act that can be approved with an intentional nod; e.g., torture a prisoner. In this instance the bodily movement lacks the necessary accompaniment of one's intention to make it one's action, even though it has been interpreted as such by those who witnessed only the movement without possessing the equally necessary but elusive insight into his thought processes to realize that the bodily movement was an involuntary twitch and not a voluntary nod. Hence, as far as we are able to, we should always distinguish between x as an action that I do intentionally and x as a mere happening. In the former instance, we are urged to believe that the will moved the muscles to produce the intended effect of nodding, and that without the intervention of the will the nod would have occurred unintentionally and purposelessly or randomly without producing an action. We are not told, though, how the will descends from its ethereal domain to enter the material domain of the body to be able to effect this amazing feat without ever missing its target and triggering an unintended action, or how the spectator can differentiate between the two movements, the action and the non-action. In other situations, however, failure of the agent to act decisively, like taking control of a rowdy class of school boys, could be blamed on his weak will in the metaphorical sense, just as successful execution of the same difficult task could be attributed to the strong will of another agent in exactly the same circumstances without postulating the spectre of an objective entity styled "the will".

It seems that if we postulate a role for the $will_1$ to set the process in motion, we also have to postulate another $will_2$ that will initiate or trigger the action of the $will_1$ to get things going, and another $will_3$ that will trigger $will_2$, and another $will_4$ that will trigger $will_3$, and so on retrogressively, *ad infinitum*. But that is something we do not want to do, because then we would never get started with our intended action. We would always be on the verge of acting as one will triggers the next will, starting all the way back from infinity, if that is even possible. Besides, if we can describe human action adequately without introducing the superfluous element of a will into the description, why do we need to postulate many more entities than we need to explain an already complex and incompletely understood process that involves selective nerves that supply and activate the parts of the body that are involved in producing a particular action, i.e., the muscles, tendons, and joints, and quite often the cerebral functions of discretion that accompany this process? William of Ockham[8] would dissuade us from this venture with his principle of parsimony—not to increase unnecessarily the number of entities required to explain anything. So we must dispense with the will and any role for it in action, unless we also want to face the dilemma of generating the problem of having to explain how mind moves matter[9] and how the ontological gap between these two distinct logical categories is spanned, since one cannot be functionally substituted for the other (see page 20). In response to the idea that there are no uncaused actions under the above definition of "action", and in an effort to avoid the infinite regress already mentioned, Danto argues that we perform what he calls "basic actions" non-causally, i.e., to perform action φ one does not first have to do δ, one can do φ directly; otherwise if every action becomes the result of a preceding causal event such as another action or "will", we will end up with the same kind of infinite regress of causes of events that are the effects of preceding causes, which in turn are the effects of preceding causes, that happen to be the effects of preceding causes, all leading up to the present effects that result from the wills that caused them from all the way back to infinity where the series of causes and effects originated (originated? Does infinity have a point of origin?). The series is illustrated as follows:

$cause_1 \rightarrow effect_1 = cause_2 \rightarrow effect_2 = cause_3 \rightarrow effect_3 = cause_4, \rightarrow effect_4$, etc.

As Danto says, "Moving an arm is not then the result of an act of will; it *is* an act of will."[10]

We have said that desires do not imply motives, but a muscular movement that results in a desired bodily event becomes an action when a motive is added to it so that it promotes the formulation of an intention to do something; e.g., waving arms after a certain pattern is basically only a bodily movement, but it may be interpreted as any one of the following: beckoning, dismissing, or saluting, all of which are actions with intended results that were motivated by certain desires. Motive, as we have already determined, explains non-causally how the action came about or why it was undertaken; it is not the cause of the action, although it may reflect on the desire and reasons for undertaking the action. In some situations, however, motive is neither a necessary nor a sufficient condition for action — some actions happen without a motive on the part of the agent, as long as the intention to carry them out existed in her mind. I may engage in the intentional action of slipping on my moccasins without any motive, but simply because that is what I do every morning when I go out into the yard. In other situations I may do x intentionally, or I may do y in its place with the intention of achieving x, because y is easily achievable and y happens to be a reasonable or equivalent substitute for x, which is not as easily achievable in the circumstances; e.g., I may catch a plane in Toronto with the intention of flying to Miami (x), or I may drive to Buffalo to fly from there (y) with the same intention (x), because the fares are cheaper from there and driving to and flying from Buffalo is a reasonable and equivalent substitute for flying from Toronto (x), which I cannot afford quite as easily, since the latter costs thrice as much as the former, even with the cost of driving included. In the end, I achieve what I intentionally set out to achieve by doing any one of x or y, except that I save a lot of money by choosing to do y.

We have also seen that not all intending materializes in action, since unintended actions occur all the time, and that intention can also characterize my state of mind (intending to do x) or my action (doing x intentionally), even though it is difficult to tell how that state of mind is related to intentional action, because not all intentional action is the execution of a prior intention; we often perform intentional actions spontaneously by what John Searle calls intention-in-action without having formed a prior intention to perform them; e.g., intentionally breaking a sudden fall, in the absence of a prior intention, by stretching out our arms with the immediate intention of preventing injury to the rest of the body. On the other hand, we also perform (or fail to perform) actions for which we had prior intentions and for which we succeeded (or failed) to carry out the necessary intentions-in-action. Jill may sincerely form the intention to raise her arm, because she desires to do so and has good reason to believe that she can do so after she confidently predicted that she could do so by assessing her physical situation and seeing that it would be possible for her to do so, and she may succeed in doing so. On the other hand she may fail to do so because of restricting or disabling circumstances of which she was not aware, i.e., her arm is tied down or it has suddenly become paralyzed and she cannot move it. From this experience she learns that intention is not equivalent to prediction. On the obverse side of this relationship between intention and prediction, Jim predicts that he will go to town tomorrow at Bob's request without having the prior intention of doing so; but knowing how successfully Bob can twist arms, he feels certain that he will yield to Bob's pressure to go to town with him unintentionally, but of his own free choice. His acquiescence in Bob's request and entreaty does not in any way undermine his freedom of choice, because he can still choose, for given reasons, to emphatically say no to Bob and not go to town with him, even if Bob stands on his head to try to convince him to go with him.

For Searle, "a successfully performed intentional action" is one that consists of "an intention-in-action, and, typically, a bodily movement."[11] Jim's raising his arm in action (to strike Bob) qualifies as intention-in-action. The intention-in-action is caused and satisfied by the going up of the arm to achieve his objective, the object being to strike Bob. But he cannot strike Bob unless he creates a situation in the world that will conform to his intention, i.e., he must raise his arm. If he cannot raise his arm, then he cannot create the situation in the world that will enable him to achieve his objective of striking Bob. The satisfaction of Jim's intention therefore depends on the world conforming to the way it is represented by his intention, which is the way his intention causes it to be. He summarizes the sequence of events that attends most of our actions as follows: "deliberation on beliefs and desires→ prior intention→ intention-in-action→ bodily movement (action = intention-in-action+bodily movement)."[12] So far, there seems to be general agreement among discussants of the nature of agent action that bodily movements constitute actions only if they are accompanied by prior intentions or intentions-in-action. Stuart Hampshire expresses this aptly when he says, "At any moment of my waking life, there are always things that I intend to do in the future and there are always things that I am doing with intention at that moment."[13]

When lawyers attach responsibility and blame for actions, they do not consider the physical action (*actus reus*) alone; they also take into account its mental component (*mens rea*), which consists of the subject's motives and intentions in executing the action. Such motives are generally born of desires seeking gratification through actions intended to achieve those ends, and from this relationship it is patently evident that intentions are not motives for action, although they may emanate from desires to have certain states of affairs prevail. A robber's intention to break into a store is motivated by his desire to take off with money, his desire being to have enough cash to support his life-style, whatever its nature, or a to have a few items of jewelry or other goods to pawn so that he can have enough cash for the same purpose. But such mental components and processes can be known to observers only if he expresses them in words; otherwise any conclusion on their part to his intentions from his actions is mere guesswork. Nevertheless, observers still claim that when they have to deal with emotions, they can deduce them from their observable and recognizable concomitants, which constitute the overt behaviour of the subject, although that does not guarantee them the ability to deduce intentions from actions. What they probably mean is that they can inductively conclude from several past observations of what is now common knowledge to them that certain physical components of behaviour in certain situations are constantly associated with particular expressions of emotion to what they do not know and can never be certain of or have any assurances of, that this causal relationship will always hold in future observations of different subjects with different temperaments in similar circumstances. They also claim that motive = explanation; but we believe that the explanation of what happens in and during an action need not include the motive for the action, e.g., no motive is implied in the explanation that the cause of the quarrel between Jim and Bob is that Jim annoyed Bob by stepping on his toe and not apologizing for his action, thus unleashing a quarrel. On the other hand, the motive for the action can often provide an explanation for it where the reason for the action is not apparent. If we are wondering why Bob is quarrelling with Jim, we can understand the situation if we know that Jim intentionally caused the quarrel by stepping on Bob's toe to settle an old grudge; his motive (to settle an old grudge) explains his action, although it is not the explanation of the action *per se,* viz., to annoy or injure Bob with a view to settling an old grudge.

On this question of motive and intent, we note also that the relationship between intention and act is further evidenced by the fact that intention (*mens rea*) by itself does not constitute a crime, nor does the act (*actus reus*) without the intent, because one can think of committing a crime without actually going on to do so, and no one should be punished for merely entertaining any kind of thoughts, as the Orwellian Thought Police would do, in as much as no one should bear blame for not doing anything where something could be done to remedy a situation, unless the inactive person has voluntarily or otherwise assumed prior responsibility for the performance of corrective action in such situations or for the welfare of the affected person(s). According to the related principle of acts and omissions, one who chooses inactivity in a situation where he could have acted and prevented dire consequences is as morally culpable as he who acted and produced the same dire consequences. Besides, as we observed before, who can prove *mens rea* or what thoughts anyone is entertaining unless the subject is willing to vocalize them? Not even the charlatan mind readers and psychics who claim to have the power to fathom the thoughts of other persons through extrasensory perception and mental telepathy can honestly lay claim to that capability. There are no ways of divining people's thoughts, not with the use of truth serum with its dubious reputation of extracting information from subjects who will not part with it voluntarily nor with brain scans that can figure out the words that a person is thinking about from the nature of her brain waves. Even the sadistic practice of waterboarding has failed to read the mind of an "enemy combatant" who will not talk.

Finally, an interesting question is whether actions can be carried out in words as much as they can be in physical activity? I can holler in a room of sleeping cadets to get them to jump out of bed, and I can whistle to get my dog to come to me and avoid being run over by a car. In both situations I am doing something with the intention or for the purpose of achieving something else, instead of dragging the cadets out of their beds or grabbing my dog to qualify my act of hollering or whistling for the honour of being called an action. John. L. Austin has described "performative utterances" in which by sincerely uttering certain words in the appropriate context, one can also be said to be doing something, and one of the examples he gives is that of naming a ship: "suppose that I have a bottle of champagne in my hand and say 'I name this ship Queen Elizabeth'. . . . in saying what I do, I actually perform that action . . . I do not describe the christening ceremony, I actually perform the christening."[14] The words do not only describe the agent's verbal performance, nor are they a report of some internal spiritual act that he is performing; but they are the act of naming; i.e., they are utterance and performance all in one, or one action with two inseparable interpretations, just as looking at an object is also seeing the object. One does not first look at an object and then see it after looking at it; one sees it as soon as one looks at it. One can, of course, call a heap of sand many things: one heap of grains of sand, or millions of specific grains of sand, or billions of non-specific atoms of sand, or trillions of non-specific protons and neutrons, all the way down to trillions of non-specific quarks and beyond, if that is possible, depending on the pragmatic interest that one has in it, much as the planet Venus is both the morning star and the evening star, depending on when it is seen in the sky — in the morning or in the evening; but such a dichotomy does not apply to the case of looking and seeing; one sees as soon as one looks in the same way as one hears as soon as one hears or tastes as soon as one tastes. Seeing does not have to be a procedurally different process from tasting, smelling, feeling, and hearing or even apprehending for that matter; all of them are instantaneous processes. Beyond the act of verbalization, the agent can complete the ceremonious action of naming by smashing (not hurling) a bottle of champagne on the ship as he says these words, as long as he is the rightfully designated person to perform this ceremony. But to smash the bottle against the ship without the proper authority or accidentally and without uttering the ceremonious words does not constitute the authentic naming of the ship, because the actions are not part of the authentically constituted ceremony of naming a ship. Also, to report on what someone else said in carrying out a performative utterance is not to carry out one, because these utterances can be valid only if executed in the first person, "I ... " When I say "I apologize", I have completed the act of apologizing; nothing more is required of me by way of other physical action than that confined to my utterance of these words. But saying "he apologizes" or he said, "I apologize" is not making a performative utterance; it is simply talking or reporting what he said without executing the performative utterance for him. Performative utterance is constituted by doing one thing (naming, apologizing, etc.) by doing something else (uttering the appropriate words in the appropriate circumstances). The same conditions apply, *mutatis mutandis*, to statements like "I promise", "I declare", etc. Absence of authority, proper procedure, and sincere intention in all these performatives renders them void or invalid rather than untrue or false.

Many actions are carried out only in words uttered and recorded, such as when states declare war against other states, or when oppressive statutes and verbally proclaimed practices are enacted that physically confine certain sections of the community to specified areas (reserves, locations, and ghettos) without anyone actually carrying these people and locking them in those confined areas, but simply by denying them ownership of land and dwellings or rental privileges in areas that have been set aside for preferred groups. These verbal acts have been executed via state laws like the infamous "Group Areas Act No. 41 of 1950" (South Africa) by which racially segregated areas were created outside of which original owners of the country could travel only if they has a "pass", and occupying land in an area designated "white" was a punishable criminal offence. The same law obtained in Canada "put in place in 1885 to control the movements of First Nation people, and enforced until the 1940s."[15] The spirit of that law and the discriminatory treatment of aboriginal peoples are still evident in "first world" states that hypocritically criticize the human rights practices of other states. These are all verbal acts that are equivalent to any physically restrictive actions to which people might have been subjected at the expense of their welfare without reasonable justification, barring crass inhumanity.

The field of action is vast and controversial, because human beings (persons) are active every waking moment of their lives. They are always engaged in doing something, proper or improper, beneficial or hurtful, intentional or unintentional. But we must now move on to consider other aspects of human agency.

Chapter 6

Is Agent Action Free or Determined?

As we have seen, action occurs when the agent uses his power to cause the occurrence of an event by purposeful choices; but when the event happens without agent choice, accidentally, or as a result of misapprehension, carelessness, or miscalculation, the agent is no longer considered to have instituted an action, although he has caused the occurrence of the event by virtue of his doing, which lacked the appropriate purpose or intention. On the other hand, in the situation where he performs the same action that he would otherwise have freely intended and executed, but under duress, his action cannot be categorized as intentional, purposeful, or deliberate from his point of view. The person who is coercing him to perform that action and using him as his tool might thus categorize it, and some others might argue that even under duress he still has the option to refuse to comply and face the consequences of his refusal. But that is to give him only a theoretical choice, because the consequences of not complying might be lethal and not worth the risk, besides the fact that such a choice could also be irrational or irresponsible, and likely to cause more overall trouble than it can resolve. Such is the case when someone is tortured to extract information out of him and he reacts by providing misleading information, implicating innocent persons, while the sadistic fools who condone this inhumane act boast about their erratic methods of acquiring information that cannot be trusted; but they still swear by it and act on it, or so the bluffers say. Such a person does not have the liberty to choose to act otherwise than he is acting. Only compliance is demanded of him, and that is why he complies by providing erroneous information for the sake of gratifying his torturers and escaping the hell to which they are subjecting him. His action, though, is still purposeful, deliberate, and intentional — to mislead.

Purposeful human agent acting is thus always intentional (directed at the goal that persons aim to achieve) and accompanied or preceded by careful thinking and well calculated but sometimes hasty deliberation. It does not, as a rule, occur unintentionally, instinctively, or spontaneously. But when we are confronted with what appears to be purposeful action on the part of animals that are presumed to be devoid of minds, and hence the power of thought, we are at a loss to answer such questions as "why did the chicken cross the road?" Did it do so because the road happened to be there and invited crossing, or was it intending to achieve a goal? Did it have a purpose, i.e., to get to the other side and join its family? If it had a purpose in crossing the road, then it is an active agent by our definition of agency, despite our reticence to credit it with a mind and the capacity to act by choice. Perhaps if it could communicate with us in a language that we understood, we would know whether or not it entertained the intention to act in a certain way, rather than in another; e.g., going in the opposite direction and breaking ranks with the group. The possession of such a faculty would settle it with responsibility for its actions, which is consistent with what we see happening (an oncoming car runs over it), and which we feel compelled, but are resisting, to call agency. To all intents and purposes, what we see looks like the result of the chicken deliberating and deciding to follow the herd rather than drift away from it and suffering exposure to attack by other animals.

Anyone who has ever observed squirrels reacting to the sound of an approaching motor vehicle cannot but be impressed with how they stop to listen intently to localize the source of the sound, and then "decide" to run off to safety in a direction opposite to the source of the sound. We call it instinct, the instinct of survival that accrues to these creatures of necessity, but we don't call similar behaviour on our part instinct; we call it choice or intentional behaviour, because it is based on knowledge of what we are doing — a capacity that we deny the squirrel and the chicken, presumably because they don't know what they are doing since they lack the faculty of knowledge. We say their "choices" are not genuine intentional choices but pseudo-choices that are mere expressions of instinctual behaviour. Regrettably, when we examine the brains of these animals we do not garner any information about their function, although we can dissect their form to the finest levels of the electron microscope; but nothing tells us that they don't have intentions or that they don't make decisions to act in one way or another as we do — not that we can see evidence of our capacity to make choices from the ultra-structure of our brains either. Since we do not have any evidence to the contrary, the best credit that we choose to give to these creatures is that they are naturally pre-determined to seek the company of other chickens, in one case, and to run instinctively to safety, in the other case, without justifying our position convincingly, seeing that we also make the same choices most, if not all, of the time. In our lopsidedly anthropocentric stance, we base our thinking about these matters on the human reaction to events in our environment; but in their situations and in bird and squirrel languages, or whatever we want to call their means of communication (which we can't deny), their responses to situations in their world will probably prove to be their intentional actions, similar to those of human animals in their own situations. To drive this point home, Hampshire states that "it might seem that the intention behind the activity is being stated. But the more intellectual word 'intention', since it is associated with the possibility of a declaration of intention, is out of place in the context of animal behaviour; the word 'purpose' certainly is not out of place."[1] But purpose =goal=aim=intention. So what's the difference?

From the preceding discussion, it is evident that we ordinarily believe that the actions of an agent are not determined in the sense of being set to follow a particular course from which they are destined never to deviate and must, therefore, be automatic to the end. We believe with good reason that she is autonomous and free to act otherwise than as she is actually doing when circumstances permit her to do so; she did not of necessity have to act the way she did, and this makes her action voluntary as opposed to being coerced. We believe that she has the ability to choose how she will act as a free agent who is therefore morally and legally responsible for her actions, with the occasional exceptions that are necessitated by precluding factors in herself (cognitive incompetence, mental ineptitude, ignorance of facts, absence of mind) or her environment (duress, physical restraint, dire threat to her life). So, when we claim free choice for the agent in the same circumstances surrounding her action, with the many positive and negative factors that entered into the formulation of her intentions and the making of her decisions at that time, including all the available, incomplete knowledge of prevailing facts and conditions, i.e., logical and epistemic possibilities, we mistakenly assume that she had the liberty to transcend her circumstances to make a choice that is not determined by them. But that in no way suggests that if she could not do otherwise, she is condemned to a determined life, since we know that our behaviour and ordinary relations do not hinge on the truth or falsity of determinism; we live our daily lives perfectly well without even thinking about its alleged pivotal role in them, unless we happen to be engaged in philosophical rumination. It seems, therefore, that those who maintain that we are a race of automatons who cannot act freely in the face of the determinism that prevails in nature are barking up the wrong tree, because most of the time we do act freely, except in the special circumstances referred to above; but those circumstances do not define our freedom, only the exceptions to it, and exceptions are not the gist of definition.

We realize, however, that the mechanics of human physical action are amenable to the mechanistic principles of Physics, which in turn are consistent with natural laws that dictate the necessary succession of physical events according to established mechanistic principles: if x occurs under specified conditions, then y will inevitably and invariably occur under the same conditions: the same input into different organisms with the same organizational state undergoes the same processing, producing the same output or result; e.g., a tap on the biceps tendon of any living human being with uninterrupted neuromuscular connections will cause contraction of her biceps muscles and resultant flexion of her arm. Nowhere in this scenario is there room for choice or variation, except when "chaos" supervenes to alter the course of events, also mechanically, thus defeating our efforts and limited ability to make precise and water tight predictions about subsequent states of the universe from our knowledge of its preceding states. But the human mind has the ability to break this mechanistic chain and impose the element of choice on it, thereby altering the course of events to suit the agent's purposes.

Every agent is a being in time; when she acts voluntarily, i.e., by choice and without coercion, she does what she wants, freely but not randomly, although she might sometimes not be aware of what it is she will do until just before she does it. Certain specific conditions, past and present, of which she may or may not be fully cognizant or have any control, and certain of her projections for the future influence and constrain her deliberation, choice, and action. If that were not the case, her course of action would always be predetermined for her to follow and deliberation about the propriety and possible effects of her actions would lose its purpose and become a pointless pursuit for her, as I indicated above and also argued in *Mind Your Ps and Qs*:

> Nellie, "Whether on this occasion or on a prior occasion, you must have made a conscious decision to have the crackers, and not the sweets, after you deliberated on the merits and demerits of eating each snack. You had to have exercised your choice only after deliberating; you cannot claim, as you are trying to do, to have been predetermined to choose the crackers without having to stop to deliberate first before you made your choice. If that is the case, you have no reason to deliberate when your course of action has already been determined; your deliberation becomes a sham. When you make a decision you are exercising your freedom to act one way or the other, not to follow a predetermined course of action from which you cannot deviate. . . ."
>
> Jacob, "I agree that it would be unsettling; but I still believe that everything that happens is caused and determined by something else that happened earlier, including what you call your freedom to choose. What you call my freedom to choose cheese is not a choice but the only possible course of action in my circumstances, taking into account the nutritious value of cheese and other non-apparent reasons. The fact that I am not able to find all the causes of my action does not mean that they are not there to influence my choice. My freedom to choose is not the real cause of my action. There has to be something else with more appeal than all other considerations causing me to choose cheese at this particular time. That non-apparent something, with all its antecedents, is the determining factor for my choice."[2]

By and large, every agent is able to choose freely how she will act. But this capacity to choose her actions freely has nothing to do with what has been dubbed her will that is free, nor does it entail that this will is something, a necessary and sufficient instrument that the agent uses to translate her intentions into action. All the evidence points to the fact that limiting factors consisting of her internal capacity, including the pivotal contribution of her genetic make-up, and the external circumstances surrounding her, are what confer on her the defined ability to act and achieve realization for the characterizing wishes and desires that prompt her actions. Hence when she says, "I willed my hand to go up", she does not mean any more than, "I raised my hand"; she means that she made a conscious effort to raise it by her own reasoned choice, and, in the absence of all sorts of impediments, she succeeded in that effort without invoking the use of a mysterious instrument named the will. Such free and undetermined or contingent action is still compatible with its being causally necessary, though, since all events are caused, and the cause can be the agent *per se* at her discretion, or other factors over which she has no control but which determine how subsequent events will unfold around her. Thus determinism of the causal variety is logically consistent with freedom and the causally determined agent can still act freely, as long as her action is free of duress and has its origins in her personal desires to which it can be attributed. Therefore the agent's action does not necessarily have to conform to a rigidly determined pattern from which there can be no deviation, otherwise life would be really insipid and pointless, since our every intention and action would be ruefully determined and predictable, thereby rendering otiose even our systems of justice that depend on the agent's free choice of his actions.

Nevertheless, there are those who still insist that determinism has a decisive role in human action, attributing their position to the undeniable influence of the genetic constitution of persons on their natures and, therefore, their actions. If Jim happens to be the driver of the engine involved in the fatal crash mentioned on pages 40- 41 in which he was faced with Hobson's choice, we will be reluctant to castigate him and hold him culpable for not exercising his power to choose to avert the accident, since he did not really have a choice. On the other hand, if we know that he caused the accident in a state of inebriation, disregarding warning signs that prohibited him from moving on until the tracks had been cleared, we will feel justified to castigate him for his irresponsibility; but he might say that his genetic constitution is the one that predisposes him to drunkenness, and it is to blame for his deeds, not him. He is the victim of his circumstances, and true to situation ethics, which is sensitive to the uniqueness of every case to which moral judgment is applied, permitting the end to justify the means, he should be judged in that context, rather than on the basis of universally prescribed ethical rules and moral standards that by their nature cannot apply equally precisely to specific cases, being relevant in some but irrelevant in others. So in the circumstances that prevailed, that was the only possible route of action open to him; i.e., he was predetermined to act as he did by antecedent [other] events—notably his genes, over which he and subsequent events had no control; he could not have chosen to act otherwise, because he did not have that liberty; his genes constrained his action in the same way that a man with a gun pointed to his head has no choice but to do as he is told, unless he does not value his life. He is not given a choice to act one way or another, and the mysterious pilot of his actions styled "the will" is totally irrelevant in these circumstances, regardless of its presumed causal role in agent action; it had no part in the luck of the draw that shaped his life.

As to the origin of acts of willing *de novo* that drive the actions of agents other than our gene-controlled man, Abraham Melden[3] observed that if acts of willing can arise in that manner, then the raising of arms and other actions can also arise *de novo*. Besides, as already indicated, acts of willing, otherwise defined as volitions or as mental states of being favourably disposed to certain actions, do not have discernible features that help to distinguish one act from another and thereby also help to relate them to the different actions that they cause. In addition, how many wills will one have to possess to be able to direct each one consistently at every action that one undertakes with every part of the body and every single element of that part that is involved in performing any action whatsoever: all the neurons, chemical transmitters, muscle fibres, bones, and joints? And how will one know which specific will to trigger, if one cannot even delineate the true nature of the will in general? What distinguishing features should one look for to be able to recognize any will, and to tell one will from another? "Will" λ for moving muscle φ in my hand, "will" γ for moving muscle β in the same hand, and "will" Ω for moving muscle δ in the same hand, and so on up to will Σ for coordinating all the wills and movements that are needed to make a fist, in addition to the wills directed to the other bodily elements mentioned above. Similarly, how is one to know that volition v_1 causes action a_1, volition v_2 causes action a_2 regularly and not randomly, with volition v_1 sometimes unexpectedly causing actions a_2, a_3, a_4, etc. Again, willing cannot be random; it has to be related to its intended result, e.g., if I will to raise my arm, my arm should go up as intended by my willing; it should not go down or sideways, and my leg should not be the one going up instead. So, to the question how do I raise my arm in this scenario, the simple answer seems to be: by moving my muscles. And how do I move those muscles? By raising my arm. But an electrical current applied to the relevant muscles can also raise my arm by moving those muscles. Is this a vicious circle? Yes, it is. So the cop out is to say that I raise my arm by volition. But what is volition? It is something-we-know-not-what that raises my arm, but has no distinguishing features. That being the case then, rather than hitch our belief to the fantasy wagon of volition, we should instead say that one raises one's arm by raising it, not by executing two processes, volition or willing and raising, since we cannot tell what volition is and how it works. Appealing to the physiology of movement still does not answer the question of how volition or will triggers the physiological sequence involved in action, and it does not facilitate the action—most people raise their arms without knowing the physiological and biochemical intricacies of neuromuscular connections and activity and without bothering to attribute the initiation of their action to the will or to volition. They simply raise their arms when they want to, if they can.

In this connection, when Wittgenstein asks the pivotal question of agent action, "When 'I raise my arm', my arm goes up. And the question arises: what is left over if I subtract the fact that my arm goes up from the fact that I raise my arm?"[4], the quick answer to distinguish between these two movements, which may be identical in some cases, cannot be the will, [(I raise my arm/action)$_a$ minus (my arm goes up/event of my arm going up)$_b$ = (my will)$_c$: i.e., a-b=c], because no such animal can be found anywhere that is responsible for making me raise my arm. It is as elusive as the self that Hume had a problem trying to define when he said, "For my part, when I enter most intimately into what I call myself, I always stumble on some particular perception or other, of heat or cold, light or shade, love or hatred, pain or pleasure. I never can catch myself at any time without a perception, and never can observe anything but the perception."[5]

Of course, one might ask Hume the question: who is it that enters into what he calls himself? Answer: it is "I". But who is this "I"? It is the one who has my experiences over the years and makes me the same person at time t_1 as at time t_2, t_3, t_4; the one whose body has changed over this period of time without affecting his numerical identity; the one whose "soul" remains the same over the years to make him the same person. Here we have a nondescript mysterious entity (soul) replacing another one (self); but that does not help to resolve the problem; it is just pushing it further into the background, because we have to explain what this soul is that has miraculously replaced the self or "I" that persists from time t_1 to time t_n as the bearer of the connected memories and experiences that are labelled my memories and experiences, centred around and belonging to this "I". It should be evident that to define this "I" by its memories and experiences is either to put the cart before the horse, using these faculties as predicates that identify the self or "I" before defining the self whose faculties and predicates they are, or else utilizing their compresence to define the existence of the transient "I" where these predicates are assembled and systematized at that time with no guarantee that they will continue to be thus assembled at subsequent times in the same or another place. Confronted with these insurmountable difficulties in our quest for the self, could we then say that the self is the brain and the integrated body in which it is lodged as the source of mental activity and driver of physical activity, in contrast with Descartes' "ghost in the machine" referred to on page 17? It seems that we might have to settle for that choice, since without the brain to generate them, there cannot be any of the experiences that are being proffered as the sources of self-identity through time. "I" can then be relegated to the role of a lexical tool (indexical) referring to the person now speaking from where this body is, as opposed to the person speaking from where the living body that is called "you" is speaking from. That allows you to be a self in your own right, in the same way as I claim to be a self. You do not always have to be only the object of the first person that I call "I", since the object that is "you" is thereby placed in the precarious position where it can sometimes be degraded to the non-person status of "it" by the "I" that considers itself the only subject in the world of objects, as Martin Buber has indicated (see page 104). You should occupy a position where you can also retain your selfhood, your "I" status, unlike the person with Cotard syndrome who does not use the designation "I", because he does not acknowledge his body or his existence.

Indeed, even though Hume could not put his finger on this elusive entity, most people speak about it as if it is both the originator and the focus of the sum total of the vast array of changing social experiences that belong to a particular body and mind through the years, in a variety of environments that shape the person's character, as well as the thread that binds those experiences by remaining constant amidst this change. (Mind is here regarded as a function of the brain, which it uses as its instrument for thinking and without which there can be no mind or thinking, in the same way as sight is a function of the eyes and hearing that of the ears, but not of thinking. Without the relevant organs with which they are intimately connected, these functions cannot be executed—sight cannot see without the eyes, nor can hearing hear without the ears, and mismatching these organs with their functions is not possible, e.g., using eyes to hear and ears to see). Needless to say, this belief in a self or "I" is based on mere speculation for which empirical evidence does not exist, and it is also flies in the face of Hume's own advice that "A wise man . . . proportions his belief to the evidence"[6;] nevertheless, it is a pragmatic concept that is here to stay.

When my or I's arm goes up, a movement occurs. In one instance, a movement caused by my agency occurs actively, behaviourally, consciously, intentionally, and teleologically; in the other instance it occurs passively, mechanically, unconsciously, involuntarily, and unintentionally, but also causally. The first movement is designated an action and the second movement does not qualify for that designation according to the definition stated above, and yet when I raise my arm I do not have to first perform certain rituals that do not occur when my arm just goes up, as would be the case where I have to write a note and must first get a pen and paper to be able to start writing the note. The processes are the same, except for the element of voluntariness in one situation and involuntariness in the other situation, but this circumstance does not by itself justify the positing of a mysterious entity called the will that constitutes the critical difference between the two processes and permits me to label the will as the sufficient cause of my first action. The action takes place without the intervention of the will as precursor or causal explanation. Besides I never catch myself going through the motions of first willing and then acting; I just act. I might deliberate or steel myself into performing a challenging task, but I don't employ the will to set the physical process in motion, in as much as I can't ever cause any object to move by applying my will to it. Can we then say that when I raise my arm I do so in direct, mass response to the activation of certain propensities or dispositions in me by events that impinge on me at that time? That way we avoid problems with a will that allegedly causes actions but is not even triggered by intentions, which are logically related to actions only as antecedents are to consequents, explaining actions on the basis of preceding desires and the beliefs that cause them. In this schema desires and beliefs are in turn succeeded by deliberations and decisions to institute or not to institute the actions that will satisfy them, unless the agent acts robotically and thoughtlessly in knee-jerk fashion. In deliberating and deciding on a course of action, the subject should assume a rational outlook to ensure that she does not first entertain outlandish desires that could give rise to equally outlandish beliefs and lead to decisions to perform actions that defy reason and decency. So desires should not be followed blindly without anticipating their potential outcomes. No room is left for the will in these relationships, and so we have to settle for using the term "will" in context as a noun to embellish the verb that adequately performs its function of signifying what the agent is doing intentionally, i.e., raising his arm, in the expression: raising his arm by an act of will. What the expression really means is that he is raising his arm by the use of a figment of the imagination created to fill a gap (also a figment) that does not have to exist but should be characterized as a state of mind or capacity for decision making or the volitional faculty that entails the desire for action, not an existent with the ability to direct the agent's actions.

Therefore, to the question did the "I" that is my will cause my arm to move or did the "I" that is not my will simply move my arm, we can reply that in both cases some nondescript "I" did something that caused my arm to move; i.e., it moved my arm when it wanted to move it. But the "I" that is I can also try and fail to initiate an action or movement with a paralyzed arm, in spite of entertaining the will or volition to move the arm in order to move it, proving that trying to move my arm is not equivalent to moving my arm and willing to move my arm is not a sufficient condition for moving it. Attempting to move my arm may, however, be a necessary condition of moving it in the sense that I thought of moving my arm with the intention of accomplishing something, as opposed to the case where my arm is moved by someone else accidentally or it moved as a result of a convulsive seizure without my entertaining the intention to move it. Nothing physical happens in the former case when I simply entertain the will to move my arm, but something does in the latter case when I move my arm for some reason. Since an act of will without possession of the requisite physical ability will never move any arm, no amount or degree of willing will ever move a paralyzed arm or achieve anything physical unless the subject already has the power to effect the intended action. Waiting for the will to initiate any physical movements is more like waiting for the sky to fall than waiting for the cows to come home, which often happens; but this "will" business will never happen — period. No blind man has ever been able to see by willing while lacking the complete, functioning optical tools to facilitate the process, or while settled with inefficient tools like corneal opacities (which can be corrected with corneal transplants), cataracts (which can be corrected with artificial lens implants), optic nerve head atrophy (which cannot yet be corrected), or some other deficiency along his optic pathways. Willing has never done anything that the subject did not already have the tools to do it with, not even if he knows the physics and the physiology that underlies his willed movements. Such knowledge only helps him to understand how his arm goes up; but neither it nor his will can ever move his arm.

Some philosophers still insist that the actions of will that we allegedly perform before we undertake physical actions serve as "action-generating actions of decision, such as deciding to go to the bank or deciding to stay home"[7] before actually going or staying. The taking of such decisions, they maintain, counts as actions in their own right—voluntary "actions that are wanted or willed and decided on – because they can and do result from the prior operation of a *voluntas* or will to perform them"[8] in keeping with our abilities, intentions, goals, and purposes. The only problem with this trend is that it generates an infinite regress of decisions: the action being based on the decision to act, which is based on the decision to decide to act, which in turn is based on the decision to decide on the decision to decide to act, etc.

A peculiar situation in this relationship of agents with their actions is that of the Alien or Anarchic Hand syndrome in which a subject who has suffered brain injury may subsequently feel as if her hand does not belong to her and that it acts independently of her control, although the movements that she performs with it are purposeful rather than random. This situation raises the obvious problem of how to characterize these movements? Should they be characterized as "agentless" actions, which is an oxymoron, since every action is caused by an agent and uncaused actions can't be attributed to an agent, or should they be characterized as unintentional intentional actions, which is a negation of the definition of "action" as intentional movement and a contradiction in terms that amounts to nonsense? But, as Thomas Pink also points out in *Free will*, actions can occur without being random or determined, since they can be caused by a freely acting agent who controls their occurrence or non-occurrence. Pink says it is a power of the agent to determine which events he performs and what effects they cause, but it is not a causal power, because many things that have the causal power to produce certain effects do not exercise control over the wielding of that power, e.g., a sizeable stone thrown at a window with sufficient force can produce only one result: the shattering of the window; but the same stone in my hand, under my control produces only the effect that I choose. I can bang it hard enough to break the window or just lightly to produce a musical sound without causing any damage to the glass; the discretion is mine, not the stone's.

Since we are hamstrung by our circumstances, and yet we live with the impression that we always make free choices, we will set aside the extreme skepticism generated by the deterministic attitude and assume that we really do enjoy freedom of choice. Hence we can say that freedom of choice promotes free action and imposes moral praise, responsibility, or culpability on the one who acts—that he should have acted otherwise, because he could have chosen to do so, unless he was the subject of a compulsive disorder or was coerced to choose the way he chose; e.g., at the risk of his life, where he also still had a choice to sacrifice it for the truth. This sequence of events is not unusual, and no one believes that he has a will that causes him to do things or act in certain ways, over and above these prompting dispositions, nor does anyone believe that he always acts out of necessity and outside of his ability to decide how he will act in most circumstances. As we have already noted, we naturally do what we want to do in spite of the prevalence of universal causality, which would tend towards determining our actions against our intentions and will or else automatically producing the effects of our intentions without us having to undertake any actions to bring about the goals that we intend. Hence our initial reactions to those who misbehave is to blame them for the harm that results from their actions, in spite of the claims of determinism, until we become aware of mitigating circumstances e.g., they are caught in situations where they cannot choose how they will act through ignorance, restraint, cognitive inability, etc.; only then do we exculpate them.

That is just the pragmatic way we function and have functioned for centuries, although some people would have us believe that we are fooling ourselves if we think that we are free to choose how we will act in the face of natural causal laws that determine the behaviour of the universe and its contents, including persons. In that kind of situation, no one has the power to alter the course of events to his choice and liking; the trends are set and nothing short of a cataclysmic change in the order of the universe will permit that change to allow anyone to exercise his rational free choice. This perspective of cause and effect reaching back to the beginning of the world disregards the essential point that causality is an observed sequence that is not absolutely necessary as happens to be the case with the fact that if I am 6feet tall and Jack is shorter than I, he can't also be 6ft or 6ft and 1inch tall. But we also know that events occur in our lives that seem to defy this overarching law of nature that is alleged to regulate every process and phenomenon in the universe, and physicists have described quantum jumps by particles that bear witness to this fact. These are variations from the expected course in the behaviour of particles that occur without apparent cause, but whose existence has been questioned seriously by some people who claim that "they are theoretical entities in a special sense of that term, not events".[9] Whatever their nature, they are still entities that behave randomly.

If determinism is true, then all the actions that we claim to have undertaken freely have instead been necessitated by preceding conditions, just like every other causal event. In that case, we could not have exercised free choice to act otherwise, i.e., in a manner that is automatically excluded by determinism (by definition), since that would be an abrogation of causal laws, and causal laws do not allow free choice. On the other hand, the truth of indeterminism, which allows events to happen without being determined, still does not permit free choice, because such events can be random, and randomness is not free choice. So, neither determinism nor indeterminism allows free choice; but this situation does not affect the capacity of the human agent to carry out free actions that are hurtful to other human agents, and for which he must bear moral responsibility and culpability, in spite of hiding behind elaborate networks of protection like the non-human persons that are constituted by some of the same individuals, viz., corporations and the governments that they control. In these roles they collectively relegate responsibility for the welfare of other persons to the lowest rungs of their ladder of concern while elevating self-aggrandizement and personal material gain to priority status on the higher rungs. In their hierarchical organizations, the burden of blame for recklessness with the lives of other persons is shifted to those who occupy the lower rungs of the same ladder of privilege that all of them are climbing, away from where it rightly belongs, which is right at the top where the monopoly is on the kudos only—they don't like to pass these on to others in the organization who also deserve them, perhaps even more than they do; they keep the kudos and pass on the blames. The acts of the organization are entailed in the actions of its personnel, but these human elements have structured these other persons (their organizations) in such a way that they can legally divorce the acts of the organization from the actions of its personnel, as if this abstract entity can think and act on its own with purpose and moral or immoral intent, apart from the personnel who constitute it—the frustrating reality with which the victims of these organizations have to deal as we indicated on pages 10-11.

In this context where determinism rules the universe and its contents, it seems that religious persons who are forever engaged in prayers for one thing or another to be made available to them (alone) are wasting their time, as Spinoza maintained, because, if the cosmic plan is fixed and determined, no amount of prayer to alter the order of the universe or the course of events to accommodate their whims, wishes, desires, and prejudices will be of any avail; what will happen will happen in keeping with already determined preconditions that are all part of the master plan on which the universe is founded. By comparison, imagine what would happen if NASA altered the structure and function of even a single element in the shuttle space craft or its booster rockets to gratify the selfish and uninformed wishes of someone who fancied a change in the operative parameters of these intricate machines without realizing the complexity of first initiating this arrangement and then maintaining the relationships among its various components for the ongoing harmonious operation of the entire system. To heed and gratify such a grossly ignorant request would be to commit literal homicide on those who are scheduled to take the trip into outer space in such a vehicle. No one in his right mind would agree to such a wish. So what is the point of prayer for determinists and indeterminists alike, if the order of the universe is already preordained?

Common sense suggests that if everything is caused, one of those causes is the human agent himself who is the sole source of his own actions and the entertainer of the thoughts, desires, wishes, needs, etc. that give rise to those actions (hoping that these will prompt moral choices), instead of other actions, and therefore the responsible subject for their outcomes. After all, every causal sequence must have a beginning or point of initiation before which it did not exist, and the human agent is one such initiating cause, as proponents of agent causality will argue. In response, determinists will argue that his thoughts and actions are caused, and so what he causes to happen will eventually be caused too, and then they will jump to the conclusion that his actions are determined, as if cause implies determination. It may be true that cause is vital to determinism, but, as we have seen, quantum mechanics teaches that some events cannot be predicted with certainty from other prior events, since quantum events happen without any apparent cause but function well in the existing cosmic structure. In itself, however, determinism is a useful concept that is essential to all cases of probability; e.g., the probability that an airplane will lift off and keep flying, rather than just rise and fall, is close to 1 (100%). This is made possible by the mechanical aspects of its structure and function that follow causal laws, according to which causes determine the occurrence of their effects with increased probability. Without this relationship, or within a world of quanta, nothing could be undertaken with any anticipation of success, since chaos would reign supreme in such a world where events occur of their own accord.

Hence we can easily understand how things are caused outside of the sphere of the random occurrence of events in quantum mechanics where the randomness of events would leave us uncertain that the plane will take off and remain airborne barring human error and mechanical failure. Luckily, events on the micro level of particles (quanta) do not necessarily represent what will occur on the macro level, otherwise life would be unpredictable and knowledge as truth would be further out of our reach, since we could neither begin to predict nor lay the reasonable foundations of certainty about anything that is within our cognitive and practical reach. Already, most, if not all, of what we self-assuredly call our knowledge of "facts" is perennially provisional, since it can change very easily with new information and discoveries replacing previous erroneous beliefs, as is the case with theories about the centre of the solar system, phlogiston, and diseases linked to the human genome. As it is, our actions are unpredictable, because they are free and undetermined, but they are not so random that we could not hazard guesses about how certain persons will react in certain situations; we often say, "I know that my parents will disapprove of action x, but they will be delighted with action y, so I will resist the temptation to do x". They are also not mechanical; they depend on our agency, which psychologists are still studying intensely to be able to delineate personality types whose behaviour can be predicted with a degree of certainty — determinism? Such information has lately been used to attempt to fix elections by disseminating particular messaging to previously profiled individuals (perhaps with an appreciable measure of success).

From the foregoing outline of determinism, it seems that appeal to determinism is an uncertain venture that is bound to fail in some places, while it shows evidence of success in others and appears to be haphazard in still others. Nevertheless, it cannot be completely excluded from our lives as we saw in the last two paragraphs, since a person's genetic constitution of character and physique is determined, but it does not completely override the corrective influence of his environment as reflected in those around him who try to instil certain desirable values into him, nor does it constrain him to the degree that he can act only in particular pre-determined ways that do not allow him to make choices, unless he is severely cognitively challenged. So, most people cannot blame their genetic make up for their deviant actions that result from making bad choices, because in most such cases they did actually choose and decide to fulfill their intention to act in the way they did without giving sober thought to their choices and decisions and to the anticipated results of their actions. The lure of the pleasure of the moment eclipsed this kind of thoughtful consideration, resulting in irrational and culpable activity that cannot be excused by misapplication of the law of universal causality. The genetic argument further casts the blame on persons all along the track and as far back as the person's ancestry can be traced; i.e., someone or everyone else in this genealogy is to blame for his misdeeds; equally, therefore, someone or everyone else but he should deserve praise for his achievements. But genetic constitution A does not mandate the occurrence of behaviour B that would not have occurred if that genetic make-up had not been present, since A doesn't contain the germ of B that steers the individual's behaviour in only certain directions. The import of this is that while A may be necessary for the occurrence of B in the sense of offering an explanation why B is occurring, it is not sufficient for the occurrence of B in the sense of being the sole determining factor, among a host of other possible factors, for the occurrence of B. The upshot is that genetic constitution can't claim justification for determinism as annulling free choice, nor can it tie us down to fatalism, since determinism is not fatalism or constraint. The only kind of determinism in action that is acceptable is one that admits of a freedom of choice, which presumes rationality in action and the elimination of beliefs and desires alone as its sole determinants.Despite the preceding line of reasoning, this is the argument that people advance to exculpate themselves when their actions have placed them in tight spots. They admit that genes may be necessary for the formation of behaviour patterns but not sufficient for their expression, and they claim that they cannot help who they are, because they did not choose the genes and the parents they have, and that they would have been different if they had had different parents passing on different genes to them and raising them in environments that are different from those in which they were raised. So how can we blame them for their determined actions? They blame fate for their characters, and so should we.

The fatalist maintains that if it was true before-hand that event A will happen at time t_1, then it will happen, regardless of the choices we try to make to avoid it; we are bound to make only those choices that will bring event A to pass, thereby proving that what we call our free choice is a mere illusion – we never did have a choice and the moral responsibility that accompanies it. But we know that the contrary is true in real life; events can be anticipated and action taken to avoid them, if they are deemed to be undesirable. They are not predetermined to occur as the necessary consequents of the antecedent truth of their prediction, regardless of the actions that we take to prevent their occurrence, since the truth of their prediction depends on their occurrence; i.e., they are not true before they happen as predicted, because prediction does not necessitate their certain occurrence but only its possibility and probability that we have the power to control. They are not as necessary as the truth of if $A=B$ and $B=C$, then $A=C$. So making their occurrence depend on the truth of their prediction is like putting the cart before the horse in an attempt to make the cart pull the horse. As we have noted before, their other argument is that since every action is either caused necessarily by factors other than the agent, and, therefore, not freely chosen by him, or else it is uncaused (random), the agent never bears moral responsibility or culpability for his actions, as the case may be – an untenable situation by all counts, which can surely not be right, because the rational agent must have a way of anticipating the outcomes of most of his actions so that he can be settled with responsibility for them. This is made possible by the determined regularity of courses of events in the universe that also makes it possible for us to predict the safety of undertaking ventures into space without fear of untimely and frequent random occurrences that can be fatal to our tasks and us. When calculations and engineering have been done meticulously to prevent error, we anticipate that the spacecraft will perform as predicted and not randomly, and so, when we act we do so with the purpose of achieving certain intended goals, not any eventuality that comes up spontaneously—we freely choose the determinate way that we want events to unfold.

It may be true that we lack choice, because the courses of all events are determined by antecedent conditions that have deprived us of autonomy, reducing us to objects and processes in the universe that do not have minds with which to assess situations and then decide how to react or respond to them, but the available evidence does not support this point of view that disregards the incompletely understood cogitative capacities of persons. So, those theorists who extrapolate from mechanistic principles of cause and effect in the non-human world to causally predetermined actions in the behaviour of persons simply because many of the functions of their bodies (limb actions with muscles, tendons, and joints forming pulleys and fulcrums, nerve trunks and their arborizations presenting the same fractal structure as electrical systems and conducting impulses in the same way as those systems, eyes that function like box cameras, lungs that function like bellows, etc.) can be explained in mechanical terms are barking up the wrong tree, because the human mind that regulates all these functions does not operate on the same plane as those mechanical principles; no one can predict or tell with certainty how any person will react in any situation, although they can do so in the case of chemical reactions and physical phenomena; we can only surmise how other persons will react, as mentioned on page 90. Physical determinism does not imply psychic determinism; we may claim to know practically all the physical conditions that are necessary for the realization of an action, but we can never fathom the depths of the human mind that directs those actions, and that alone is sufficient to incline us to absolve some agents of blame on purely arbitrary considerations. No one wants to see someone else hang for a capital crime that he committed when he was not fully aware of the nature and implications of his action, including its lethal consequences, simply because he cannot fathom the workings of the offenders enigmatic mind; but few would object to meting out that kind of punishment to someone who knowingly and callously killed other people for reasons other than self-defence. This argument and the one from genetics are meant to absolve us of culpability by denying our responsibility for our actions. It says that if we act according to our natures, we cannot be responsible for how we act, because we did not fashion our natures or cause ourselves. But the truth is that human endeavour at achieving a moral existence is entirely up to humans and cannot be offloaded on anyone else, including a postulated supreme being, and it is time that humans started bearing responsibility (and culpability, where it is merited) for their actions instead of passing the buck on to others or blaming unyielding fate, genetics, and God for their failures, as is their wont.

To summarize the preceding maze of arguments, free action entails the ability to choose and subsequently decide to act otherwise than how one has acted in the face of determinism whose influence is to ostensibly make such a choice impossible, since every event is supposed to have its determining cause. But such a hurdle is only apparent, because the human agent himself can be such a cause. At the root of all choices of action, one's goals and intentions play a crucial role. Behind them are one's desires whose satisfaction one is free to block at any moment, if, after deliberating freely on them, one finds them to be irrational, thus rendering them incapable of having any effect on the actions that in turn have the capacity to determine which ones of our desires will satisfy their direction of fit, as Searle has indicated in his *Rationality in Action* (pages 37-39), and as Melden has also argued. At the same time, we recognize that the world does not always answer to our desires and wishes, and we have to modify them to conform with conditions imposed on us by inflexible reality, or else risk precipitating chaos by acting obdurately and imprudently. Furthermore, if our actions are not determined or causally related to antecedent events, and if our choices, motivations, and reasons for action are not causally determined by the same circumstances in which those events occur, the possibility exists that some of them may be random. But even in this case we can argue that although they are random, they are still caused (since every event has a cause i.e., there are no uncaused events, even if their causes are not known as in quantum mechanics), but not by us, and we can therefore not be blamed for them as much as we cannot be blamed for predetermined actions over which we had no control and no choice, because they were necessary sequels of rigidly determined preceding events; i.e., given that event A occurred, event B could not but follow it in those particular circumstances of place and time; although this is not to say that B must occur in any situation where A has occurred. If B had not followed A in the first case, the situation would have been irregular to the point of challenging existing "natural" laws about the behaviour of these entities in the circumstances under consideration.

The dilemma created by the foregoing consideration can be avoided by claiming that this is the exception that proves the rule; i.e., no such rules apply to human behaviour. Even if someone has followed a particular behavioural pattern in similar past situations, we will not accuse her of having broken a "natural" law if she behaved differently on the present occasion, although we might wonder why she behaved that way. After all, she is free to choose and decide how she will respond to the same situations at different times by the exercise of her power of initiating actions that answer to the needs or demands of the moment. Using her agency powers, she can vary at will and spontaneously curb her actions and reactions at any point in their progress, unlike the inert object that must follow its fixed and programmed course, unless it just fails to function as designed and intended by its architect, the human agent. The agent's free action is explicable "in terms of justifying reasons and purposes" and much more, since while the popular feeling is that she could still have chosen otherwise than she did in the same circumstances where she was possibly presented with a multiplicity of choices, such a choice was not open to her in the particular circumstances in which her choice was made; she chose the only way she could at that time and in that place, without committing to necessity about her actions. That is why an agent can opt for performing an action that is less optimal than the one that she strongly believes is the better one, or even the right one, in the circumstances of her action—a case of weakness of will, so-called, seen best in the addict who acknowledges the harmful effects of her smoking habit, but still chooses to smoke cigarettes. (Discussed in chapter 5 of my *Mind Your Ps and Qs*).

In the end, even with these foregoing limitations, we can still choose how to act, unless we are physically or cognitively restricted and disabled from acting or making those choices. Sometimes, even threats of physical harm to ourselves or our families may fail to restrict our determination to exercise our free will and choice of action in those circumstances, because we are guided by the desire to do what is good and right, rather than what is expedient; otherwise our intellect loses its relevancy. These considerations of goodness and rightness serve to direct our focus on the concept of value, which has been the undercurrent of our discussion from the start. So we will now devote some time to a discussion of the role of value in human agency.

Chapter 7

Persons as Moral Agents

When we evaluate the chosen actions of the human agent, we not only pay attention to his intentions, which are often unknown to us, since we are not able to read minds and intentions can be dissembled, but we also and mostly look at the effects that those actions have produced or are likely to produce on the subject at whom they are directed and at the example that they are setting, if not the code of conduct that they are helping to prescribe. Therefore the good agent should, at all times, exercise good reason in choosing to bring about or cause to happen those conditions that will promote the good of the individuals and the whole community in which he is domiciled. His actions should also be the kind that bring benefit to humankind at large, while he is promoting his own interests without hindrance, but unselfishly; and that is not to say he should necessarily be extremely altruistic or supererogatory at all times. To this end, he is also expected to reject those actions that have the potential to result in hardship, misery, and unhappiness to those individuals on whom they will have their effects. If he does not make rational choices but instead chooses to make irrational and irresponsible choices that make him an instrument for these and other evils in the community, his actions stand to be condemned as immoral, because, as is often the case in such situations, he is conveying the unpalatable message that he is prepared to sacrifice the welfare of the rest of the people on the altar of his self-service and selfish interests, which, in this modern age, are guided mostly by an overwhelming and irresistible motivation of the combination of pecuniary greed and crass inhumanity.

The norm in modern human societies seems to be that wherever money can be made—honestly and often dishonestly—even at the cost of some human lives, people will always be found plying their trade of exploiting situations to squeeze the last dollar out of those situations. Such is the ascendency and hold of money over human values. Its ardent worshippers are oblivious to the harm that ensues from their unscrupulous pursuit of it; they are happy as long as they can get their hands on it, amass it, and use it to enhance their social standing and their handle on power over the rest of their community that stands to suffer immense harm from the uncontrolled greed of the highly sophistic characters that it breeds in both the economic and political arenas. For example, they will not hesitate to lie to the electorate about their noble intentions (draining the swamp), which run counter to their track records and their pronouncements uttered in secret, or to hypocritically rail against the pork that they also enjoy, if only to impress the citizens about their ostensible fiscal conservative credentials, which they tout for show but are really a gateway to their destination, the seat of power. Once comfortably settled with the reins in their hands, they are able to create favourable tax and other conditions for their rich friends and supporters in their declared war against the naïve electorate that votes them into office on a whim, but still continues to bear the tax burden alone while their exploiters contribute only a pittance and stash their money offshore as indicated on page 148.

To show the power that money wields over human affairs, unequal applications of the laws of the land to citizens are not hard to find, where the rich have been treated lightly for crimes for which the poor would have been incarcerated and vilified for who they are by the persons who made them what they are through their selfishness and greed. So-called celebrities of favoured lineage have often got away with slaps on the wrist where non-celebrities and celebrities of disfavoured lineages have been made to pay dearly for the same kinds of misdeeds—ask those who promote dog fights. Swindlers (who unfortunately include "men of God", as some crooked priests have been labeled) of hard working middle class clients and senior citizens who have made off with their life-time savings and investments have mostly been treated gingerly in contrast with the harsh treatment meted out to poor persons who take food without permission, even discarded treats from the trash cans of their employers. Persons belonging to the latter category are given the third degree treatment by the law, mercilessly dragged before the courts, indicted, prosecuted, invariably found guilty of theft, and slapped with a sentence of some kind. Meanwhile, the real criminals who are a menace to society are roaming freely and may even escape punishment if and when their days of reckoning ever come around. In these respects, human agency has failed humanity, because it operates with contrived values that have no regard for the moral equality of all human beings and their right to equal, fair, and humane treatment. Whether these ignominious practices are a cultural defect is difficult to tell, but they certainly don't speak well of those sections of the community that habitually engage in them.

In Ubuntu culture (discussed in chapter 4) all are treated equally on the basis of their equal humanity, even granting that differences in the physical make-up and circumstances, both historical and extant, of different persons render them unequal. No one is treated as a second or third class citizen, as long as she observes the values and universally accepted norms of her society. So every effort is made to ensure that no one is selectively oppressed, discriminated against, or treated unfairly or inhumanely. One would like to think that the theory of Ubuntu always translates into practice in the forging of relationships among peoples, but unfortunately, that is not the case. Far too many people are choosing to exercise their power and privilege by making life in this world hell for others whose freedom they have chosen to erode and restrict. They deprive them of their freedom of choice by first relegating them to the lowest rungs of the socio-economic ladder, and then they use them by subjecting them willy-nilly to the ravages and destruction of self-serving wars, disrupting their family lives and forcing them to flee their homes to seek shelter in foreign lands and in makeshift dwellings where their dignity is lost in the dust of the earth in which they roll day and night while their persecutors are enjoying the comforts of their own luxurious homes with their precious children. Many others are forced to endure hunger and starvation, because those who would save them from these evils have chosen to accelerate their effects by doing nothing, as if trying to realize their goal of eliminating the pestilence that these poor people constitute in their sight. It does not matter how much they try to absolve themselves of blame for the hardship that befalls poor people by claiming that they did not do anything to bring about that hardship, the fact remains that by choosing to do nothing they have chosen to stand by idly and let nature take its course and thereby do for them what they often refrain from doing themselves for fear of being seen and branded as inhumane. Who can blame them now when these same people are perishing from the hand of nature and not from theirs? No one.

Others simply kill their subjects for their audacity in demanding their right to be treated fairly by their self-appointed rulers who shamelessly engage in peddling scurrilous lies about being compelled to murder innocent children, women, and men by the need to curb armed rebels and foreign agencies from trying to disrupt the complacent lives of all the citizens of their states, including the malcontents—strange logic. Some other cowards who are afraid of facing the truth suppress legitimate dissent against their selfish, heartless, and inhumane treatment of the masses of people by disrespectfully throwing dissenters in jail and keeping them confined in their tiny hell holes against their will for many years, without the decency of a trial to afford them an opportunity to prove the lies under which they have been detained. Others just flatly and selectively deny certain populations entry into their states, or else devise other means of keeping them out with tough immigration laws and other laws ostensibly meant to discourage "human trafficking". These are the same immigrants who now shun other immigrants and moan about the waning influence of their skin colour in determining the direction of elections to conform with their contemptible racist outlook or regress into puerile verbal convulsions when decisive democratic elections do not go their narrow-minded, racist way, and also descendants of the same marauders who benefited from colonizing and looting the lands from which these now undesirable immigrants and refugees have originated. They are not good enough to come and share the proceeds that have blossomed from the wealth that was and is still being reaped on their backs—thanks to globalization and its enslaving organizations.

In this execrable cesspool of positive evil, a few decent individuals and groups stand out for their benevolent actions and their respect and recognition of the moral worth and dignity of oppressed persons who are forced to eke out a bare existence on nothing; they always go out of their way to assist in making the lives of the rejected and neglected masses as tolerable as they can make them, even risking and receiving scorn from their ilk for genuinely empathizing with the vermin that the oppressed appear to be in the eyes of successive generations of privileged oppressors. They do not call those who are demanding fair and decent treatment and opportunities to be the best that they can be "wannabes" while they alone enjoy the comforts of life that are denied the wannabes by the twisted structure of the societies in which both parties have their being. They deplore the shameless greed that prompts the corporation bosses to fashion the economy in such a way that all the benefits accrue to them and little or nothing is left over for the rest of the people who labour arduously in the trenches for their pittances while the bosses are having an easy time in their board rooms and hoarding as much money as they can reward themselves with at the expense of their lives. At any time, the shabby and inhumane treatment of the real providers of wealth to the corporations only serves to reveal the moral bankruptcy of those who exploit their labour for their own benefit without rewarding the labourers adequately and fairly for their services and even depriving them of their tips. We should not make the mistake of labeling their actions as ignoble and immoral *per se*, because actions by themselves are simply complexes of happenings that do not carry any moral implications, until benevolent or malevolent motives and intentions have been added to them by their perpetrators, at which point they acquire a characterizing label from the character of the person whose motives and intentions they are and to whom it rightly belongs. Evil people always harbour evil motives and intentions, and they carry out evil deeds, because good deeds are foreign to their evil natures. Their so-called evil actions are only manifestations of how they express their evil natures in their inhumane relationships with those around them. It is these evil dispositions that are perpetuating the gargantuan, ever widening gap between rich and poor that is so much on everyone's lips and hardly deserves any more flogging but happens to be a disturbing feature of our world that we cannot help mentioning, if only to remind ourselves not to forget the evil that is being perpetrated and perpetuated on humanity by humanity.

If these people were of noble character, they would know that they should not treat other human beings like animals—not their pets that receive special treatment, nor even other animals for which animal rights activists would haul them over the coals (that's another strange lot of people who will raise dust to protect animals while they remain mum when other human beings are being dehumanized and desecrated). As Arthur Schopenhauer so wisely observed, "the happiness of any given life is to be measured, not by its joys and pleasures, but by the extent to which it has been free from suffering from positive evil. If this is the true standpoint, the lower animals appear to enjoy a happier destiny than man."[1] It is sad to admit that the suffering of the wannabes does not compare with the happy destiny of the pets of the rich, but it is also very sad to see animal rights activists displaying perverse values that thrive on the welfare of these people, as if to corroborate the statement attributed to Voltaire (François-Marie d'Arouet), quoted by Schopenhauer in the introduction to his essay, "The Wisdom of Life", that "we shall leave this world as foolish and as wicked as we found it on our arrival."[2] Raising a stink over the mistreatment of lower ranking animals while condoning ill-treatment of the highest ranking animals on the tree of evolution, the ones endowed with rationality and autonomy, is nothing but a reflection of the foolishness and wickedness that rules our world and will doom it to self-destruction, because it cannot go on forever; somewhere, sometime this madness with its distorted values must come to a cataclysmic termination, and woe betide those who will try to stop the cataclysm in the same manner as they have been engineering its advent with their inhumanity. They will be crushed by the truth that they have been suppressing for centuries while living the lie that makes them think that they are better persons than the rest of humanity who are their moral equals, if not their moral superiors in many respects.

Our world may be the best of all possible worlds in the terminology of Leibniz, but it certainly is not inhabited by the best of all possible creatures, if we exclude the lower animals that have been given a place far above some sections of the society of humans that are regarded as subhuman. The human animal, the highest species of animal that constitutes the most valued element of this world, foolishly roams the face of the earth in endless search of elusive happiness and the means to purchase it. But he is also the very same one who is degrading this habitation and turning it into the human jungle of evil, misery, and infelicity that it is, because he is never content with what he has (always wanting more to hoard), and he can't find what he is naïvely busy destroying but thinks that he can purchase it with money, even when it sometimes accrues to him solely from the accidental goodness that he condescendingly bestows on his neighbour—he does not have the grace and vision to see that he achieved his elusive quest by simply being human and not by purchasing it with his degrading money and high social status. All of these deviants of nature lack some of the most essential ingredients of life: forbearance, benevolence, respect, empathy, and simple love of fellow humans. They are content with the images that they see when they look in their mirrors, believing them to represent the only creatures on this earth and in this world that matter. Besides, in this egotistical lack of respect for the personhood of other people and the suffering that they inflict on them, they live as if they are the centre of the universe who are exempt from the clutches of the leveller, death, which reduces their self-made god-like image to dust and dirt with the rest of the lowly folk on whom they have been trampling for decades without as much as a twinge of guilty conscience.

Whoever has the freedom, ability, and prerogative to act in ways that he chooses is also free to bring about any result that he chooses to suit himself only, even in the absence of justifying reasons. He disregards the restricting reasons that obtain and claims to have made a "hard choice" to subject millions of people to hardship for selfish reasons. We have seen this kind of behaviour repeatedly in the careers of some human agents. Thus the self-absorbed warmongers who bellow the desire for, and ring the bells of, war on the slightest provocation have assumed the prerogative of invading other states by virtue of their positions of leadership in the nation state, and, more often than not, do not pay any attention to the entreaties of citizens to refrain from gratifying their selfish desires and aspirations for "greatness" at immense expense to those on either side that they are dragging into this despicable state of immoral, disabling, and fatal conflict. Any talk of moral responsibility is wasted on these types, because they are always ready to lie and pass the buck to those whom they victimize, or to those who are serving under them and carrying out their disreputable and depraved orders, like torturing the prisoners that they round up in their wars or denying any knowledge of actions that were carried out under their watch (only when their lies come back to bite them), and they will slither out of their responsibilities as serpents slither out of tight situations. Being the ardent religious believers that they are, they are probably also staunch adherents of the misconception that death in battle is part of God's plan for populating the kingdom of heaven, or that God intended life to begin in the "horrible situation of rape". Their advice, a kind of far-fetched wish-fulfillment, to the rest of the people is to hang in there, because this world is and will continue to be a vale of tears for the underdog, and they should, therefore, rather look forward to abundant recompense in a realm beyond this mundane one. They will say this while absolving themselves of responsibility for these inhuman acts for which they deny all culpability—it is always the other guy, or the poor have only themselves to blame, because they don't work as hard as we do for what we have. Baloney! What they should be saying is, "we don't work as hard as we make them work for us to own what we have; the only hard work that we do is that of sucking blood and nutrients out of their systems like vampires and parasites." They also apply the same tactic among those citizens who are too vocal in criticizing their actions or appear to be poised to retaliate for the indignities that are imposed on them. These critics are summarily thrown in jail in the name of national security and left there to rot without being granted the decency of proper due process; and they call that justice. Plato, save us.

Similarly, when the so-called leader who has been elected to serve the people wants to appear tough with those who do not want to be servile to him, he mobilizes goon squads to harass them and subject them to third degree tactics, which are meant to bring them to their knees, his flattering hope being to render them so docile that they will give him free reign to act as he chooses to bring about the kind of disguised state dictatorship that he would like to establish to suit his own purposes of being the unquestioned boss and the self-crowned non-regal king. (Make no mistake, this last phrase is not meant to endorse royalty, that detestable practice of leeching on other people under the lame guise of being their God-appointed lineage of rulers endorsed by their accomplices in the church, but more precisely their exploiters, of whom Denis Diderot said, "Men will never be free until the last king is strangled in the entrails of the last priest!"[3]). Some others spend their time in office, not on the affairs of the nation state, but berating and vilifying everyone else who has the audacity to criticize their incompetence, ignorance, greed, and amorality.

So what should be the guiding posts to personal and group behaviour toward other persons? The choice is wide, but in each case the theme is that of doing what will benefit them and never doing anything that will hurt them; i.e., doing what is good for them. (See chapter 3 of *Our World and its Values*) The concept "good" that we will follow is that stated by William Frankenna: "in order to come to a judgment about whether something is good . . . we must first determine what its intrinsic value [value in itself as a desirable end in itself as such, not as a means to another value] is, what the intrinsic value of its consequences or of the experience of contemplating it is, or how much it contributes to the intrinsically good life."[4] We will therefore consider some of the many ways in which people have theorized about achieving this goal, bearing in mind that every decision to act on every situation in life is subject to different directive moral codes and principles, which sometimes advocate conflicting responses, thus making it difficult for the subject to decide which one to follow. She therefore has to either ignore the theoretical injunctions of some of the guiding principles or combine them to synthesize a rational course of action from their product; e.g., morality per Kant prohibits lying, while holy book morality prohibits killing. So should one still not lie to a pursuer about the whereabouts of someone that he wishes to kill for whatever reason? In this kind of situation most rational persons would lie without the least hesitation, because the harm that would result from the killing of someone is far greater than that of telling a lie, no matter what the reason might be for the intended killing. The person$_1$ who wants to avenge a killing with another killing (as some barbaric states still do) is only starting an infinite regress, because his act of killing will be avenged by another person$_2$, and that other person's act of killing will be avenged by yet another person$_3$, and so on, *ad infinitum*. So there is never a good reason to tell the truth to a killer in these and similar circumstances, but every reason to tell a well sanctioned lie. Regrettably, some people cannot distinguish between these kinds of cases and most of the daily situations where telling the truth is the right thing to do and they make a habit of lying most of the time; and as I have indicated in my other writings, when lying replaces truth as the norm in human relations and communication, life becomes difficult to the point of being unliveable, because on the rare occasion when someone decides to tell the truth, we will assume that he is still lying and we will neglect to carry out the requisite life-saving action that he is advocating on the basis of a wrong assumption. Every school child knows the illustrative story of the boy who cried wolf for no good reason so many times that on the one occasion when his cry should have been heeded, it went unheeded on the assumption that it was the usual false alarm, and he landed in trouble with no one to help him — his own fault.

In other situations, as we will see on page 105, the choice facing the subject is between the duty to any single individual, again *à la* Kant, or to the happiness (also styled "maximum satisfaction of interests or of preferences") of the majority of individuals at the cost of the one. Nothing outside of the ethical codes or principles of deontology and utilitarianism[5] dictates that the life and happiness of one will be worth less than the lives and total happiness of many, because many situations unknown to the observer enter into determining the value of each human life, and no person has the right to use another person as a tool to promote the happiness of other persons on the basis of his assessment of the relative values of their lives, or for any other reason. People can also choose to follow sheepishly the rigid injunctions of their inviolate holy books, which are no more authentic than the often biased and contradictory opinions of fallible ancient moralists and some gurus from within their own communities who claim to be advised by their different gods to instruct the people. Gurus sometimes urge them to engage in such absurdities as participating in ritualistic and other exterminations of sections of some foreign communities that they claim are possessed by demons that only they have the power to exorcise, and also to participate in other senseless rituals that amount to insults to the intellects of clear thinking persons. These outlandish instructions are not lost on those modern religious fanatics who claim to be the select few who can communicate with their gods when they are embarking on insane ventures and claiming to be following the instructions of the supreme beings or gods depicted in their holy books who chose to whisper ambiguous, contradictory, and controversial orders for wrong actions into their ears alone (like waging wars and destroying the habitations of innocent people, or taking them on suicidal missions to Waco or Jonestown) — a claim that is heard often from persons suffering from paranoia who also claim to have heard God's voice telling them to kill the devil who is represented by their children or the next person. Poor God, he has to bear the blame for all kinds of genuine human insanity and frankly stupid behaviour. The ambiguity of their orders allows them the liberty to interpret them as they see fit, and that is why they can quote from their holy books to justify actions that constitute an affront to the dignity of other persons. They elect to claim that their gods command them to perform certain actions because they (gods) have made them right, instead of saying that their gods have so ordered them because those actions are the ones that they instructed their gods to decree as the right ones to perform in those particular circumstances, and their gods have obeyed their decree and turned around to issue it as a holy order to them. (Not unlike some spineless, sneaking politicians who pretend that they are bringing fresh news but are in fact regurgitating their accomplice's words back to him to befuddle citizens) Their fear is that the latter stand would eliminate from the equation the gods behind whom they are hiding, making their warped standard of "rightness" purely self-initiated and subject to the condemning judgment of rational persons, thus nullifying their misguided, warped, and self-serving interpretations of right and wrong. In another respect, this choice is practically the same as living by the injunctions of worldly authorities who claim to know best how everyone should conduct himself, and whose stipulations provide an excellent route of escape from responsibility for their own actions. After all, when the code of conduct and procedure has been laid down by the gods or by the self-proclaimed gurus, what right do mere mortals have to question them? They must only follow orders thoughtlessly and leave questions of justification of, and responsibility for, their actions to their superiors who are always running away from those responsibilities and passing the buck back to them.

If they are unhappy with this arrangement that sends the ball back into their court, they can decide to follow their own consciences, which will tell them how to differentiate right from wrong and incline them in the right direction; and that is what they eventually have to do with every injunction that is imposed on them by other persons and their holy books—they must learn to think for themselves and make their own choices and decisions, not be led like sheep. Religious affiliation *per se* will not make an immoral person moral; he can stand on a soapbox and proclaim his religion as zealously as he likes, but that alone, without the deeds to match his words, will leave him as evil as the many who hold the fate of the underprivileged in their murderous hands. He has to be moral and virtuous before he embraces his religion, which he does not need to make him so, but which he may use to show (not tell) others what it means to be virtuous. No ethical codes will ever help them to decide between right and wrong, and no sanctified theoretical knowledge of the same codes, however detailed and sophisticated, will ever fashion them into moral beings. They should learn to recognize the absurdity in some of the alleged "truths" contained in their holy books, such as that

a) what the holy book says it is true; (no proof required)
b) the holy book says injunction ψ is true,
c) therefore injunction ψ is true. QED.

The truth of a) is not self-evident; so it cannot be accepted without proof, and b) cannot be accepted on that basis. c) is therefore an invalid conclusion, even though the structure of the argument is valid. The argument itself is not sound, but people who call themselves the true believers who have seen the way to salvation accept this kind of illogical argument glibly and will stake their lives on it. That is all very well, because they are free to do as they like with their own lives, but they don't only stop there, they want to force other people to see life through their distorting eyeglasses and to act as irrationally as they are doing. Why can't they live and let live as Humanists do with other people?

They should learn to realize that they will be truly happy only if they live in peace and harmony with other persons without necessarily obeying a divine command in doing so, because without that command they will live in perpetual war of all against all even as they are doing today under it—Catholics versus Protestants, Sunni versus Shiites, and Christians versus Muslims, Presidents versus citizens. But the snag is that some people have the most warped consciences; all they ever think about is how much evil they can wreak to reap what is good for themselves, and that is why they will exploit any and every situation in which they are involved to suit their own ends, regardless of how costly and hurtful it is to other persons. As the saying goes, they are always looking out for number one; everything starts and ends with them. For them, happiness means their own happiness; they do not accept the challenge posed by others who have elected to act only in a way that will potentially or actually result in the most good and the least evil for everyone everywhere by promoting their maximum individual happiness and best interests, helping to reduce their suffering to the minimum that is tolerable, pending its complete elimination, nor do they ever think of going beyond attending only to the welfare of number one, number two, number three, number four — me, myself, my wife, and my five children — to include all of humanity, present and future, in the benefits that will accrue from their actions now and in the years to come. They demand unconditional loyalty from everyone associated with them, but they are so disloyal to them that they will readily sacrifice them to save their hides.

Even so, many who are thus inclined tend to limit their utilitarianism strictly to parochial boundaries and to situations in which they stand to gain immediate benefits of prestige or money, forgetting the incalculable harm that is being wrought on millions of disadvantaged peoples by the policies of their friends in high places, which they are always ready to condone, even if it is disinterestedly, when they could and should be condemning them plangently. They are still wrapped in their cocoons of selfishness that do not recognize the moral being of others around them, whether near or far. They claim rightly that they cannot be expected to be responsible for the wellbeing of everyone in their world, because charity begins at home. But their home is restricted to their own home, and they will not do anything to curb their own actions or those of other persons like them that are meant to hurt everyone else and to exploit their happiness to ensure their own happiness and advantage in life. To them, the other is an object, an "it" rather than a "you", to be used as means for the realization of their own ends, contrary to the wise words of Martin Buber:

> The basic word I-You can only be spoken with one's whole being.
> The basic word I-It can never be spoken with one's whole being.[6]

The unseemly behaviour of these people leaves no doubt that they believe in a world of us and them. "[They] do not know association; [they] only know the feverish world out there and [their] feverish desire to use it. When [they] say You, [they] mean: You, my ability to use!"[7] and, of course, they don't want to go on a limb to incur the displeasure of their ilk by acting in sympathy with the underdogs and risking all the vilification that goes with the expression of that displeasure when they are enjoying the same comforts and privileges as those who will vilify them for being deviants. Yes, standing up for the rights of the underprivileged is being a deviant, a kaffir-boetie or nigger lover. So, they curb their ostensibly benevolent activities and confine them to acceptably safe limits where they can in turn be condoned by the hawks and misanthropes, very much against the demands of their prototype ethical maxim that urges them to pursue the course of bringing high quality pleasure to everyone regardless of the cost to themselves, sometimes, if not always. Being mere human beings they cannot see themselves sacrificing their well-being for the welfare of complete strangers at home and far abroad, and worse still, of future generations whose wants and needs they cannot anticipate. Such altruism, they claim, is the preserve of special beings of whom there are very limited numbers in their world; it cannot be expected of them and everyone else who is living for the present and living well. And these are followers of the greatest altruists, Confucius, Jesus, and Mohammad.

From these types, one can expect only a readiness to sacrifice vulnerable but innocent individuals for the gratification, pacification, or appeasement of the many in their midst who may be clamouring for revenge for anti-social deeds committed by unknown persons. On the other hand, if their actions had been guided by a sense of justice, and the duty of respecting the rights of other persons, they would not have flinched from taking the right decision only after they had diligently investigated their cases to find the right culprits. But they are always in such a hurry to pacify and to advance their own careers that they will incriminate innocent persons with crimes that they know very well that they did not commit, especially if they are from less privileged sections of the community. What they need is to hang placards on their walls and around their necks inscribed with these words: "Act so that you treat humanity, whether in your own person or in that of another, always as an end and never as a means only"[8] or "Act as though the maxim of your action were by your will to become a universal law of nature".[9] When the misery that they inflict on others by using them inhumanely is legally inflicted on them, they should be happy and satisfied with the action, because they have established that kind of action as appropriate for all persons. But that is not what they intend when they act in a manner that rational beings would not want to see universalized, because they act under on the invalid assumption that events will not take a turn to where they also find themselves on the receiving end of similar inhumane actions, like the amoral, self-centred man described by Bernard Williams in the first chapter of his book "*Morality*" whose unbecoming behaviour is parasitic on the goodwill and sincere attempts of other persons to adhere to generally approved ethical norms of behaviour while he requites them by violating every accepted ethical code. (ring familiar?) Deliberate unconcern for the welfare of other persons as entities that deserve respect and humane treatment, coupled with the desire to bring morbid felicity to their docile base that comprises seasoned howlers and cacophonous misanthropes masquerading as the vocal majority, easily dissuades them from pursuing the noble goal that they should be embracing unreservedly. What could be nobler than redeeming the lives of millions of deprived peoples or even those of the few scapegoats who have been unjustly implicated in murders that they didn't commit or in the abduction of children whose tearful mothers were later proved to be the culprits who were guilty of disposing of them? Not promotion earned disreputably, Mr. Prosecutor, by securing the conviction of someone who is innocent of the crime with which you are calumniating him and reflecting your "lack of capacity for a sense of justice", which is an indisputable ignominy in your position. It also reflects unfavourably on the morals of the society that condones this despicable act of thus using an underprivileged member of the community for the gratification of their morbid desires, rather than finding the right culprit and "using" him to send a message to the community that will help to shape the mores that they are selfishly distorting with their treatment of an innocent victim.

Still others claim to believe in treating everyone justly and fairly, meting out rewards and punishments without bias in proportion to the actions that trigger those compensations, and ensuring that the basic goods needed for survival are available to all persons, but especially to those who have been degraded by society to the ranks of the lowest wannabes who have no hope of ameliorating their doleful circumstances. And yet, all we see is unjust justice that I discussed in *Homan Inhomanity*, blatant unfairness in trade, housing, education, employment, and the lucrative pursuit of political opportunity with access to perks that are denied the ordinary citizen who pays the taxes that provide the funds for those perks. Everything seems to be and is weighted against the wannabes in favour of the holders of the trump cards, and however much the underdogs protest about their unfair treatment, their protestations always fall on deaf ears; the people on the gravy train don't heed them; they remain selectively deaf to their clamorous demands for fairness. Besides, they have no respect for them as subhumans who are just a nuisance in their lives of comfort and excesses. The wannabes try to claim respect for their rights, but the usurpers of those rights ridicule their claims, divesting them of more of their human and other rights by passing laws that will silence them in the name of state and national security. Anyone who dares to question their inhumane actions is declared a security risk, has a file or dossier kept on him, and is spied on for the rest of his life. Everyone's rights are stripped by this ploy that gives the usurpers complete control over the citizens who are presented with the spurious choice of either enjoying their denuded rights or succumbing to decimation by phantom and inert enemies of the state from whom only the usurpers can protect them. The phantoms and bogeymen are constantly dangled before them to cow them into submission. So what do the citizens do? They opt for protection from these apparitions at the expense of their rights, and they end up in the chains that Jean-Jacques Rousseau so aptly referred to when he wrote: "Man is born free; and everywhere he is in chains."[10] Subsequently realizing how they have allowed themselves to be made serfs of their rulers, they try to reverse the situation, but the laws that they embraced in a state of intentionally induced fear now constrain them and threaten to have them thrown in jail for sedition. The rulers have triumphed and entrenched themselves.

That is how the ethics of fairness and respect for the happiness of the privileged converts into the immorality of scorn, disrespect, injustice, and unfairness to those who are owed the duty of service laid down in the holy books of all religions and nationalities. The only problem is that these injunctions are directed at persons who lack the virtue of being basically good persons and whose actions can always be counted on to be other than the right ones in any set of circumstances. Their lack of benevolence and their hard-heartedness, both of which appear to be innate, render them incapable of assuming a non-oppressive attitude toward others. They deny their role in the privations that they have caused, and so they disclaim any obligation to get involved in alleviating the lot of their victims. Meanwhile, they continue to ply their sole purpose in life, which is to hurt them as much as possible, so that they alone can prosper. These are the well-known "statesmen" and others who are nothing but villains, cutthroats, schemers, bigots, liars, thieves, opportunists, and devils whose every action is riddled with evil. They never think to put themselves in the shoes of the deprived to get a semblance of what they are experiencing as dished out by them. Looking at their works of iniquity, they see only their commendable achievements of having put the underdog in his place. Where and how much the shoe that they have compelled him to wear pinches him, they do not want to know or imagine; but they cannot escape the sight of the utter deprivation that they have wrought when it is looking them in the eye. Anyone of them who claims not to be aware of it just does not want to see it, although he continues to exploit it and to benefit from its perpetuation, like the privileged populations of past and current apartheid states and their cheerleaders with their constructive engagement policies who will lie outright to soothe their absent consciences: "we were not aware that you live under such conditions". Where have you been bozos, away on semi-permanent vacation on *Curiosity* hurtling in space to Mars after you created the oppressive conditions?

Persons who are devoid of the virtues of benevolence, compassion, fairness, justice, etc., and have not lived by them cannot be expected to exercise them in any situation, and no amount of appealing to them to alleviate the prevailing human predicament will be of any avail. They are accustomed to malevolence, callousness, partiality, injustice, exploitation, etc., that cause them to ignore the want and suffering of the wannabes and cater to the excesses of those that have more on their plate then they need to live in comfort, because they belong to the same club. All their actions are geared to diverting advantage to their club members away from the underprivileged and deprived masses of people that they are exploiting, and that is why they can say to *the occupiers*, "you have made your point; it's time to go home now", reflecting their insensitivity to the plight of the 99% that are exploited and pushed around by the 1% in whose hands the wealth of the world is concentrated and growing exponentially. These are the people who describe child poverty as inability to own hockey equipment, because parents cannot afford it. I wonder what they will call inability to place a morsel in a hungry child's empty stomach, because his parents can't afford it. But those are not the kinds of abject poverty over which they lose any sleep; they care more about the luxurious poverty of children with full tummies engaging in expensive sporting activities. What a shame.

When they go out of their way to enact statutes that ostensibly stand to assist everyone in the population who might not have the means to provide for the future of their special needs progeny, they are, in fact, paving the way to benefit themselves, their own children, and their club members who can afford to invest in such schemes, which are beyond affordability for the underprivileged. They guide their lives and actions by this sore lack of the quality of virtue, which is not entirely teachable, although some people believe that it can be taught by emulating virtuous persons so that actions can be defined as virtuous if they emulate those that virtuous persons would do in the circumstances under consideration. But this is a circular definition that defines the action by the person and the person by the action. The only way out of the circle is to allow that some person(s) initially acquired the quality *de novo* to be able to serve as the paradigms from which the definition was framed. But this is to engage in theoretical ethics in which the practicalities of ethical living are bound to be eclipsed if not lost. Trying to teach an innately callous person empathy is tantamount to changing his character by a 180^0 turnaround, which is not always possible. Faced with daily situations in which his callousness is second nature, he does not have to pretend not to be what he is (callous), but faced with exceptional situations where benevolence is called for and where callousness has no place, he struggles but fails to be what he is not (benevolent), and his real nature exposes itself for all to behold. The truly benevolent person who does not have to wait to be faced with exceptional situations to display his benevolence displays that virtue effortlessly, because that is how he lives his life and how he raises his children, which is not how the callous person raises his children. The lives of parents and children in the callous society are permeated by an odious phoniness that stinks from a mile away. Similar arguments apply to the pretence of these people to display other virtues that are alien to them, whatever the percentage of citizenry affected.

On all counts, whether the human agent acts in conformity with the principles espoused by any one or more of the above-mentioned ethical theories and practices, the virtuous person whose example is to be followed is the benevolent one who recognizes, respects, and makes a rational choice to uphold the dignity and humanity of all persons while striving at all times to allow those human values to flourish in any and every situation, and not to stifle them. He has no problem with flogging his brain trying to remember and observe ethical laws that purport to govern moral conduct, because it is not possible to frame a law and all the exceptions to it for every conceivable and inconceivable situation. He does not need to resolve the inevitable clash of recommendations from the various ethical theories, whether to promote the greatest happiness of the greatest number at the expense of one or a few; to observe the strict imperative of duty not to tell a lie, even if that will endanger many lives; or to refrain from using his powers of reasoning and obey only the commands of the gods as conveyed to him by other finite persons who have now assumed the role of authority. Meanwhile, his uncharitable counterpart will have a problem trying to act only as virtuous persons do, if he even knows any in his depraved circles, or if he will even be able to recognize the virtuous actions of these aliens when he comes across them. The good person is not obligated to stratify these laws, so that some duties implied by them take precedence over others (*prima facie* duties) in situations that require resolution, because, even in those situations he does not have any other criteria than acting in the best interests of the person(s) concerned when he is making those decisions. He does not harm anyone, but always tries to do what is morally right and best for everyone, doing for others the good that he would do or like to have done for himself, and ensuring equal access to the basic goods of life for everyone for the sake of living a decent life, not from a sense of qualifiable duty, but only because it is the right thing to do in any circumstances. He has no quarrel with persons who happen to do the right things like him for the wrong reasons, as by persuasion, his hope being that the practice will instil in them the a recognition of what is intrinsically right and do it for that reason. So he does not withhold credit from them whilst expecting others to lavish it on him for having attained his level of morality; he extends compliments to them too as a form of encouragement to persist in doing right by others, by persuasion or otherwise, until they see the true light of day that will inspire them always to do right for its own sake.

We would like to think that these demands are so obvious that they should occur intuitively to everyone who is not mentally challenged, but intuition cannot always be relied upon to convey the right judgment for the right action in every circumstance, since one can feel intuitively certain about the correctness of something that is incorrect. In such cases there is no chance of appeal to a faculty that is more basic or fundamental than intuition; only experience can correct the intuitive error in the same way that empirical errors are corrected empirically, e.g., one may see a crooked stick in the grass in poor lighting conditions, and yet feel certain that one saw a snake and react with snake-fearing behaviour, until a second look with closer scrutiny reveals one's mistake. There is no other way of correcting this mistake but to look again. With intuitive error, there is no second intuition with closer scrutiny to reveal one's mistake; only appeal to other modalities in use for acquiring knowledge will rectify the error. This lack of intuitive certainty provides a handy excuse for the bigots of this world who claim exoneration from culpability for their inhumane actions on the basis of ignorance of these demands and how to tell if any action is the virtuous one, since the criteria of virtue have also not been rigidly laid down. They argue further that duties are relative to different cultures at different times and in different circumstances as we saw on page 23 with the practices of cultures where old and frail persons who are dying are put out to die without the fanfare of ventilators, tubes, etc., as happens in other cultures where death is an unwelcome event and everything possible is done to postpone it, even at the expense of the dignity of the dying person; but they are not fooling anyone—benevolence and caring transcend the bounds of relativity in morality anywhere at any time. The good of the community outweighs by far the good of any individual in that community, and no one has the right to place in jeopardy the interests of others by acting selfishly and without due regard for those interests. Besides, the validity of this postulated relativism has to be parasitic on its own covert absolutism if it is to survive self-destruction and degeneration into amorality, since it has to possess a considerable degree of absoluteness to be able to withstand the onslaught of other relativistic viewpoints.

So in considering the truth status of relativistic viewpoints, we should be aware that the same ethical proposition (e.g., killing another person for other than self-defence) can be both right and wrong at the same time, depending on beliefs, practices, and justifications thereof by different groups of people with different cultural backgrounds, thus rendering universal morality otiose, because each side can advance what it considers good reasons for sticking with its point of view and not yielding an inch to the opposite viewpoint. On the other hand, the presence of an absolute standard would at the very least provide a focus around which arguments *pro et contra* could be centred; but who is to set that standard? Well, the standard should not be impossible for rational creatures to agree upon, although different communities may have different ways of dealing with deviations from it; but people should not allow contrived relativity to turn them into irrational, amoral beasts. Everyone should know how not to cause harm to other people but to help them to live the decent life that he wishes for himself as much as this is humanly possible; the rest will follow automatically without the need for focussing on and arguing about the meanings of theoretical ethical codes but forgetting to live by their injunctions, or by pretending instead to be following the fanciful call of transcendent divine injunctions, which the hypocrites profess but do not hesitate to violate with impunity all the time.

Chapter 8

Unveiling Transcendence

Transcendence refers to the process of actually reaching beyond the range of regular human experience and understanding, the occasional out-of-this-world into the unknown that is brought on by a variety of stimuli, of which religion is the one that we will discuss in this section of human agency. For ordinary human beings to be able to apprehend the object that is beyond their senses of seeing, touching, hearing, tasting, and smelling, they will have to rely on their imagination or on the many mystical experiences that are claimed by those who are privileged to have them. The rest of us are expected to believe them without convincing, rational evidence. Figuratively, however, transcendence is an attainable pursuit that consists of a coming out of himself and a transportation of its subject beyond the bounds of his puny ego to a realization of the being of other subjects besides himself and of a reality to life that lies outside of his circumference of limited self-regard, with the especial benefit of the entire world of human and other agents in mind. But transcendence in the religious sense is quite different and extremely challenging. It is tied to faith in the existence of an unreachable and unknowable object to which religious people perform the impossible feat of reaching out when they take temporary leave of this world to enjoy a brief sojourn in a mysterious and mythical somewhere-we-know-not-where, a place where they can escape the buffets of their daily lives, paradoxically reach the unreachable and similarly acquire knowledge of this unknowable object of their knowledge—quite a contorted feat, I must admit!

Now, since knowledge entails acquaintance by way of either experience or rational deduction, belief in this kind of transcendence brings us in direct conflict with both empiricism and rationalism. We are required to commit ourselves to a method of acquiring knowledge that is as outlandish as doing so by faith, the antithesis of evidence. Ordinarily we operate on the principle that defines knowledge as true belief that is justified by universally accessible evidence, not the kind of evidence that is the prerogative of only those select individuals to whom it has been revealed (by?) or the shaky, manufactured evidence that is often used to claim that the mere existence of the universe, whether created or spontaneous, is ultimate evidence of the existence of transcendent forces of the religious kind that brought it into being and to whose guidance we should submit our lives. Such evidence generates a regress of evidences to justify preceding evidences, besides calling for an unassailable definition of truth. Faith and its compatriot transcendence demand belief in an inaccessible and unknowable reality that constitutes a direct affront to our sense of integrity in the search for open truth, since belief in the existence of transcendent reality is belief in the hidden "truth" of that reality and what it purports to represent, which may be nothing. People have been known to yield to sufficient arm twisting and even coercion to make them believe in figments of the imagination, believing in propositions that they know can't be proved by anyone, since their proof, if there is one, is the sole prerogative of those who are positing them for general acceptance. In the face of knowledge as justified true belief, one balks at the idea of accepting this characterization of faith as knowledge: "We shall now have a full definition of faith if we say that it is a firm and sure knowledge of the divine favour toward us, founded on the truth of a free promise in Christ, and revealed to our minds, and sealed on our hearts, by the Holy Spirit. "[1] I am unable to decipher the sealing process, but whatever that means in practical terms, how can one claim firmness and certainty of knowledge that is based on faith in the truth of a promise given by someone else, as if that alone constitutes indefeasible evidence? There is no question here that faith is "contrary to reason", even though some philosophers find it necessary to favour it with a special dispensation by denying knowledge to make room for it. Such is the power of faith that it can be exempted from the rigorous evidentialism (demand that the truth of claims to knowledge be justified by evidence) to which every other claimant to truth is subjected on the basis of authoritative divine testimony—hard to swallow, unless one already believes in the divine on the basis of the same authoritative testimony$_1$, which is based on previous authoritative testimony$_2$, which is in turn based on authoritative testimony$_3$ that emanated from authoritative testimony$_4$, *ad infinitum*. But to add insult to injury, the truth of the existence of that divine authority figure can be accepted only on the prior belief in its existence, not on the prior evidence for its existence—strange logic.

As I have already indicated, we recognize two modalities of acquiring knowledge of reality, and between them they do not leave any room for faith and transcendence. The two modalities are empirical (*a posteriori*) knowledge as knowledge acquired only from our sensory experience of reality, such as by seeing, touching, hearing, smelling, or tasting something and knowledge acquired by pure reason without the intervention of prior experience (*a priori*), such as that an object cannot be red and green all over at the same time, or that if A=B and B=C, then A=C. These conceptual truths are known intuitively, and they can be entertained and accepted without any proof from sensory experience, although they are also amenable to empirical proof by demonstration. Anyone can paint a golf ball red all over and then try to paint it green all over at the same time without obscuring the red colour and noticing that the maneuver does not work; instead, one could end up with a yellowish golf ball, if the colours blended into each other appropriately. Similarly, anyone can confirm (visually, by measurement) that object A's weight and volume are the same as those of object B, and then do the same for objects B and C; from which it then becomes apparent that A=B=C, proving the intuitive fact that if A=B and B=C, then A=C. At the other extreme, which is the empirical extreme of sensory experience, there is no way that we can deduce the properties of objects from merely thinking about them as we can in the examples quoted above. The only way that we can tell that dough is soft is by touching it, and we can tell that the sky is blue only by looking at it, or that a loud and piercing sound hurts the ears only by hearing it, or that sugar is sweet only by tasting it; i.e. only through perception via the appropriate or relevant sensory modality, even taking into account the fact that we sometimes misperceive reality. But that should not be a problem, because we can recognize misperceptions from knowing authentic perceptions, and hence we can rectify them when they occur, as Gilbert Ryle observed: "There can be false coins only where there are coins made of the proper materials by the proper authorities. . . . there remains one proposition which he cannot entertain, the proposition, namely, that it is possible that all coins are counterfeits. For there must be an answer to the question 'Counterfeits of what?'"[2] No one can taste the sweetness of sugar with her ears or smell the aroma of roses with her eyes, unless she has been endowed with presumed special powers to transcend the sensory limitations imposed on mere mortals by their constitution; but anyone is free to run the relevant tests to prove or disprove these facts. On the other hand, no one has the liberty to do the same with the claims of the preachers of transcendence, because there are no rational methods of testing those claims besides appeal to blind faith. One either has to take that incredible leap or just flatly refuse to venture into that uncertain and inaccessible territory on a factual basis.

Sense perceptions are the final port of call on our journey to acquaint ourselves with and to get to know reality; they are "the ultimate evidence" for the justification of our beliefs. No amount of mulling over the physico-chemical properties of these objects and phenomena will reveal those sensations to us; we have to experience them. Between these two extremes are those truths that pass both tests for intuitive and empirical truths, e.g., 2+2=4, or the whole is bigger than its part—if a slice of cake has been cut from a particular slab of cake, then that slab must be bigger than that slice, although it is conceivable that a really thick slice from one cake can be bigger than a small slab of another cake; but certainly not a slice from the same slab. Of course one can still argue that experience has taught us that two horses + two horses = four horses, since such a conclusion does not come inscribed on any combination of horses; it is arrived at by definition, and definition is a mental maneuver that is the result of consensus on the use of terms, not a result of experiencing such packages in nature. Consensus could just as easily have settled on a different concept, i.e., 2 +2 = 5. Similarly, visual and tactile experience (measurement) can teach us that the slice is smaller than its parent slab, although we might not need this kind of experience to know such an obvious fact. We need not delve too deeply into the complexities of arguments about the authenticity of measurements and the possibility of errors in perception, because errors also occur in conceptual procedures. We can make mistakes about what we see as much as we can also make mistakes in mathematical calculations, passing successive generations of false beliefs as truths and all our false beliefs generally as knowledge, and thus living a lie, much as we often do under the influence of lying politicians and others who trade freely in mendacities. But in all cases we have ways of discovering and correcting our errors of perception and conception, and this is aside from questions about using the wrong words to describe what we perceive or conceive correctly; it is about the actual processes of perception and conception *per se*. Ultimately, we must live with our perceptual and conceptual capacities and abilities, regardless of the fact that they sometimes mislead us; no others are available to us as long as we belong to the Homo sapiens species of mundane animals. So much for this necessary, orienting digression; now back to the subject of transcendence.

The word "transcendence" is derived from the Latin trans = beyond or over + scandere = to climb. Transcendence therefore implies existence or being beyond the coordinates of space and time The concept *transcendence* is evident in Plato's Theory of Forms in which he referred to a supra-sensible, unattainable realm of ideal Forms that can be appreciated only via the mind's ability to reach beyond the limits of the material body whose reach is limited to its immediate narrow or wider circumference. The Forms, in contrast to all the ever changing and disintegrating material substances of our world, human beings included, are eternal "spiritual" substances that retain their stability through time. In our experience, our bodies are undergoing constant physical change as their cells perish with time and are replaced by newly generated ones. Simultaneously, our identities seem to persist through time by virtue of whatever is responsible for them—call it soul, mind, or what you will. The extraterrestrial Forms, like the soul or mind, on the other hand, are imperishable, and it is this stability that makes them the independently existing prototypes for the predicates of the discourses that we employ in the subject-predicate sentences of this world, e.g., x is beautiful, or just, or good means that x participates in the Forms of the Beautiful, the Just, or the Good. x can only participate in the Form; it can never exhaust it, because other objects, a, y, z, etc., that are beautiful, just, or good are called that by virtue of their participation in the same inexhaustible Forms. The objects (subjects of subject-predicate sentences) may perish, but the qualities that describe them (predicates of subject-predicate sentences = Forms) endure through time. In modern parlance, the relationship between transcendent Forms and their mundane counterparts can be equated with that existing between concept and object on one hand, and universal and particular on the other. Several particular objects can all fall under the same universal concept, like all blue objects that participate in or share the colour blue without ever exhausting it.

At no time, however, did Plato ever produce any concrete evidence of the existence of these transcendent forms or of the soul that allows us to communicate with them and thereby "obtain a foretaste of immortality."

They remained mere postulates existing in an imaginary world, and yet from this Platonic postulate of a faculty that facilitates communication with the Forms to the existence of an immaterial soul that communicates with a divine being who cannot be apprehended by human senses and who also provides an eternal abode for this soul, Descartes found it easy to postulate his own theory of personhood as a compound of body and soul (mind), with the latter being able to leave the body and exist in detached form as a disembodied mind. In so doing, he set the stage for the religious dogma of fictitious souls that leave the body when the person dies to inhabit equally fictitious celestial abodes for whose existence there was and still is no evidence whatsoever beyond the creaky insistence of mystics; they who can pit the hypothetical and unknown against the proved and known and still opt for the hypothetical .

From these daring speculations and bold ventures into a mysterious and inaccessible realm, religious people found reason to formulate and promote their belief that humanity can never comprehend the gods that they have created for their comfort, because, being transcendent and therefore out of contact with this world, they cannot possibly be known by any of the means for the acquisition of knowledge that we have detailed above. But that claim does not make sense, because their gods are products of their own making, and hence must be knowable; and that is borne out by the fact that they have endowed them with omnipotence, omnibenevolence, omniscience, omnipresence, etc. Either they know that their gods have these characteristics, in which case they are knowable, or they don't know the real qualities of their gods and they dress them up in human qualities for convenience, because their true nature is beyond the reach of common human knowledge and understanding. As St. Augustine said, apprehension of eternal truths (which religious folk claim through divine revelation) doesn't equate with knowledge of God's nature in this life, but is possible only after death. So, are these phony gods, these perishable products of human imagination, of any use to us? It seems that whatever their presumed nature may be, we do not need them for solving our problems of living, and on that account we do not need them in our lives. Being irrelevant, they might as well not exist for us.

To repair this damaging situation, mystics and others have made efforts to bridge this gap between the mundane and the transcendent by claiming immanence in transcendence for their gods, thus conferring on their nature the inconsistency of being here and not being here at the same time and thereby making them as contradictory as round squares. But they have also dared to claim for themselves possession of special powers that enable them to engage in privileged communication with the gods and then tried to make the rest of us believe in their fantasies, as if we cannot reason that godly transcendence is intrinsically incompatible with godly immanence and with their inability to bridge the gaping chasm between the transcendent and the mundane logically, ontologically, and epistemologically. They prefer not to listen to Spinoza when he tells them that ". . . knowledge of G-D, is not the consequence of something else, but immediate, . . . since there is such a close union between G-D and us, it is evident that we cannot know Him except directly."[3] Spinoza repeatedly stresses that knowledge of God whom he regards as immanent, rather than transcendent, is immediate and direct, even if it entails knowing him to some degree only, because without such knowledge we cannot possess any other knowledge. So the architects of the transcendence theory have only succeeded in shooting themselves in the foot, according to Spinoza, since their transcendent and unknowable god is knowable, after all. But the proponents of immanence are no better than those who believe in transcendence, because they also engage in wishful thinking, besides kissing and worshipping statues, which they apparently regard as the two way street that simultaneously facilitates ready access to immanent transcendence and transcendent immanence. If Zeno had had the privilege of hearing these arguments he would have included them in his paradoxes of plurality and motion, like his famous example of Achilles and the tortoise where he gives the tortoise a head-start in their race, but never catches up to or overtakes the tortoise, because each time he reaches the point where the tortoise was, it has already moved on, regardless of how small the distance is. In practice this situation is as much a howler as the one outlined above.

In contrast to these excursions into fairyland, while agreeing with the concept of the transcendent as that which is not real but ideal because it is beyond the bounds of experience and hence inaccessible to all human knowledge, Kant did not go so far as to equate the transcendent with deity or to link it with a mysterious soul that alone has been accorded the ability to comprehend that deity. He distinguished it from the transcendental, which is that which we can conceive but cannot experience via perception, such as the thing in itself (*ding an sich*) that we can only conceive from our experience of objects that we perceive, e.g., the apple that we see and eat is a mere representation of the real apple or thing-in-itself that is beyond the reach of our sensory perception. So what are we eating if not the real thing that we can see, touch, taste, smell, bite and chew? Perhaps we are eating sense-data, as the phenomenalist would assert, since he interposes sense-data between real objects and us, claiming that we never experience objects *per se*, but only the representative data (visual, auditory, tactile, olfactory, or gustatory) that result from the interaction of our sensory apparatus and the objects that we are perceiving; to which we reply with the questions: data from objects apart from us via our sense data or from our sense organs by self-generation, and data that are variable and impossible to re-identify and change their character with the changing states of the same perceiver and with different perceivers and their changing states?

We cannot follow these conundrums without going into discussions about Hilary Putnam's brains in vats and the experiments of Dr. Wilder Penfield, which demonstrated how easily we can be deceived into thinking that we are experiencing an outside world when we are only experiencing stimulation of certain sensory areas of our brains that give us the feeling of perceiving things external to our bodies. Suffice it to say, however, that even these experiments do not dispose of the outside world of common sense, because the responses of the stimulated brain produce consistent pictures of what both the experimenters and other persons who have not been similarly treated claim to experience in their ordinary awake states. (Of course Putnam's argument is more complicated than I have simplistically portrayed it). Georg W. Hegel's simple rejoinder and counter-argument to this hazy concept of transcendence was that a boundary cannot be known without knowing the nature of the entities on either side of it that it separates. That means we must already know the nature of those entities that are believed to be beyond the reach of human accessibility, acquaintance, and knowledge to be able to draw the line of demarcation between them and entities that are accessible to our sensory experiences. Without such prior knowledge, it is impossible to know where to draw the line.

As mentioned above, Kant also held that appearances of reality and our interpretations of them are all we can ever know, but we will never know reality as it is, or the objects that cause those appearances—which leads one to ask how we know that those appearances are caused by the objects that they purport to represent without distortions, omissions, or additions, and why we should not be content with how we perceive our world, which is the only way that we will ever perceive and know it. After all, we are still able to distinguish between apparitions and perceptions of real external objects out there that cause those perceptions in us. Besides, since different persons perceive and interpret appearances differently, the worlds that they construct will of necessity be different, and yet we claim to see and discourse about the same things. We claim factual perceptions of oranges, bananas, and apples, because under standard conditions that exclude optical illusions caused by subjective factors like defective vision and external influences like inadequate lighting, real oranges, bananas, and apples cause those perceptions in us, not misrepresentations of unknowable Forms that could, without our knowing it, be other things like worms, snakes, and crocodiles. But since we can't step outside ourselves to eliminate the subjective point of view, and we also cannot know if things as such$_1$ have another and true nature (things as such$_2$) as well; they might, in fact, also be representations of other things as such$_3$, which are representations of things as such$_4$, and so on *ad infinitum,* all of which we can and will never know. Besides, our perceptions are the only means of contact with our surroundings, and we have to rely on them to convey to us what is out there, as long as we are aware of pitfalls of illusion and other limitations, which we come to know by knowing how authentic objects present to our perceptions. So when do we get to know these authentic objects to be able to correct our misperceptions, and how else can we tell that there are objects out there without using one or more of our modalities of sensation to establish that fact? Try hard as we may, we can never extinguish all our sensory modalities and still claim to experience the now experientially inaccessible world and its unknowable contents by reason or intuition or some magic. Nevertheless, this is not to deny that whatever reality happens to be, we perceive it subjectively, and we add that subjective viewpoint to how we interpret it—that is an unavoidable fact, and that is why our accounts and valuations of the same situations are more often than not as many as there are perceivers or observers; don't they say beauty is in the eye of the beholder?

Taking all these and many more considerations into account, it is surely pertinent to ask how believers in religious transcendence know what is beyond their capacity to know either empirically or rationally, but by blind faith, unless they are trying to pull wool over our eyes. True, they can conjure up any mental picture of what their wishful thinking can muster, as much as a child can conjure up mental pictures of fictitious persons, including Santa Claus and the tooth fairy, but that doesn't prove the existence of these objects. If it did, we could also conjure up pictures of golden mountains that we will spend our next summer vacation scaling. Wouldn't that be exciting? We imagine something, and, abracadabra, it becomes a reality. We imagine that if deceased persons are nominally baptized (by proxy) by us, they will be salvaged from where they have been languishing for decades or even centuries, so that they can finally find their way into the kingdom of heaven. Finally, they are emancipated from one form of temporary oblivion to enter the next one where they can await further emancipation or else resign themselves to what will now be their ultimate oblivion.

In the previous chapter, we were concerned with questions of right and wrong actions; but as we noted at the end of the chapter, transcendence beyond utilitarian, deontological, and other theories of action is more often than not called for in selecting those right actions that will be useful in establishing loving human relationships. Often, the best relationships are those that cannot be categorized as utilitarian or deontological, since they do not spring from any desire to delight or to fulfill a duty, but from a deeper sense of innate love of fellow human beings. I call it innate love to emphasize the point that it has nothing to do with what allegedly lies beyond the confines of our world and knowledge and resides in celestial realms about which we know and can prove nothing. Most of us have acquired the bad habit of speculating about the nature of the next world, which we claim that we will inhabit after the expiry of our lifespans in the only world that we know; and we even go so far as to describe it as a city whose streets are paved with gold—a daring bit of overreach, confidently describing what we have not seen. But we have no business to overextend our wishful thinking and flights of airy fancy to such absurd limits as to conjure up these outrageous fabrications that we sell as reality, claiming at the same time that they have been revealed to some of us alone in private communication with the deity that resides in those select gilded realms. The proselytizers would have us believe that their experiences are as self-authenticating as our daily perceptual experiences of the world around us, of the existence of other people and their impenetrable minds, and of the fact that night will not persist for ever without any chance of daylight succeeding it—facts that lie beyond the bounds of the challenge to which their unreal figments of transcendence are subject. They fail to distinguish between what might have actually happened (objectively) and what they thought or wish had happened (subjectively). But they are so bold as to objectify their subjective experiences, insisting that we should believe in their fantasy trips and regard religious belief as axiomatic or foundational as the fact that in Euclidian Geometry the shortest distance between two points is a straight line, a fact for which we have no formal proof other than that it is basic and self-evident. It has also stood the test of time as the solid rock on which we have constructed theorems involving the use of straight lines in the form of isosceles, right angled, scalene, and other triangles that have always proved to be true, and we have used this information practically and authentically in daily life, as in this example from my *Our World and its Values*.[4] They want us to believe in the truth of unfounded religious beliefs based on other unfounded beliefs, *ad infinitum,* in spite of the insubstantial nature of the results of such beliefs. The problem is that if the initial beliefs were unjustified, lacking evidence, and even the results of wishful thinking, then all subsequent beliefs based on them will be false and not worthy of being believed, because they all form an intricate web of inexactitudes in which the unwary can be trapped at any point.

To those who are not convinced that the religious experiences of believers are proof enough of the existence of their Deity, their only response is that any efforts to prove his existence by argument will be wasted on non-believers; they have to go through religious experiences to be able to believe in the existence of Deity. And yet, the same believers have devised proofs for the existence of their Deity to convince non-believers: the ontological argument should claim that if merely thinking of Deity proves his existence, then the thought of a golden mountain should also prove its existence, which we know is outrageous logic; the cosmological argument should claim that if Deity is uncaused, being the first cause (why?), so should everything else, contrary to the postulate that everything has a cause; and the argument from design should allow that Deity must have a designer$_1$ who must also have had his designer$_2$, who must have had his designer$_3$, and so on *ad infinitum*. Do their tactics work? There is no evidence that they do, and more that they don't. That is why Blaise Pascal devised his theistic gamble: believe in Deity and you will enjoy eternal bliss in the afterlife. If the belief happens to be unfounded, you have nothing to lose, and you will at least have led a fruitful life. But if you disbelieve, you stand the chance of everlasting damnation in your afterlife, if there happens to be a Deity, besides having led a ruinous life. So your best bet is to take the chance of believing in Deity, since objective, rational, justified, and conclusive evidence for belief in the same Deity is not forthcoming; i.e., be a fideist in defiance of all evidence to the contrary. I will not even mention the problem of all the evil in this world that I dealt with on pages 44-45 of *Homan Inhomanity*, which theodicies can't adequately dispose of. I am not persuaded to believe that it exists as a form of punishment for humans for misusing their freedom of choice by going for the bad things in life, or as Deity's means of maximizing human happiness in utilitarian fashion.

We are left in a quandary, because one is supposed to be committed to

the truth of what one believes; but we are called upon to believe in what is most likely not true. Consider the following statements:
1. "The view that there is a God explains *everything* we observe."[5]
2. The view that there is a pumpkin explains everything we observe.
3. The view that there is no God explains everything we observe.
4. The view that there is a Santa Claus explains everything we observe.

Why should anyone believe statement 1 in preference to the other statements, unless the proof that has been produced for it is overwhelming? Even so, the categorical character of all these statements does not justify any kinds of conclusions from them without evidence to support those conclusions. Anyone can make wild claims that he expects other people to believe simply because he has made those claims, like the claims in quotations [5]above and [6 & 7] below. Reasons have not been produced thus far by the promoters of view #1 above to make us believe that theism adequately explains the observed data when evolution does an incomparably better and evidence-supported job of explaining the same observed data. So when they go on to ascribe infinite powers and other attributes to their god that they deny Santa Claus and the pumpkin, they are making sweeping arbitrary assumptions that cannot even be justified by the proffered evidence. They say he can "make gunpowder explode when we set a match to it"[6], as if we don't know the chemistry of the reaction that we have set off by so doing, and as if we cannot claim the same for Santa Claus or the pumpkin without, like them, also proffering any proof. They say the he can do anything, and he can change or suspend the laws of nature that we discussed on page 32, creating horrendous and inexcusable havoc and chaos in the universe, but he can't do what is logically impossible, like making it untrue that if all men are mortal, and Jim is a man, then Jim is mortal; Jim is still as mortal as all other men like him. They say he knows everything, but not what we will do tomorrow—everything? They say he is everlasting; he had no beginning, and he is "something that exists under its own steam, not dependent on anything else."[7] So what stops the universe and life as we know it from also having arisen spontaneously and existing under its own steam, rather than having been created and now being sustained by him, and what prevents the laws of nature, as we formulated them from observing the regularity with which natural events happen, from being self-maintaining, instead of being maintained by him? Besides, why should he choose for us how we will act, if we have freedom of choice, unless we are, in fact, automatons that have no control over our actions, in which case all the hoopla about sinning is just hot air and we should not be held responsible and culpable for actions that hurt other persons; the responsibility should be placed right where it belongs, with him.

What is strange about these arbitrary claims is that they are being promoted as the ultimate facts about what obtains in our universe. People encountered these inexplicable mysteries of reality and life and in their eagerness to fill the gaps in their knowledge just decided that they will invent a deity to serve as the explanation for the inexplicable, and they declared that that is indeed how things are, and the rest of us should accept their fantasies and live by them, as if we can't think for ourselves and make our own informed and reasoned decisions about these matters that they have dreamt up for us. Advances in Science and new knowledge are proving daily that we don't have to accept dubious dogma imposed on us in ignorance. Theism does not, as claimed, provide "the simplest explanation of all phenomena"[8], as much as *msieht* (theism spelled backwards) also fails to do the same, however much we may wish that it should and claim that it does, but science explains most of the *how* of natural phenomena, even though it may, for now, still fail to explain their *what*, like the interface between brain states and thoughts, feelings, etc., which theism also can't explain. Finally, the laws and postulates of science, including evolution by natural selection, are open to confirmation, refutation, or amendment by anyone who cares to do so, as long as she has convincing and conclusive evidence to confirm or disprove prevailing beliefs; but the same cannot be said about theism and *msieht*. They come as a package that must be accepted *in toto* and recited without amendment or any kind of variation; they discourage and forbid critical analysis of their tenets, calling the attempts heresy for which they anathematize the perpetrator. What are they afraid of? Is intellectual enquiry such a big threat?

Ordinarily, we do not disbelieve the authenticity of what we sense (hear, smell etc.), in the appropriate circumstances, until we have good reason to doubt our senses, as in the case of illusions like the stick that is partially immersed at an angle in water appearing to be bent, or the mirage that appears in the middle of the road and disappears as we approach it, or the same pool of cool water that feels warm to the touch after we have immersed our hands in ice-cold water and cold after immersing them in very warm water. The difference is, of course, that experience has taught us that these particular aberrations can be explained logically according to the laws of Physics, whereas religious belief, which blinds people to the truth of factual evidence, demands automatic acceptance of its dubious dogma without evidence of its rationality and without offering any justification for it; and that, to say the least, is asking too much of us, expecting us to act against such wise advice as that we should swear by only those beliefs for which we have unassailable evidence. People often believe propositions for which they have only insufficiently researched or no evidence, and which they therefore have no business to believe as firmly as they do, simply because someone claims to have exclusive access to what he represents and whose truth the people have no means of verifying. As a result, they engage in wrong actions that form the shaky foundations of a concatenation of further wrong actions that unfairly engulf other people over prolonged periods of time, if they are not rectified in a timely fashion. In this situation, they must be held culpable for any ill effects on other persons that result from their unjustified beliefs and the misguided actions that result from them. That would not be the case if their actions were based on beliefs based on the best possible evidence — what could be better than the best, even though it may be a temporary best, pending the possible discovery of a better best.

It is our common experience that the final word on any matter at hand often turns out not to be so, because new evidence often discredits old evidence, accounting for the notable advances in human endeavour that have become the hallmarks of the present age? Besides, knowing the limits of our percipience, when our senses have deceived us, we remain open to correction and to accepting contrary ideas, if they are reasonable, in our search for truth; but religious folk will not brook the contradiction or amendment that will threaten to dismantle their dogmas. Anyone who cannot accept and recite them as they have been articulated must stand aside until he has been brainwashed by them to think like them and accept the same dogma as they do or stay out of their fold. They even take serious issue with those of their fold who use their exclusive ranking to wrestle with issues of social justice in the community instead of devoting their service to plying the dogma of their church, which vilifies and condemns birth control, homosexuality, abortion, etc., while doing nothing to assist in resolving the societal plight of those who are faced with problems centred around these issues. They do not have room for dissenters like those who believe that transubstantiation, for example, is a physical absurdity and logical howler; only the brain-washed who accept and believe such absurdities are welcome within their circles. They anathematize any thinker who questions their irrational beliefs that they propagate without any shred of evidence, because they are afraid that exposing their hollow beliefs will deprive them of the magic that attracts credulous and gullible people to them and also cause the untimely collapse of the empires of exploitation and bigotry that some of them have built around the sale of those beliefs. That's what they are afraid of. They are as afraid of people who think as politicians and their corporate friends are of the same kinds of people who do not fall for the puerile distractions on television that divert other minds from the serious concerns of life or the incurable lying that characterizes their communication, allowing the duo to enslave them and strip them of their rights.

The rational person therefore feels justified in regarding these claims about divine revelation in religion as simply what certain members of the human race, often wiser than their comrades, decide is the truth as manifested to them during these periods of special insight as the opiate that they use to allay the people's troubled minds about the injustices of life in this world and to dissuade them from trying to change it. Meanwhile, they are assuring them of justice in a world to come, after they are dead and buried, of course, if they can just hold out a little longer for now until the dawn of that catastrophic day when all these promises come to naught in the oblivion that will follow their demise. But this is just the kind of fiction that religious folk who would have us believe in their hocus-pocus that there is life after death for themselves and their pets delight in spreading, in addition to claiming that the only source of truth is to be found in their domain of dogmatic disciplines and fundamentalism based on unsubstantiated belief in a divinely revealed transcendent existence conjured up by them to fill the void that will result from their earthly demise.

They foist these beliefs on the rest of us without producing rational and convincing evidence for their hunches, hunches that are based, not on a concatenation of past statistically relevant occurrences that approach the certainty of established facts, but on their fear of death and its oblivion and their wish to continue to live well beyond their allotted time in years. So they have decided that the best way to do it is to magically create this transcendent existence that is awaiting them in never-never land where they will not be overtaken by this oblivion that has been haunting them all their lives, in the same way as all of us are alleged to create our own reality by the way we interpret what we perceive — our interpretations can never exhaust reality, and no one can ever claim to have complete knowledge of it.

Even if one were tempted to believe their hoax, granting that some of our beliefs are based on provisional evidence that has yet to be confirmed, they bedevil the picture by bringing in a devil that has existed from the beginning of time and will persist through time in the same way as their god. Now how is that possible? How can the timeless life span of omnipotence, omniscience, omnibenevolence, and omnipresence be co-extensive with that of the evil that this devil fellow represents in the world and the universe? Why is he allowed to challenge Deity by hanging around for as long as Deity has been around and will be around? Does he do this by his own omnipotence etc., or is he receiving preferential treatment to outlive all the generations of equally sinful humankind when every bone in his body is bad to the core, unlike some humans who exude and epitomize goodness but exist for finite periods? This is a very strange arrangement that should not be allowed to continue unchecked; good guys should not finish last. Perhaps that is why some people engage in absurdities like stomping the devil out or stoning him. They have decided to deal with this menace of a man (or a woman — who knows?) by taking things into their own hands to eliminate him once and for all, regardless of how fatuous or ludicrous their actions may appear to be.

As for the fear of oblivion after death, who can derive comfort from the thought of it, especially when all the available evidence indicates that it will succeed our earthly life, in as much as oblivion also preceded it? And yet we do not fret about our pre-birth oblivion, because we were not yet alive to think and fret about it, as Thomas Nagel has said. So why don't we wait until we are no more (i.e., dead) to see if we will still display or express solicitude about that stretch of oblivion to the extent of inventing a fictitious refuge from it! We won't do that, because we have no physical assurance that anything awaits us beyond the boundary of death, and yet we still believe firmly that we will still be alive in a different world, in a different form, and exempt from the awe that oblivion inspires. So, instead of living in fearful anticipation of this uncertain end of the bliss of a life to come, as proselytized by organized religion, we are trying hard to smother the uncertainty with our other certain and instant bliss, the bliss of this life that we are enjoying now (only some of us privileged ones) by worshipping the god of money, even though that particular refuge has brought more unhappiness than contentment with our lot as the greedy ones among us grab more and more at the expense of the lives of the deprived who have now begun to resist victimization by oppressors at great cost to their own lives. But the endpoint will come, with or without the cooperation of the oppressors; justice will eventually prevail. As one gentleman of the cloth, a transcendentalist, put it, "I do not pretend to understand the moral universe; the arc is a long one, my eye reaches but little ways; I cannot calculate the curve and complete the figure by the experience of sight; I can divine it by conscience. And from what I see I am sure it bends towards justice ".[9]

What is required to amend this doleful situation is for us to engage in the practical and plausible pursuit of trying to transcend our puny egos and their limitations, instead of trying to transcend present life in search of will-o'-the-wisps; to be involved with others so that we can find meaning in our otherwise empty lives, because life cannot be lived in isolation, even in the lower levels of the animal kingdom that we see living, hunting, moving around, and sporting together. Moral ideals don't have to be founded on something beyond our cognitive reach; we should not be striving to establish contact with the unknown and unknowable, leaving the known and knowable to languish from lack of our attention. What is known and knowable are tangible flesh and blood human agents like us, not the ethereal elements that many human agents feel proud to be chasing after and some human agents claim to be mystically acquainted with to the exclusion of others of their kind. We delight in pursuing the transcendent ideal and forget to live in peace and love and peace with our neighbours who do not yield to the pressure to engage in this fruitless pursuit with us, but even with those who are similarly deluded. Seeking eternal life, we forget to live this life in love and peace with our neighbours, and we end up empty-handed in the end, because we sacrificed the welfare of our fellow human agents on the altar of our quest for our own gratification, as usual. But by then it is too late to go back and try to recover what we were given but either despised because everyone else possessed it equally with us or were dissatisfied with and ignored for something better that we conjured up in our minds to conform with our elite status.

It behooves us to steer away from imaginary future abodes in the sky and rather rely on honourable human endeavour to make life worthwhile here and now, as long as the rights of all persons are equitably recognized for reaping the benefits that will accrue from those endeavours. The kind of unjustified discriminations that I have already discussed at length in *Homan Inhomanity* should have no place in this scheme of things where the utilitarian happiness of all should be the governing motivation—serving, giving, and helping. Truth and happiness will be found only in mutual respect and fellowship with one another and not in outlandish figments of the imagination riding on a transcendence that has no foundation in reality. What is required is simple mental and existential self-transcendence: going beyond our egoism, being true to ourselves so that we will not be false to others, and heeding the golden rule in our relationships with other people, being more a part of the only world that we know and will ever know, instead of deceiving ourselves by trying to live beyond it in another fantasy world that is inhabited by spirits, souls, angels, and other imaginary subjects. Owen Flanagan said the same thing when he wrote: "if you wish that your life had prospects for transcendent meaning, for more than personal satisfaction and contentment you can achieve while you are alive, and more than what you will have contributed to the well-being of this world after you die, then you are still in the grip of illusions."[10]

Of course, the holy mob can accuse the secular crowd of committing the logical fallacy of appealing to ignorance by pointing out that their ignorance and denial of the existence of evidence of the hereafter is just another case that illustrates the truth of the fact that absence of evidence for any x does not equate with absence of that x, since the bounds of knowledge exceed by far the capability of the human mind to traverse them. They may argue for the adoption of their belief in transcendent existence by pointing to the adoption of many scientific truths that are beyond dispute today but were the prior subjects of mere speculation with scanty evidence and only a balance of accumulated mathematical probabilities in their favour. They may also argue for their point of view while admitting that scientific hypotheses, by dint of their construction in an atmosphere where they have been rendered more probable and exempt from any possibility of error by genuine efforts to cover all areas where error could possibly arise, face fewer counterarguments with the ability to neutralize them and disprove their claim to authenticity, while refusing to admit that their claims are devoid of such redeeming advantage by virtue of their improbability. They may claim that we and they are the victims of the ubiquitous tendency to error that can't be excluded or eliminated completely from any venture, especially since our ability to know everything and to act on the basis of all the relevant information is limited by our cognitive powers, but still insist that their error is more apparent than real and that we suffer from the paralysis in action that characterizes skeptics who refrain from initiating any venture until we are assured that all possibility of error has been decisively excluded. But the error of their postulated transcendent abode is one humongous fatal error that is based on the word of fallible authorities who claim to be infallible, as if there ever was or ever will be an infallible human being, and to have come by that information and "evidence" by transcendent powers, which are themselves in question as being unverifiable—there is, in fact, no method of verifying their claim, which is part of the dogma used to hijack and ensure perpetuation of the allegiance of the already duped millions of faithful followers.

Their claims, which they want us to accept on face value, are permeated by far too many negatives and lack of strength of evidence to be accepted as indubitable knowledge. So why not reject them on face value, if not on the absence of their amenability to any degree of rational substantiation and their susceptibility to attenuation with every counterargument? Whatever rigorous standards are demanded for belief in the postulates of science must apply equally to the postulates of religious belief, especially since its proselytizers are hell bent on making it everyone's business, instead of keeping it strictly to themselves as believers in its claims. They try hard to base secular government on its unfounded tenets, and they vilify anyone who espouses common sense humanist beliefs. To shield it from being ravished by pure reason, they argue that rational scientific standards cannot be justly applied to religious belief, and that religious proof should be held to the same less austere standards as civil legal evidence and those philosophical beliefs that hinge on an accumulation of circumstantial evidence, like belief in other persons and their minds or belief in the external world *per se*, except that in religion the evidence is of the extraterrestrial, supernatural, mystic, and hearsay kind that hinges on ineffable, transfiguring, and overpowering revelations that cannot even be witnessed or captured by other people, because they occur spontaneously, privately, and unexpectedly to their subjects, as I wrote in *Our World and its Values* chapter 11, pp158-60. So if every effort by would-be believers is being thwarted by the need to wait for the uncertain descent of divine revelation to which they cannot reach out and acquire for the salvation of their souls, how can they even begin to entertain any thoughts of embracing it? Their best bet is to take to heart the words of Bertrand Russell: "Science can teach us, and I think our own hearts can teach us, no longer to look around for imaginary supports, no longer to invent allies in the sky, but rather to look to our own efforts here below to make this world a better place to live in, instead of the sort of place that the churches in all these centuries have made it."[11] True, Mr. Russell, they have made it a den of vainglorious thieves, pedophiles, liars, and murderers — it is churchmen who wage wars that wantonly destroy other people's habitations and their lives, steal their lands, put their children at risk of molestation, and then lie about all their misdeeds.

In any case, why should the rest of humanity be made subject to the religious whims and superstitions of some? Why can't the religious folk live and let live? What do they stand to lose if other people don't subscribe to their esoteric fancies? The other people do not go out of their way to dissuade them from their trips into fairyland, in as much as they let them make their own decisions what to do with their bodies, like staying out of their choices to have abortions for reasons that appeal to them; who knows what they do when no one is looking — like the hypocrites who rail against the pork that they solicit privately? They probably have as many abortions as the people that they are harassing for undergoing the same procedures, as long as no one of the objects of their hypocrisy finds out, but unholy persons don't harass or murder them for participating in or facilitating these procedures for themselves in the name and under the direction of their deity. These religious bigots and hypocrites certainly do not make their hobby attractive to the non-religious with their murderous ways; they rather turn them off, since the latter do not advocate violence as a means of making the other see and appreciate their point of view. They claim to love God whom they have never seen and simultaneously hate their neighbour that they see and persecute every day, but they fail to see that they have missed the whole point of their religiosity, which is not only to stand on soap boxes and passionately beat on their chests, hypocritically, fanatically, and self-righteously blaring their immense love for God in deafening tones, but also and more so to show kindness to their neighbour and respect him and his life without reservation, if only for also being their God's child. But no, only they or their tribal group are their God's children, the true god, as their priests so arrogantly claim, and that is why they will not brook to see God's other children, the ones with an excess of melanin pigment, get married in *their* churches — Christianity at its best. These are the same Christians who will derogatively replace an African child's "heathen" name (given to him by his African parents) with a Christian name like Paul (St. Paul), but will do nothing to replace the unchristian names of their tribe's children like Rodney or Tiffany (St. Rodney or St. Tiffany!) with Christian names like Peter or Mary (St. Peter or St. Mary?). One religion accuses the other of pandering to violence, but no one stops to find out who cast the first stone. Each one wipes its murk off the other and then claims to be the clean one while pointing its dirty finger at the other that it smeared with the murk that came from that same finger. As things stand, there is no hope that they will ever clean their act and come together in search of the truth that eludes them continually because of their arrogance and vain self-regard, with each one of its priests quite happy to preach and promote sacerdotalism among his flock (of sheep) and each religion claiming to be the true religion that has privileged access to the truth — huffishly denying their holy communion to those who do not belong to their rabble but worship the same God. So which one should we believe? Are they a curse to humanity and living proof of the opinion that "men never do evil so completely and cheerfully as when they do it from religious conviction"?[12]

In spite of this despicable show of hypocrisy and misanthropy, we still draw considerable courage from Sartre who assures us that transcendence also refers to what the human agent is attempting as he struggles to live above his animal self to prove that his existence precedes his essence — he first exists as the animal man of Thomas Hobbes, and then makes himself what he wants to be as moral man with all the wonderful attributes that we described before, without giving in to the inevitable difficulties entailed in realizing his quest to be the best that he can be, which is always better than he was before. This fact alone fills him with hope, optimism, and courage to persevere in the face of different existential odds to make, not only his own life, but also the lives of other persons, worthwhile, in spite of having to contend with religious hypocrites. Humanity does not have any clue what is in store for it in the decades to come, because our knowledge is finite and the extent of reality remains a hidden mystery that we are forever trying to fathom with dreams of transcendence, even as we seem to be driving ourselves to the brink of self-annihilation with our nuclear weapons that can incinerate us instantaneously in a moment of the insanity of hegemony with which we are possessed. The race for weapons that can wipe out the entire human race is gathering pace all the time as states are working feverishly to acquire them for their own protection against the bullies who have been stockpiling them for many years. Puerile "leaders" of states are also playing chicken like little boys, intimidating each other with these highly destructive weapons, leaving us all shaking in our boots as we hold our breaths until we turn blue while we search frantically for an avenue of escape from this potential Armageddon.

Does this situation call for embracing transcendence that is based on the faith that the religious folk would have us embrace in their bigoted fashion, without evidence, if we are to realize our yearning for a better human race? I hardly think so. What else would they have us embrace that will be a blight on human welfare in the name of irrational faith? Richard Norman was right when, realizing the terrible things that have been done in the name of religion and the church: inquisitions, burnings at the stake, misuse of secular statutes by church hierarchy to harass critics of their moral standards who are considered to be a menace when they should be praying hard for help to mend their own ways, death-inflicting opposition to espousers of scientific facts that cut against religious dogma, castrations of boys for no good reason, one-man prohibitions of all forms of birth control regardless of surrounding circumstances, etc., he wrote that "Religion has blighted people's lives, imposing restrictions and inhibitions in the name of divine commands which thwart people's aspirations to happiness, filling them with guilt for innocent pleasures and fear of eternal damnation".[13] Long before him, Friedrich Nietzsche also wrote, after studying the ways of these hypocrites, that he had need to wash his contaminated hand after shaking hands with any of them; that is how venomous they are and how lethal they can be for anyone who does not tow their dogmatic line. They even follow and harass those who walk far away from them or have forsaken their fold and now have nothing to do with them, because they have lots to hide.

For religious folk to excuse their multitude of heinous deeds (to date) by pointing accusing fingers at scientists and hiding behind the atrocities of science, like the incineration of people with atomic bombs, maiming and killing children and adults with cluster and other kinds of bombs, and suffocating them with poisonous gases, amounts to a lame cop-out, because they should be setting a better example, simply by virtue of who and what they claim to be. They should be leading the uproar against these inhumane uses of scientific knowledge, instead of being its cheerleaders, simply because these atrocities are committed on persons that they regard as their inferior subhuman co-inhabitants of this planet. In their failure to be the conscience of their world religious people have let the human race down, but they have also made it possible for the non-religious to fill the gap with their benevolent actions that put these zealots to shame.

Ultimately, religion has proved to be the force that awakens people to the stark realization that they can still lead upright lives without having any religious affiliations or becoming the victims of hogwash. Religious practices through the years have driven them that way and are still driving them that way at the same speed, if not faster. They no longer give a credulous ear to fanciful promises of the world to come, nor do they still needlessly expend their energies pursuing phantasmagorias that purport to represent that world. We can therefore thank religion for its contribution to the person's discovery of herself, instead of the miserable, damned, self-condemning sinner that it has made her out to be, and for its unintended but continuing endorsement of secular Humanism, which we will examine in the next chapter.

Chapter 9

The Challenge from Humanism

And now back from uncharted celestial wanderings and day dreaming about imaginary palatial abodes, where streets are paved with glittering gold, to the reality of terra firma, where shanties or the open starry or weeping sky are the only abode for many, and where the streets are paved by dust for some and with lowly asphalt and concrete slabs for others; back from fanciful sites, where harems of winged females are ruled by one male archangel, to the prototype for this captivating myth, which is the world of Homo sapiens sapiens and male chauvinism, where binders full of females are still largely subservient to males in church and state, presumably on orders from the sky —orders that were fictitiously bounced back from there by their earthly fabricators to suit their own devious purposes. Let's talk about life as we know it first hand and as we live it. Let's talk about Humanism of the secular variety, the living challenge to all the phantasy that we have just been discussing; let's talk about how we can lead upright, useful, and genuinely happy lives on our own, without invoking the inaccessible myths that mysticism has imposed on us, making us think like the ancient Greeks and Romans who made up gods and goddesses that they worshipped and revered, and to whom they deferred for wisdom, strength, and fortune; e.g., Zeus, the supreme Greek god of the sky who controlled lightning and thunder from Mount Olympus and was worshiped by all ancient Greeks; and Apollo, the roman god of healing, light, truth and other virtues that he dispensed via his oracle at Delphi. Let's talk about our own ability to decide to do one thing or another ourselves without praying and waiting for the hosts of angels to come and do it for us; about how it is up to us to stop the persecution and slaughter of other humans by heartless autocrats and by equally heartless leaders of the most civilized and democratic states of our world who think nothing of killing old people, women, and children—let alone other men—for self-serving reasons; about how the fate of our world rests in our hands and not with the whim of some unknown deity that we have created and to whom we have entrusted our well-being. We are the ones who will save this world with our caring or else destroy it with our foolishness; no one else will do it for us. So let us stop kidding ourselves and be realistic, assume the Humanist attitude, and stop wreaking havoc on everyone and everything and then praying for forgiveness for our transgressions, as we often do to assuage our consciences (those who claim to have any left), only to return to the same foolishness and inhumanity, proving that we never had any consciences left in us, in the first place.

Let us realize and acknowledge that excellence of character is to be achieved, not by hypocritical religiosity, lust for power, or closed-mindedness, but only by personal responsibility and devotion to humanistic ideals, and by honest efforts to be true to our own selves and to others with whom we should be sharing our common values and morally motivated aspirations. Let us talk about Humanism.

To introduce the subject of Humanism, I cannot do better than quote from Corliss Lamont's *The Philosophy of Humanism*; but before I do that, let me introduce my adaptation of Wittgenstein's question stated on page 83: what is left over if I subtract organized religion from humanity? The answer is, Humanism. But what is left after I subtract Humanism from Humanity? Nothing. Now to Lamont:

> Humanism is the viewpoint that people have but one life to lead and should make the most of it in terms of creative work and happiness; that human happiness is its own justification and requires no sanction or support from supernatural sources; that in any case the supernatural, usually conceived of in the form of heavenly gods or immortal heavens, does not exist; and that human beings, using their own intelligence and cooperating liberally with one another, can build an enduring citadel of peace and beauty upon this earth."[1]

It should be quite evident from the above quotation that Humanism is not a religion, less still a religion based on dogma that derives its authority from some other-worldly source that insists on sacrificing the happiness of the actual life of now—in this known world—to the potential and uncertain bliss of life after death in another, unknown world whose existence is an unthinkable mystery that we can never hope to solve and must accept on faith. Even its protagonists admit that it lies beyond the reach of the most elemental factual evidence and our ability to apply any rational methods (including scientific) to its elucidation and substantiation. In contrast, scientific theories and hypotheses, which are also not a form of dogma-based religion, are creative products of cooperation among people who trust in and use their own intelligence, instead of reaching out to transcendent phantoms while they sit around and wait for things to happen; they stand or fall on the evidence, not on emotional appeal to human longings of immortality and the commitment of their lives to chimeras. As it has been said, "Humanists encourage us to make the best of our lives, lives containing meaning and purpose, without resort to superstition and the supernatural."[2]

Humanism, by emphasizing the capability of human beings to lead full and meaningful lives in a godless world through the use of reason, presents a stark contrast with religion's trust in dogma and fantasies like miracles and revelations; intolerance of non-conformists; obsession with the fallacy that they alone know all the answers to worldly problems of living; and faith in all types of vindictive, repressive, and murderous, but God-anointed and thus sanctified human leaders of both secular and religious persuasion.

The morality of humanists does not spring from self-proclaimed infallibility, or from divine commandment without which they would be amoral torturers, oppressors, and murderers like many religious persons who are still torturers, oppressors, and murderers in spite of being subservient to divine commandment, as they mendaciously claim. So if divine commandment does not have any positive influence on morality, who needs it? One might as well depend on her humanist morality than entrust herself to religious ethical practices whose moral basis is a mixture of defiance and fear, defiance of their god's commandment to love others and not do them harm, and fear of the wrath of their god for all the destabilization of communities and heinous crimes that they still continue to commit. The morality of humanists originates from their own sense of values relating to right and wrong, good and bad, and from the "social inter-relations" that enable them to recognize the evil that dwells in inhumane religious folk and their matching deeds that are allegedly divinely ordered by a benevolent Deity—a contradiction in concepts that amounts to nonsense and by implication eliminates the need for that Deity. Humanism does, however, demand a certain measure of altruism from us, a genuine interest in the wellbeing of all people regardless of domicile or rank, as opposed to the prevailing philosophy of Egoism that puts the subject ahead of everyone else in the baseless hope that his self-concern will spill over to other persons and bestow equal good on them—a kind of "trickle down" morality. That, of course, will never happen, so no one should waste her time waiting for that miracle to happen, not even people who believe in miracles in which Hume said we should believe only if their contraries happen to come into being, like a dead man coming to life on the order of another mortal—once dead, always dead; that is the law of nature whose violation will constitute a real miracle. For us to believe the miracle of a dead man coming to life in this manner, we would first have to believe the miracle of the man dying, which is no miracle but the normal course of events. In this case, it will be the egoist keeping everything for himself that will be miraculous, which is no miracle, because that is his nature, and once we have lived through that miracle, we can then face the miracle of him sharing his superfluous possessions.

Humanism relies entirely on the inherent power and authority of the freely thinking, rational human being to shape his own life and altruistic morality for today and for the days and years following, without any fear of offending a supreme architect of his life as ostensibly represented by yesteryear's and today's dogma-ridden church with its opposition to free, rational thinking and its encouragement of the self-denigration of its credulous members as cursed sinners who are unfairly forced by other sinners to carry the disabling burden of the guilt of the original sinners (whatever that means) for the rest of their lives, at the same time as it condones their hoarding of worldly treasures, which are exposed to destruction by moth and rust and break-and-enter, and for which they should be feeling guilty instead. What else can one expect when some of the churches are richer than some existing worldly kingdoms and states? The demeanour of the church through its leaders is not surprising, considering that these are the same self-denigrating, guilty, and cursed sinners who own the church and who robbed free-thinking persons of their productive lives, burning them at the stake for their non-conformist views and for refusing to be railroaded by its "holy" devils in celestial garb, the same church that is still permeated by reason-suppressing, inflexible dogma supervised by some of the most irrational bigots of all descriptions who preach their own warped morality of oppression, violence, exploitation, and racism. How can any rational person believe and live by anything they preach when they and truth are riding galloping horses that are moving farther and farther away from each other in opposite directions on their flat earth where there is no chance that they might meet at the antipodes, if they are prepared to move and seek out others with whom they can commune about their common fate that rests squarely in their hands. Only people who live on a spherical earth stand a chance of meeting and reconciling with others at the antipodes after they have separated from them and gone in opposite directions. These folk don't stand that chance; theirs is a life of perpetual separation, of "I-It", never "I-You".

Some religious persons continue to oppose the reasoned postulates of science in favour of their fantasies that spring from their unholy prejudices and ignorance, their reason being that these scientific facts are not written in their holy books. They "discourse like angels" but live like sinful mortals, and they forget that some of the exploitative sexual practices in which they engage are also not written in or sanctioned by their holy books. These dishonest, bible-clutching, holier-than-thou members of the church who control secular affairs are the ones who pressure honest scientists to lie about the ill effects of chemical products (e.g., growth hormone) that they want to introduce into the population's food, directly or indirectly, for the monetary gain of their friends and masters in the money world at the risk of people's health; who withdraw their research funding for refusing to propagate their ideological lies as scientific facts, contrary to the truths revealed by their research; and who muzzle scientists and punish them mercilessly for blowing the whistle on them for their disreputable deeds. But that is not all; some of them have embarked on enacting legislations that will condemn whistle blowers on their immoral and illegal deeds to incarceration for many years. I will not even mention their reprehensible pretence that the pollutants that they and their friends generate are not harmful to the world's populations. They have the power to shield their misdemeanours from exposure (so they think) and public condemnation with their laws, and they do not consider it immoral to protect immoral actions with immoral laws, impelling one to ask: where did they leave their religion-driven morality?

Such actions compel any person with intelligence to doubt their claim to divine guidance in whatever they do, and to deny credence to the divine force that they claim is guiding them. Many of them have claimed divine guidance through revelation and faith in the unknown, not their hatred and ill will, for the murders, unjust wars, oppression, and other atrocities that they have committed. They still burn other people's religious books and kill those who do not subscribe and submit to their bigoted religious viewpoints, e.g. abortion; they preach against the scientifically established facts of evolution and the finality of death against the background of baseless creationism and assumed transcendent abilities of a nebulous human entity called the "soul", and they display a pathetic lack of the mutual respect that can allow them to live and let live. They don't want to know that the essence of nature is diversity with minimal conflict, because they believe in uniformity with maximal conflict to enable them to divide, antagonize, and rule conflicting parties that reject their hypocritical ways and railroad them into subjugation to any of their bigoted ideas. That, I presume, is to be expected when intelligent people are dealing with egocentric fanatics who fight among themselves on both levels — religion and denomination — with each group promoting itself as the only authentic one that leads to a place called heaven, implying that the others are false and misleading, but failing to produce any evidence to prove their case. Some of their arrogant ones who claim to be the true church, but are also the most tainted, firmly believe their fantasies that only they know the truth, unlike the really wise Socrates who said that true knowledge is knowing that you know nothing. Meanwhile, each one of their sects is trying hard to convince everyone of us to reject the others for demanding belief in their teachings by faith, which they all preach, instead of exhorting them to look for the convincing evidence that all of them have failed to produce, because that would amount to shooting themselves in the foot. So what and whom should we believe? These people still have the audacity to think that their religions and denominations have the right to divest people of their autonomy and free choice and dictate to them how they shall live — in accordance with their selfish, hypocritical religious way. If anything, their inhumane conduct only succeeds in providing enough justification for rejecting them and their pious claims, until they can decide to show some humanism and consistency, come together, speak with one holy voice and present concordant, credible, and rational claims, instead of taking discordant, contradictory, implausible, and irrational positions and expecting rational persons to accept and live with their contradictions without being repulsed by them. Minor cultural and regional differences in how they do things are to be expected, and they are not in question; but it is the arrogance with which some of them proclaim themselves the authentic holy rabble that irks and turns off onlookers.

Throughout the years, religious instructors of prominence have sprung up among the people, but their messages, while largely ethically sound, have not done enough to uphold and accord undisputed primacy to the human agent as the beginning and the end of human life with all the problems that he has created for his species, and for which he is seeking asylum elsewhere. Humanism discourages attempts to find refuge in figments conjured up to substitute for the necessary courage and fortitude required to solve our own problems, instead of offloading them on a mysterious spirit; to determine our own future, instead of abandoning it to unknown fate. Humanists believe in laying the foundations that will serve as tracks along which they also plant beacons to guide present and future generations in the continuing quest by conscience-endowed persons for a better life on earth for all peoples. The idealistic red herring of transcendent existence does not feature in humanist aspirations, although it passes in religious circles as the source of their security and the impetus that is supposed to keep believers on the straight and narrow path from which they wander freely all the time. Unlike authentic ideals toward which people strive with the full knowledge that they are lodestars that are unattainable, transcendent existence misleads them by pretending to attainability, requiring a blind, giant leap of faith into the unknown and unknowable, against all the dictates of common sense and fact, whilst also pretending that faith can create fact—believe, and abracadabra, it becomes true. Humanists do not, therefore, base their lives' policies on the chimera of transcendence, which is also used by many religious folk to selectively exclude less favoured persons form enjoying the good things of this life on the empty promise of abundance in the life to come. They believe in ensuring that everyone lives well in the world that they know, instead of letting life pass them by solely on the basis of unfounded and empty promises of life after death. If people make this life worthwhile for everyone, they do not have to spend their time slavishly trying to prepare themselves for another life after this one while treating other people shabbily in the process, because, if there is such a life, they will never be admitted into it with their putrid track records.

Humanists do not, unlike religious fanatics who disparage science and offer some infallible fantasy in its place, claim that science provides all the answers to all the questions, as the other people do for their discipline. They acknowledge that in its coldness and strict objectivity it does not and cannot answer questions of morality and values, and they also acknowledge that its principles are subject to change with new conclusive evidence for alternative theories, as the jettisoning of phlogiston and other theories that laid the foundations for modern scientific theories has proved. These other people try to match their baseless postulates with the indisputably logical methods of science, which lays open its pronouncements to verification or refutation by anyone with the know-how, placing it on firmer ground in the search for truth than blind faith which is shielded from counter-argument by its rigidity and dogmatism from which nothing can be logically deduced or predicted. As Diderot so wisely remarked, "I was lost in a great forest at night, with only a small flickering light to guide me. A stranger came and said to me 'My friend, put out your candle, so that you will find the way better'. That man was a theologian."[3] This is as much a compliment as the one attributed to a drunk man who had lost his car keys in the dark part of a parking lot but was looking for them in the lit up area, because, he said, he would never be able to see them in the dark area, so it was pointless to look for them there.

Science studies Nature, of which arrogant human beings are but an infinitesimal part, a tiny, highly vulnerable speck and not a favoured one at that. It keeps its candle lit so that it can discover what is and what ought to be from what is and what will likely be, with the full knowledge that chasing after mystery and myth will not yield any returns and is time and effort wasted. It recognizes Nature's credentials as it presents itself in daily living, without assuming the existence of a supra-sensory, inaccessible, and mythical secret to life that can be "known" only through faith. Little wonder that the ardent protagonists of faith—the ones who are using it to further their own ends—are often eager to undermine those scientific postulates that expose the bankruptcy of their skewed views of the place of humans in the world. They are like governments that undermine their own legislative committees by encouraging witnesses who might divulge damaging information about them to defy any calls by the committees to get them to testify. Typical of the challenge posed by non-humanist irrational thinking that has no basis in science is the outlandish and unbridled, but self-comforting belief that the earth was made only 6,000 years ago and the advent of humans in their present shape and form, which is allegedly the original form in which they were created, dates back to only 6,000 years, on the same day as the creation of the heavens and the earth, or 6,000 years minus 6 days, whichever version one chooses to believe. The appearance of humans at the end of creation, before the 7th day of rest; i.e., the end of the week (our seven-day week was reverently acknowledged back then by the creator), is consistent with evolutionary facts, but it is inconsistent with and contrary to geological evidence that the world is more than one billion years old and humans appeared more than seven million years ago, after evolving from lower animal forms. Charles Darwin demonstrated this fact clearly and convincingly, and modern palaeontologists are constantly demonstrating it with discoveries of fossils that can be dated back to more than 550million years ago (like Pacaia gracilens the eel-like creature that is estimated to have lived before that time and is supposed to be the ancestor of all animals that possess a backbone, including humans). But the unyielding mystics and spiritualists of our world still ardently contest and reject these facts in favour of biblical communication from "above" about the origins of humans and the world that they inhabit; they pretend to be blind also to the obtrusive evidence from teleonomy that they encounter in their daily lives and that is not as cognitively challenging as palaeontology, which requires erudite interpretation of fossils. Their dogmatism is unshakable.

In my discussion of persons in chapter 2, I referred to Descartes' body-mind dichotomy as having given added impetus to the unfounded religious belief in the existence of a soul—the "ghost in the machine" called the human body—that is capable of an independent and timeless existence in a transcendent world, the one that our friends claim has streets paved with gold. In my other works, I have referred to the common tendency of humans to anthropomorphize their deities—Christian, Islamist, Judaic, etc.,—for the sake of draping them with their own physical and psychic characteristics to gratify their unfulfilled, competitive yearnings for infinite power and wisdom over the populace and over each other, but strangely not for infinite benevolence. All of these mental gymnastics are just that, fictitious contortions; they lack factual, scientific corroboration to make them even worthy of competition with the truth that the demise of the person marks the end of his bodily functions, including the mental functions that depend entirely on the brain, which also disintegrates with the body after death. At no time can a soul be tracked departing from the body, soaring to celestial heights where it will make its timeless abode with all other souls that have preceded it and are indistinguishable from it in the overcrowded city where all the departed make their abode, otherwise the advocates and protagonists of this fanciful idea would have shoved such evidence in our faces long ago to decisively silence skepticism about their dogma.

Humanists do not believe in the divine ethics referred to on page 102. To them, moral life is not one of prayer for guidance by Deity and ultimate salvation from hell-fire by the same Deity for disobeying his commandments but confessing their sins twenty times a day to another human for the twenty times that they commit them every day; that contradictory and outlandish practice does not make sense to minds that are unencumbered by enslaving religious dogma. Their morality stems from their cordial and caring personal relationships with other people and their desire to see everyone flourish, not from commands issued from the sky or from vassal adherence to dogma that has been conjured up by others under the transparent guise of conveying privileged communications from a superior being regarding the acceptable manner of human behaviour that is, in fact, regulated by them. In any case, if Deity has already decreed the inflexible course of events in a tightly regulated universe where even the slightest deviation will derail the entire works, what is the point of still praying for a change in the order of things and expecting Deity to risk the cataclysmic disarray of his meticulous creation for the sake of gratifying one selfish petitioner? Most of the time these people pray for their own advantage, instead of getting up and doing something to save themselves from whatever it is that they are afraid of, which they want their god to deflect from hurting them and direct to other people. The problem with them is that they are cowards who do not have the guts to shape their own destiny by acting and taking responsibility for their actions, but instead choose to become easy prey for unprincipled opportunists among them who in turn use the rest of them to achieve their own ends whilst encouraging them to sit or kneel and pray for salvation (from being used by them?).

Such slavish and close-minded adherence to ancient, unchanging, and unenlightened religious dogma is responsible for the nasty animosity that exists today among so-called Christians who have partitioned themselves into warring factions of the right, the middle, and the left, and who are engaged in sacrilegious battles that can only be described, in their language, as fit for heathens. Some of these pious, lovelorn, holier-than-thou, starved-for-attention egotists are "teachers of morality [who] discourse like angels, but live like men".[4] In the language of Samuel Johnson, they deny with their tongues what they confess by their deeds. They fail to see the personifications of phoniness that stare at them when they look in their mirrors; they claim to see its reflection from others toward whom they have turned their mirrors, because they lack the guts to face the parody of truth that they will see in those mirrors when they face them; that includes their bigoted evangelists who have the nerve to question the faith of other Christians by looking at the motes in their eyes with mammoth beams that obscure the defective vision in their own eyes. Humanists abhor this irrational conduct as much as they reject the fright inducing Christian concept of eternal agony inflicted by the physical hell fires that await those who have disobeyed alleged divine commands like them. As freethinkers, they believe that hell and heaven are created in the minds of inhumane and humane persons alike according to how they use their talents to shape the world for all its inhabitants, rather than for themselves as Milton's Satan consoled himself when he was being consumed by the fires of hell; they believe that

> The mind is its own place, and in itself
> Can make a Heav'n of Hell, a Hell of Heav'n.[5]

Therefore senseless talk of a place called hell manned by someone named the devil deserves to be dismissed with the contempt that it has earned itself.

In the social arena, Humanists are dedicated to promoting justice and fairness of opportunity. They do not believe in depriving people of the basic opportunities that will equip them with the tools to qualify them to engage fairly in competition for the good things that make other people's lives worthwhile; they do not believe in making other people's lives hell on earth while exhorting them to focus on going to heaven to enjoy future endless bliss, as David. H. Lawrence so wisely observed in this excerpt about people saving themselves and not depending on a saviour who sells them out:

> They say: we are saved, but we are starving.
> He says: the sooner will you eat imaginary cake in the mansions of my father.
> They say: can't we have a loaf of common bread?
> He says: No, you must go to heaven, and eat the most marvellous cake.-[6]

They also do not believe in exhortations that tell the poor to derive comfort from offensive and insensitive pronouncements like these from churchmen:

> And let the poor, and all those who at this time are facing the hard trial of unemployment and scarcity of food, let them in a like spirit of penance offer with greater resignation the privations imposed on them by these hard times and the state of society, which *divine Providence in its inscrutable but ever-loving plan has assigned them.* Let them *accept with a humble and trustful heart from the hand of God the effects of poverty,* rendered harder by the distress in which

mankind is now struggling; let them rise more generously even to the divine sublimity of the Cross of Christ, reflecting on the fact, that if work is among the greatest values of life, it was nevertheless love of a suffering God that saved the world; let them take comfort in the certainty that *their sacrifices and their trials borne in a Christian spirit will concur efficaciously to hasten the hour of mercy and peace.*[7] (my italics throughout the quote).

After seriously taking to heart all these brave, comforting, and putatively hope-infusing but insulting words, the deprived crowd for whose pacification and presumed spiritual upliftment they are intended find themselves still wallowing in their miserable circumstances while the rest of their world (including their very comfortably placed exhorter who wrote those words) continues to live it up. For them, equal access to higher education and equal opportunity in the workplace, in the absence of prior equality of preparation, is a remote dream that can never convert into reality, unless they are granted special privileges to prevent their exclusion from these basic opportunities.

With that kind of background, these vain promises of a better life to come from people who do not show the slightest inclination to share the plenty that they have with them or have the power to ensure that these empty promises that they are making can ever come about are only an affront that they do not deserve and can do well without. Nevertheless, even when opportunities are created for the disadvantaged to improve their situation and hence their chances for survival in this cruel world, the self-preoccupied opponents of affirmative action who have enjoyed historically easy access to all available opportunities prefer not to see things that way. They still want to monopolize every field from which the underdogs will be shut out by their traditions that are geared to maintaining and increasing the socio-economic gap between the privileged and the deprived. They are content to let social inequality with widening of the already gaping chasm between rich and poor continue to belie the wishful thinking of equality optimists, as much as they are letting crass racial, ethnic, class, religious, and gender bigotry thrive like weeds in a cornfield, choking up all the plants that are trying to bear a good crop for fruitful harvesting. Insincere politicians with sinister motives that reflect their strict variance with the purposes of humanism oppose the making of a college education available to all young people who want to seize that opportunity for self-improvement and positioning for the best chances at obtaining a decent job and standard of living as being a snobbish pursuit, but they send their own children to college to take advantage of the same opportunities, and they and other members of their families have a college education. Are they snobs? The very rich still swear that they will withdraw the extension of health care benefits to poor people so that their corporate friends can continue to exploit them while they enjoy the benefits of insured health care paid for by the same poor people. Where is the honesty of purpose? Where is the devotion to the quest for truth? Where is the goodwill? What are they afraid of? Are they afraid of equipping the discriminated against, underprivileged, oppressed underdogs with the wherewithal to raise their heads from serfdom and the scourge of ill health and premature death so that they can claim the *de facto* equality that they have been denied for centuries under the disreputable guise of the sham *de jure* equality of opportunity with which they have been distracted? If not, what is their problem? Come out clean from behind the smoke screens and dust that you are stirring up to conceal your intentions, guys. Are they so disreputable that you are ashamed of declaring them openly?

These are the same people who do not take kindly to cordial handling of irritants between their nation and other nations, because in their arrogance, they believe in "kicking ass" to show the other people that they despise who is the self-positioned boss of the world. Like religious persons who shun Humanists and would like to make them disappear from the face of the earth for exposing the pointlessness of their obsession with chimeras, they also shun the extension of olive branches to would be adversaries as a sign of weakness, not humanism. Little wonder that unlike humanists and the rest of the clear thinking people who support democracy as the best form of government, since "democratic societies provide more freedom and equality of concern, less duplicity and cruelty, more opportunities for cultural enrichment, creativity, and shared experiences, and higher standards of living"[8], these pretenders and hypocrites pay the most yawping homage to democracy, and yet they practice the worst form of surreptitious but transparent dictatorship at home and proxy dictatorship abroad through their many puppets in foreign lands that they prop unequivocally with the tax dollars of humanist citizens. Unfortunately the tax payers are letting them get away with this indirect murder of foreign citizens, because they have been conditioned to regard their nation states as more civilized than the barbarians who are being oppressed and massacred with their tax dollars to sustain the vested interests of their civilized states that are no better than plutocracies and oligarchies parading arrogantly as democracies. The truth is that modern states are complexes of selfishness, suppression, duplicity, cruelty, lowering of living standards, disregard for the wishes of the majority by governments that have hijacked the concept of majority rule with a majority of the minority of voters who have characteristically been sufficiently duped to vote them into office to pursue their own ruinous agendas. They conduct costly wars that benefit no one else but them and their corporate friends who manufacture the implements of war or those who come in to mop up their mess after they have callously destroyed other people's property for reasons of greed and hegemony. Ironically enough, the so-called leaders who are riding on minority mandates are so deluded that they act as if they have majority mandates and even remind others who are in the same boat that they do not have a majority mandate to institute their ruinous programs like them.

Governments and their political cronies think nothing of stooping to the low level of rigging votes by misdirecting voters away from legitimate polling stations or tampering with ballots to ensure their victory in elections; they cannot resist the greed for power and access to money by the use of underhanded and sometimes legitimized (by them) means that will enable them to board and remain anchored on the gravy train for the rest of their miserable lives. Those who are not on the train but are dying to get on to promote their nefarious policies do their best to disqualify voters who are unlikely to vote for them by passing restrictive and hostile regional laws to achieve their purpose (disenfranchising minorities who are unlikely to vote for them) or by giving them wrong dates for polling, while their favoured candidates lie shamelessly and endlessly to seduce the sometimes credulous electorate. The irony of the situation is that these are the holier-than-thou who have the audacity to go out like saints to monitor the elections of other nation states to ensure fairness in the process; i.e., that they are free of the different kinds of fraud and sleaze in which they themselves engage with impunity, and then lie about them and point accusing fingers at their victims by uttering the most asinine statements. Who ever heard of someone with intelligence shooting his own foot, crippling himself and suffering defeat in the race against his opponent, and then crying foul? But some of these bright sparks will shoot their opponent's foot, manage to achieve success over him, and then accuse him of having disabled himself and engineered his own defeat by shooting himself in the foot. That is the deplorable cognitive caliber of some persons who are supposed to be managing the affairs of intelligent citizens and to have their social, political, educational, and economic fate in their hands. Frankly, this kind of illogical and dishonest maneuvering is scary, because the dolt who engages in it thinks and believes that he has put up a convincing argument that is enough to silence his legitimate accusers. He knows that he will get away with it, because many of the electorate are gullible sheep.

They do not or cannot think; their minds are perpetually clouded by propaganda beyond which they cannot look to discern reality, the reality of the chicanery that goes on around them and even dupes them into believing that multimillionaires are men of the people who are fighting for the people's rights when they are squarely in the corner of their rich friends fighting against the people, as they have so boldly stated; but the people never learn; they still follow them like the sheep that they are. They swear by con men who demonstrate to everyone that they do not have a single moral fibre in their constitution or any understanding of government and its workings; all they know is that they are there to rip them off as they have done with many others in their disreputable careers of lies, fraud, and debauchery — certainly not the kind of behaviour to hold up as an example for children and youth to follow.

Due process of law is a joke with these governments that can jail these same people arbitrarily and deny them *habeas corpus* at will for extended periods of time, while they also subject them to inhumane torture on the mere suspicion that they intend to change the existing systems of misgovernment by means other than those that the same delinquent governments use to usurp their rights and civil liberties with the help of foreign governments and the free media. Some of these media, rather than being free, have become extensions of corrupt governments and special interest groups that manipulate them so well that they have now become mere propaganda machines that should be approached with extreme caution. These myth media can be used to pound political opponents and smear them with fictitious accusations every minute of the day to the advantage of those who are in league with their owners with the full knowledge that the naïve electorate will believe everything they read or see on their television screens that are employed effectively to disseminate this kind of trash. In the midst of all this evil, the crying lack of economic democracy that is represented by the corporations and various types of local and international money lending vultures stands in sharp contrast to what democracy should mean and be to the people for whom and by whom it should be exercised. Couple this with the unfair taxation of the middle class that is hounded for a few cents owing in taxes while the rich enjoy free rides under the pretext that they provide jobs, which they are withholding for unsavoury reasons and for which they offer minimum compensation but scoop up the rest in their huge pay cheques and bonuses totalling trillions of dollars, while they simultaneously raise the prices of commodities well above the ability of poor people to afford them, and we have the most despicable form of governmental oppression and exploitation. I will not enter into a discussion of the unjust, undemocratic, inhumane, and homicidal distribution of material goods amongst the people, which is a historically sore point that I have dealt with fully in chapter 9 of *Our World and its Values*, except to say that giving much (tax cuts, wages or salaries, pay raises, and bonuses, lower tax rates, off shore tax havens) to those who already have much and little to those who have little or nothing is an evil that diminishes the human worth of the underprivileged citizen. I will, however, mention some other topics to which I have referred in the past, such as the separation of church and state, an indefectible situation that is being assailed and undermined relentlessly by religious fundamentalists, a pressure group that wants to dictate the conduct of affairs of state on the basis of their antiquated, biased, and narrow-minded interpretations of their unscientific holy books that they use to challenge rational, scientific facts and arguments, e.g., evolution by natural selection that I have already mentioned, expecting intelligent, clear thinking people to submit to their irrational beliefs and fancies and align themselves with them.

They are also trying hard to discredit the autonomy of individuals, challenging the right of women to decide when to interrupt the carrying of their fetuses to term, after taking thoughtful consideration of all their prevailing circumstances and making well informed decisions on their contemplated actions. Hence, in their ignorant wisdom the dolts claim that in the case of "legitimate rape", "the female body has ways to try to shut the whole thing down" to prevent pregnancy. They also prevent women from availing themselves of safe means of contraception to prevent forced or unwanted pregnancies that will, in some cases, expose innocent fetuses to infectious diseases like AIDS, which are a lifelong form of unfair and unjust punishment for the persons who will result from the full development of those fetuses in circumstances that have been cast upon them by other persons. Furthermore, they also contest the prerogative of suffering, terminally ill patients to receive professional assistance to end their suffering and die with dignity; they prefer to see them suffering for prolonged periods, enduring painfully lingering deaths, and they call that compassion. They use their hopelessly distorted interpretations of their holy books and their public offices to oppress and demonize persons who subscribe to different sexual preferences from the rest of the population that considers itself the norm. But the irony is that some of the most outspoken accusers of other persons are guilty of the same actions, leaving the impression that those actions are not as deviant as they make them appear, if they, the critics and castigators can also secretly participate in them.

Overall, therefore, governments are proving to be unreliable custodians of the people's rights, and to even think that a time will come when we can have a single world government is to entertain a dangerous and thankfully futile hope. Everyone out there is looking after parochial interests; but their parochialism is strictly limited to the circumference within which they stand as individuals or co-conspirators in the disinheritance of the peoples of the world for whose dignity and ethical worth they have no respect and for whom they do not harbour any "sympathy or compassionate concern". The values of respect and spirit of cosmopolitanism are taboo to them. They are not sworn to ending world-wide hunger, disease, and poverty; instead, they are dismantling and slashing programs for health, welfare, education, ecology, and prosperity for the people in favour of diverting available funds to their own pockets and to the pockets of their friends in the multinational corporations. They plan programs like NSSM200 (National Security Study Memorandum) to deprive certain so-called "third world" countries of food for the selfish purpose of controlling their populations and their mouthy youth who are rising against the status quo — today apartheid states use the same programs for subduing and perhaps decimating vast populations of democratic states that do not kowtow to their lordship over them. They slash programs and benefits due to aged people in their twilight years, so that they can maintain their own extravagant ways of living. Their bosom friends who boost them financially will not forgo their immense profits from drugs that would otherwise save millions of lives in poor countries if they were made affordable to them at a price that they could afford, seeing that their co-conspirators in the task of making fortunes on the backs of these same and other people will not forgive the debt that they have imposed on poor countries in the despicable guise of helping them to solve their financial problems with loans that have enslaved them and are severely inhibiting their already meagre economic growth, denying them healthy lifestyles, education potential, ability to afford life-saving drugs, and crippling their survival. They think nothing of aiding their corporate friends in devastating the ecology of poor people for the sake of establishing commercial concerns that will earn them tons of money, while they offer the owners of the land peanuts, and of dispossessing the people outright to make room for their friends. A friend once challenged me to name even one poor politician or bureaucrat. I couldn't; and that speaks volumes.

In the face of all these negative factors and the additional crimes of stealing elections, stooping so low as to send letter or parcelled bombs to selected individuals who are hated for their criticism of mismanagement of state affairs, refusing to give up power after losing elections, selectively hauling only some wrong doers before their international criminal courts, but protecting other freely roaming criminals from arrest and prosecution, etc., it is difficult to envisage "an effective new World Parliament elected by the people of the world . . . a worldwide security system to resolve military conflicts; an effective world court with enforcement powers . . . a transnational environmental protection agency . . . universal education and health care . . . some procedures for regulating multinational corporations . . . "[9] and other universal agencies when existing global agencies of control are failing to contain arrogant nations that flout United Nations resolutions while pointing fingers at others in the same boat with the connivance of powerful friends, and some others choose to place themselves above the jurisdiction of existing international courts of justice. Anyone who argues that these iniquities could be eliminated if the people involved in their perpetration were all Christians is obviously naïve, because the Christians and others who are guilty of these misdeeds are no better than the rest, if not worse, as their histories testify, and to even think that they could lead a world government is to engage in phantasy, as I have argued in *Homan Inhomanity* about Krustans, their doubles of twin world, and as present day Christians are demonstrating so clearly and unequivocally. And so I say to our Christian and other "brothers": if you love life so much for yourselves, then love it for others too, because they also love it for themselves; don't deprive them of it. And when you think of starving or otherwise killing off all the gay people, because you believe that they have lost their way in your world of phony purity and trumped-up righteousness, remember that your founder said: "For the Son of man is come to seek and to save that which was lost"[10], not to destroy that whose values happen to be different from mine; and that applies to others who persecute and oppress people who are different from them in their efforts to render them stateless instead of sharing their god's land with them.

I end this chapter with a statement of the Declaration of Humanist Principles[11]: (See also Humanist Manifestos I, II, and III.)

(1) Humanism aims at the full development of every human being.
(2) Humanists uphold the broadest application of democratic principles in all human relationships.
(3) Humanists advocate the use of the scientific method, both as a guide to distinguish fact from fiction and to help develop beneficial and creative uses of science and technology.

(4) Humanists affirm the dignity of every person and the right of the individual to maximum possible freedom compatible with the rights of others.
(5) Humanists acknowledge human interdependence, the need for mutual respect and the kinship of all humanity.
(6) Humanists call for the continued improvement of society so that no one may be deprived of the basic necessities of life, and for institutions and conditions to provide every person with opportunities for developing their full potential.
(7) Humanists support the development and extension of fundamental human freedoms, as expressed in the United Nations Universal Declaration of Human Rights and supplemented by UN International Covenants comprising the United Nations Bill of Human Rights.
(8) Humanists advocate peaceful resolution of conflicts between individuals, groups, and nations.
(9) The humanist ethic encourages development of the positive potentialities in human nature, and approves conduct based on a sense of responsibility to oneself and to all other persons.
(10) A fundamental principle of humanism is the rejection of beliefs held in absence of verifiable evidence, such as beliefs based solely on dogma, revelation, mysticism or appeals to the supernatural.
(11) Humanists affirm that individual and social problems can only be resolved by means of human reason, intelligent effort, critical thinking joined with compassion and a spirit of empathy for all living beings.
(12) Humanists affirm that human beings are completely a part of nature, and that our survival is dependent upon a healthy planet which provides us and all other forms of life with a life-supporting environment.

(I have discussed the environment fully in chapters 4 and 5 of *Our World and its Values*).

This essay has been, in many respects, an exercise in the expression of humanism and the challenges that it faces from human inhumanity in its many faces of presentation: religious, political, economic, and social that I have dealt with before in *Homan Inhomanity*. The tenets laid down by Humanism are second to none in their sublimity, and more importantly, their observation by their adherents literally put to shame those who have adopted the high moral codes of their religions but practice a debased kind of morality that would make their founders hang their heads in shame at the deeds of their purported followers. We can confidently look to Humanism to redeem our world from the ravages that religion and politics have wrought on it.

Chapter 10
What's next?

The human agent has proven to be a complex mixture of contraries: greed, a smidgen of benevolence; hegemony, minimal compassion; selfishness, rare generosity; egoism, occasional altruism; mysticism, humanism; cunning, honesty; duplicity, probity; hatred, love; etc., and as difficult to fathom as the Milky Way and the totality of galaxies in space. Nevertheless, in the midst and in spite of all its contradictory positions, it is still able to achieve phenomenal progress in providing for the comforts of living for the chosen few, reaching out to explore extraterrestrial territories with a view to expanding knowledge about our universe and to possibly establishing new colonies in these territories to replace the ones in our world that have been and are being reclaimed by those from whom they were taken by brute force. One dreads to think, though, of the kinds of colonies that it will establish there, considering the odious kind of track record that it has established in this world. Such fears are not idle or foolish prattle; they are only the most appropriate conclusion to draw from that track record of inhumanity. It is a pity that the deeds of a few should stain the rest of the people who are always trying their best to be truthful, honest, and humane in their dealings with everyone; but there will always be those who see an opportunity to take undue advantage of others and their honesty, promising them greatness in the ruin that they are planning. That is how life unfolds.

Civilization, which should be a boon to human existence, will unfortunately be the death knell of humanity, as it is already proving itself to be. Empires have come and gone, and today's great and invincible empires will suffer the same fate, regardless of how much might and influence they wield in the world. Already, the writing is on the wall for some of them; but they refuse to acknowledge the truth of their steady decline and eventual decay, if not their present state of early decay, judging by their conduct and the malodorous trail of death and inhumane devastation that they leave behind everywhere they go. Contemporary events are clear enough for everyone to see the impending implosion of these empires of self-confidence and hegemony, and anyone who looks at these events with a penetrating eye that is not blinded by self-regard will readily appreciate the predicament that is about to befall humanity as it is proudly defined in those decadent societies of our world, some of which have turned to religious fanaticism, pushing their bibles into everyone's face (especially the face of their governments) but violating its injunctions every hour of their cursed lives. Regrettably, they read these bibles upside down with frosted glasses through which they see only distorted letters, exposing their foolishness, if not their hypocrisy.

Is this combination of negativism and pessimism justified, and is it the correct attitude to assume about our flourishing world? Regrettably again, yes. Despite its flourishing, the world in which we live is ruled by dictators and elected governments that are subservient to unelected back room boys and corporations that they serve diligently at the expense of their citizens; where children die by the millions from purposely engineered hunger and preventable and treatable diseases while the corporations and their pawns (governments) drain the coffers of poor nation states in contrived debts that have been imposed on them under the pretext of development, which is really a way of supporting projects from which corporations generate money for themselves and their pawns, the governments; where inanimate and unthinking (free) markets determine the fate of poor nations by facilitating their exploitation through globalization, thereby further widening the gap between soaring salaries, profits, pensions, and bonuses of the rich and the plummeting wages and meagre pensions of the poor; where corporate money lending vultures denude the natural products and modest national income of poor nations reaped from the remainder of their assets after the lenders have relieved them of the bulk of the riches of their lands—a case of the poor feeding the rich; where money is worth far more than human life and dignity; where the quest for dollars, euros, pounds, yens, etc., trounces concern over an environment that is already ravaged by pollution, global warming, genetically engineered foods, hormone treated meat, etc.; where the duo of opaque dealings and corruption of all kinds is the order of the day at many levels of government, private enterprise, and even the church; where the middle and "lesser" classes bear the brunt of taxation from which the rich are exempted—another case of the poor feeding the rich; where success by cheating is an accepted practice that does not elicit enough deserved disdain to shame the perpetrators, and where even they are hardly shamed by their immoral actions, as long as they can be number one and "qualify" for lucrative employment in positions of power or add glory to their names as the best athletes, etc. In such a world, pessimists are the only ones who will not be disappointed in their fear for the worst in life; optimists will more often than not be sorely disappointed in their hopes and aspirations, with corruption, dishonesty, inhumanity, and a hefty dose of disrespect awaiting them around every corner.

Unless the precipitous trend to self-annihilation that has produced these ruinous attitudes of mind is reversed by the expansion and persistence of activist attitudes such as those that fuel noble enterprises like the "occupy" movement and the rise of working classes against exploitation by employers, churches, and governments, the future of humanity will remain as bleak as it now appears, and we will all—the guilty and, unfortunately, the innocent as well—perish from the greed-engineered ills imposed on all of us by a few self-obsessed individuals. It is strange but true that little disappointment will overshadow one who sees this world for the moral disaster that it is than for the one who is deceived into thinking and hoping that it is the best of all possible worlds. Such is already the case with the young people who entered politics to change the corrupt ways of their elders but were disillusioned by being emasculated and placed in cold storage by the old rascals who would not brook their audacity to interfere with their sources of irregular income. But that should not be a deterrent to the younger generation to change the status quo; the future of their world depends on them. If they follow the same obscene abuse of office as their elders and they adopt the same attitudes of greed that some politicians and CEOs have adopted, then we can all despair of saving our world, because power is vested in these rascals.

It is time, therefore, that the majority, reputed to be a staggering 99+%, woke up to the havoc that the mere -1% is wreaking on their world and their lives. They must not allow the status quo to persist. They can use their votes to throw out any government that does not look after their interests and elect one that will do their bidding, instead of one that sells them out to the -1% who finance their election campaigns. But even before that, their votes can block the election of a government of the rich for the rich by the rich whose candidates for office have made no secret (in secret until the secret information leaked out into the open becoming a no-secret) of the fact that they do not care about them and their votes, unjustly besmirching them with epithets that they should justly be applying to themselves as the privileged and entitled few who can shelter their loads of money from being used to "spread the wealth around" by stashing it offshore and then having their hounds persecute the same people for whom they don't care for infinitesimal amounts in taxes that they have imposed on them. This is an unmistakable wrong and immensely heavy and inhumane burden that the 1% who are preoccupied with the growth of their fortunes and protecting them have cast on the 99%, subjecting them to hunger, deprivation, avoidable sickness, and ultimate dehumanization and blinding them to the magic of the one living world around them. Yes, one world, but also two different worlds that are miles apart from each other and from the natural beauty in which they exist, attesting to the sad truth of the sentiment that was expressed by William Henry Davies when he wrote:

> What is this life if, full of care,
> We have no time to stand and stare.
> ...
> No time to see, in broad daylight,
> Streams full of stars, like skies at night.
> ...
> A poor life this if, full of care,
> We have no time to stand and stare.[1]

Notes

Chapter 1

1. The meaning of the word "good" used in this essay is that defined by William Frankenna, quoted on page 101. Ordinarily, a good knife is one that will cut well when it is used for that purpose; i.e., one that will perform the function for which it was designed and made as expected. A good deed is one that benefits everyone and hurts no one, and a good person is one who performs such deeds or is disposed to perform them when the need arises; one who, if he can't do anything for others, will not do anything to them. In all three cases commendation is appropriate, but not enough to describe the object, the deed, or the person and to demarcate them from those that are commendable but not necessarily good in the senses defined above. Goodness is the concept that embraces these and other "goods". By "common good" we will understand a just and moral good-in-itself that should be accessible to all members of the society that is known to shape the individual (not majority against minority or vice versa with self-serving cliques claiming to serve the people); a good that respects personal autonomy while it transcends individualism, parasitism by free loaders on the willingness of others to uphold the system under which they all live and flourish, and the puerile attitude of persons (governments) who will not play their part in helping to achieve the goals that have been set by them as part of the unity of nations to save the earth and the world from the ravages of pollution, simply because the junior members (developing countries) are not ready to carry an equal share of the burden with the putative adults (developed countries). Such a good is to be found only in ethical social systems that are structured to benefit all people alike.

Jacques Maritain first enumerates the "public commodities and services" that "constitute the common good of political society" and then goes on to say, "The common good includes . . . something more profound, more concrete and more human. . . . It includes the sum or sociological integration of all the civic conscience, political virtues and sense of right and liberties, . . . material prosperity and spiritual riches, . . . of moral rectitude, justice, friendship, happiness, virtue and heroism in the individual lives of its members." See Jacques Maritain, *The Person and the Common Good*, trans. John J. Fitzgerald, (Indiana: University of Notre Dame Press, 1966), 52.

2. An action is right when it is intrinsically good and it gives greater quality of pleasure or happiness and other good effects than any other possible action could have done in the circumstances. To be intrinsically good it must be good on its own, without depending on anything else to make it so, even if it contains parts that cannot be good on their own apart from the whole in which they participate; but even they, if they are present, must be present to a minimal degree. Of course, a wrong action will be one that has opposite properties. The temptation to incorporate motives into the labelling of actions as right or wrong, while it is appropriate for characterizing their moral connotation, should be resisted, because good motives can produce unintended and unforeseen bad consequences for which the agent should

not be condemned, but which, nevertheless, are still bad for those who have to live with their consequences and must therefore be labelled as bad actions.

Chapter 2.

1. A condition is necessary if it is required for a situation to obtain; e.g., B can't be the case without A. It is sufficient if it is the one that precipitates the occurrence of B in the presence of A or by itself and in this case A can also serve as a sufficient condition for the occurrence of B. So, being a member of the human species is a necessary condition for personhood, if and only if personhood cannot be asserted without membership of the human species; i.e., non-membership of the human species deprives an entity of personhood, because personhood is defined in terms of such membership together with other qualifying conditions. But membership of the human species alone does not guarantee personhood, although personhood cannot be asserted without it. On the other hand, there are now entities that lay claim to personhood without prior membership of the human race, such as corporations, thus necessitating a broader definition of personhood. Hence, membership of the human species is no longer the sole sufficient condition for personhood, since it does not alone guarantee personhood; i.e., personhood is not solely dependent on membership of the human race, since other entities also satisfy the condition of being labeled persons (as per the new, expanded definition of persons). Each one of the necessary conditions also serves as a sufficient condition, since the other conditions do not have to co-exist with it as jointly necessary conditions to satisfy the definition of personhood. Eliminating any one of them does not disable any one of the others from satisfying the definition by itself.

2. Edward Makhene, *Philosophy for Medical Students and Practitioners*, (self-pub., 2018), 77.

3. Plato proposed a theory of Forms whereby all material objects and their mutable properties are the imperfect, sensible copies of perfect, supersensible Forms, perceived only by the intellect or reason through the intervention of the soul. The transcendent Forms, which are the true objects of knowledge, determine the essence of every existent; e.g., the good person, deed, article manifests (participates in) the universal form "Goodness", without which he/it cannot be good. Similarly, a yellow ribbon manifests (participates in) the form "Yellowness" by virtue of which it is yellow — otherwise it cannot exist as an entity with a yellow colour. The immutable Forms are to be regarded as the universal standards or paradigms on which all constantly changing particulars are modelled, in the same way that axioms are the foundations of Geometry for which no proofs are required, to avoid the infinite regress generated by the fact that an x that resembles X does so in virtue of a common characteristic c, which in turn resembles C in virtue of their common characteristic c_1, and so on ad infinitum. This third entity, a something-we-know-not-what, has given birth to the so-called Third Man argument into which we will not enter.

4. Jean-Paul Sartre, *Existentialism and Humanism*, trans. Philip Mairet, (London: Methuen, 1963), 28.

5. John Locke, *An Essay Concerning Human Understanding*, ed. Peter H. Nidditch, (Oxford: Oxford University Press, 1979), 335.

6. Arthur C. Danto, *Connections to the World*, (Berkeley: University of California Press, 1997), 219.

7. René Descartes, "Meditations on First Philosophy", in vol. 1 of *Philosophical Works of Descartes*, trans. Elizabeth S. Haldane and G.R.T. Ross, (Dover Publications Inc., 1931), 153.

8. Aristotle held that matter is the basic substance of all existing objects to which form is added to give them their distinctive identities as the kinds of things they are; e.g., humans, sheep, boats, and statues. For him matter and form cannot be primary substances independent of each other. Forms are related to the particulars in which they are manifested, and both are appreciated via sensation, unlike Plato's Forms, which transcend the five senses and exist in a realm of their own. Yellowness cannot exist apart from a yellow flower or something else that is yellow — it is found only in yellow things by means of which it comes to be known. So the form, which is the essence of the unchanging human property styled personhood, is what gives the human body (physical substance with mutable properties shared by all material things) the unique characteristics that make it the person that it is, distinguishing it from other substances and bodies with which it shares its physical attributes. Similarly, a sculptor can imposes form on a nondescript mass of marble or granite by hewing a statue at one time and headstone at another time, without the addition of any extraneous matter to achieve his end.

9. Thomas Aquinas, Summa Theologica, "Treatise on the Creation, Question 44", www.sacred-texts/chr/aquinas/summa/ sum049.htm

10. Peter Strawson, *Individuals*, (London: Methuen, 1964), 89.

11. Vegetative state refers to states in which "persons" are alive, but they lack self or environmental awareness, interaction with others, and evidence of purposeful responses to various stimuli, although their cranial and spinal nerve reflexes are preserved.

12. David Hume, *A Treatise of Human Nature*, (London: J.M. Dent & Sons Ltd., 1951), 1, 4, 6 (Of personal identity), 239.

13. Makhene, *Our World and its Values*, (self-pub., 2006), 76.

Chapter 3.

1. Gerald N. Hill, Kathleen Thompson Hill, *The People's Law Dictionary*, s.v. "Law". (New York: MJF Books, 2002), https://archive.org/stream/B-001-001-744 /B-001-001 -744_djvu.txt

2. Roger Trigg, *Morality Matters*, (Oxford: Blackwell Publishing, 2005), 163.

3. Intuition refers to the direct and immediate knowledge of truths, i.e., self-evident truths, about his world (including himself) by a subject, based solely on his beliefs, which have not inferentially been justified by any prior acquaintance with other true facts about it and which therefore fall outside of the generally accepted definition of propositional knowledge (that such and such is the case) as justified true belief. For example, that killing another person without just cause is wrong, or that the whole is bigger than its part are intuitive facts that are known readily and without inference from other facts, but whose truth is justifiable from the subsequent experiences of the subject. The evidence for them and their effects is acquired after the fact of their acceptance. Nevertheless, in adopting the definition of knowledge as justified true belief, we should not lose sight of the fact that there are some known putative facts that have been proved to be untrue; e.g., the geocentric theory of the solar system which was prevalent and pragmatic until it was replaced by the heliocentric theory, which proved to be more pragmatic; and there is "knowledge" that is based on beliefs that are in turn not justified by the facts and the evidence but

happen to be true guesses; e.g., the story was told at a certain medical school that medical students learning about the pathology of disease somehow often claimed to know that they were afflicted with one or more of those diseases, until it was proved to one of them that he was truly afflicted with the gonococcus—to his utter horror. For further discussion of intuition, see page 109.

4. Makhene, *Homan Inhomanity*, (self-pub., 2018), 80.

5. John Rawls, "The Sense of Justice", in *Moral Concepts*, ed. Joel Feinberg, (London: Oxford University Press, 1969), 136.

6. Pankaj Kumar, "Meaning and Types of Rights", http://www.slideshare.net/birubiru/meaning-and-types-of-rights

7. A real life case is described by Chris Purdy in the Toronto Star of September 4, 2012: ". . . he saw the children crossing the road and realized they were in danger. . . . The four kids, ranging in ages from 3 to 16, had the right of way. . . . all vehicles had stopped except for a silver car that was heading straight for the children. . . . the vehicle was travelling at a pretty high rate of speed. . . . made a split decision to drive into the path of the oncoming car. . . . saved the children from serious harm and possible death.

8. John Stuart Mill, *Utilitarianism, Liberty and Representative Government*, (New York: Dutton, 1922), 79.

9. Denis Diderot, https://www.goodreads.com/quotes/54491

Chapter 4.

1. Anthony O'Hear, *Philosophy in the New Century*, (London: Continuum, 2001), 10.

2. O'Hear, *New Century*, 52.

3. Heinz Kimmerle, "Ubuntu and Communalism in African Philosophy and Art", Rozenberg Quarterly, July 4, 2011, http://rozenbergquarterly.com/?p=1811

4. Dani W. Nabudere, "Ubuntu Philosophy. Memory and Reconciliation", http://nkwankwala.blogspot.com/2011/02/ Ubuntu-philosophy-and.html

5. Nabudere, "Ubuntu and Communalism"

6. Possible worlds are imaginary worlds in which conditions that obtain in this (actual) world might have been totally different but still non-contradictory and therefore logical.

7. John Donne, "Devotions Upon Emergent Occasions", Meditation xvii, http://web.cs.dal.ca/~johnston/poetry/ island.html

8. Makhene, *Our World and its Values*, 173.

Chapter 5.

1. Alan R. White, *The Philosophy of Action*, (London: Oxford University Press, 1968), 2.

2. Thomas Pink, *Free Will*, (Oxford: Oxford University Press, 2004), 100.

3. Pink, *Free will*, 5.

4. Anthony Kenny, *The Metaphysics of Mind*, (Oxford: Oxford University Press, 1992), 22.

5. Donald Davidson, *Essays on Actions and Events*, 2d. ed., (Oxford: Clarendon Press, 2001), 8.

6. Davidson, *Actions and Events*, 4.

7. John Searle, *Rationality in Action*, (Cambridge Mas: The MIT Press, 2001), 46.

8. William of Ockham - medieval monk whose basic philosophical rule states that entities should not be multiplied beyond necessity; alternatively, that we should always choose the simplest of competing theories that adequately explain any given situation.

9. Neuroscientists are now toying with experiments whereby they can record the movements of matter by means of brain power.

10. Danto, "Basic Actions" in *The Philosophy of Action*, ed. Alan R. White, (London: Oxford University, Press, 1968), 56.

11. Searle, *Rationality*, 49.

12. Searle, *Rationality*, 46.

13. Stuart Hampshire, *Thought and Action*, (Notre Dame: University of Notre Dame Press, 1983), 134.

14. John L. Austin, *Philosophical Papers*, ed. J.O. Urmson & G.J. Warnock, (London: Oxford University Press, 1961), 222.

15. Stephanie Cram, "Dark history of Canada's First Nations pass system uncovered in documentary", *CBC News*, Feb 19, 2016, https://www.cbc.ca/news/indigenous/dark-history-canada-s-passsystem-1.3454022

Chapter 6.

1. Hampshire, *Thought and Action*, 97.
2. Makhene, *Mind Your Ps and Qs*, (self-pub., 2007), 48.
3. Abraham Melden, *Free Action*, (London: Routledge and Kegan Paul, 1967).
4. Ludwig Wittgenstein, *Philosophical Investigations*, trans. G.E.M. Anscombe, (Oxford: Basil Blackwell. 1963), 161^e, §621.
5. Hume, *Treatise*, 239.
6. Hume, *On Nature and the Human Understanding*, (New York: Collier Books, 1965), 116.
7. Pink, *Free will*, 28.
8. Pink, *Free will*, 28.

Chapter 7.

1. Arthur Schopenhauer, "On the Sufferings of the World" in *The Essays of Arthur Schopenhauer Studies in Pessimism*, www.readcentral.com/chapters/Arthur-Scopenhauer-Studies-in-Pessimism/002l

2. Schopenhauer, "The Wisdom of Life" in *The Essays*, http://w2.hn.psu.edu/faculty/jmanis/schopenhauer/ Schopenhauer-7.pdf

3. Denis Diderot, https://www.libertarianism.org/encyclopedia/diderot-denis-1713-1784

4. William Frankenna, *Ethics* 2nd ed., (Englewood Cliffs NJ: Prentice Hall, 1973), 83.

5. Deontology refers to the theory that the morally right action is one done out of duty. Utilitarianism labels the morally right action as one that produces the maximum amount of happiness to the greatest number of person.

6. Martin Buber, *I and Thou*, (New York NY: Charles Scribner's Sons, 1970), 54.

7. Buber, *I and Thou*, 109.

8. Immanuel Kant, *Foundations of the Metaphysics of Morals*, trans. Lewis White Beck, (Chicago ILL: University of Chicago Press, 1950), 87.

9. Kant, *Foundations*, 80.

10. Jean-Jacques Rousseau, *The Social Contract*, trans. Maurice Cranston, (London: Penguin Books, 1968), 49.

Chapter 8.

1. John Calvin, *Institutes of the Christian Religion*, trans. Henry Beveridge, (Grand Rapids: Christian Classics Ethereal Library, 1845) 464 http://www.ccel.org/ccel/calvin/institutes.pdf
2. Gilbert Ryle, *Dilemmas*, (Cambridge: Cambridge University Press, 1994), 94-95.
3. Benedict Spinoza, *Short Treatise on G-d, Man and His Well-being*, trans. A. Wolf, (London: Adam & Charles Black, 1910), 102 http://www.yesselman.com/Short Treatise.htm
4. If I were erecting a shelter and I knew only the vertical height, a-b, and the ground level dimensions of the opening, c-d, I could calculate the length of the metal sheet needed by using the theorem of Pythagoras. But I would have to prove that the sum of the internal angles of a triangle is 180^0. I would not have to prove that a triangle has three angles, or that the three straight lines that form the triangles acd and bcd are the shortest distances between any two adjacent end-points, or that those lines consist of a series of points, because that information is basic to the system; it cannot be justified, but it can be used as justification for the theorem and its applications. Pythagoras' Theorem states that the square on the hypotenuse is equal to the sum of the squares on the shorter sides.
5. Richard Swinburne, *Is There A God?* (Oxford: Oxford University Press, 1996),
6. Swinburne, *Is There A God?* 6.
7. Swinburne, *Is There A God?* 19.
8. Swinburne, *Is There A God?* 41.
9. Theodore Parker. https://www.goodreads.com/quotes/303285-i-do-not-pretend-to-understand-the-moral-universe-the
10. Owen Flanagan, *The Problem of the Soul*, (New York NY: Basic Books, 2002), 319.
11. Bertrand Russell, *Why I am not a Christian*, (London: Unwin Books, 1967), 26.
12. Blaise Pascal, *Pensées*, trans. W.F. Trotter, section XIV, no. 895, http://oregonstate.edu/instruct/phl/1302/texts/pascal/pensees-contents.html
13. Richard Norman, *On Humanism*, (London: Routledge, 2004), 16.

Chapter 9.

1. Corliss Lamont, *The Philosophy of Humanism,* 8th ed., (Amherst NY: Humanist Press, 1997), 15 http://www.corlisslamont.org/philos8.pdf
2. Peter Cave, *Humanism*, (Oxford: One World Publications 2009), 1.
3. Diderot, *Pensées sur la Religion*, www.badnewsaboutchristianity.com/gg0_medicine.htm
4. Samuel Johnson, *The History of Rasselas Prince of Abyssinia*, ed. Thomas Keymer, (New York: Oxford University Press Inc., 2009), 45.
5. John Milton, *Paradise Lost and Paradise Regained*, ed. Christopher Ricks, (New York: Signet Classic, Penguin Books, 1968), 54, lines 254-255.
6. David H. Lawrence, "When wilt thou teach the people-?", in *The Complete Poems*, ed. Vivian De Sola Pinto and F. Warren Roberts, (New York: Penguin Books, 1964), 442.

7. "Caritate Christi Compulsi", http://www.vatican.va/holy_father/pius_xi/encyclicals/documents/hf_p-xi_enc_03051932-caritate-christi-compulsi_en.html#top

8. Paul Kurtz, *What is Secular Humanism?* (Amherst NY: Prometheus Books, 2007), 45.

9. Kurtz, *Secular Humanism,* 54.

10. Lk. 19: 10. KJV

11. What is Humanism?, http://www.humanists-london.org/What_is_Humanism.html

Chapter 10.

1. Davies, William H., "Leisure", http://www.englishverse.com/poems/leisure

Index

abortion, 122, 126, 134
act, 63-64
action: affirmative, 37; 139 definition, 62-65; free, 87, 88, 93, 94, 153; goal directed, 64-65
acts and omissions, 70, 75
acts, mental, 63, 64
actus reus, 74, 75
agency: 1, 62, 79, 90; action through, 14; free, 3; human, 6, 96, 111; movement caused by my, 85; powers, 94; Ubuntu as, 47
AIDS, 56-57, 143
Alien Hand syndrome, 87
altruism, 25, 105, 132
anencephalics, 12, 16
angels, 125, 130, 133, 138
animal, human, 1, 3, 79, 99
Anscombe, Gertrude E., 153
apparitions, 106, 117
appearances, 117
Apollo, 130
Aquinas, Thomas, 18, 19, 24, 151
argument: cosmological, 119; ontological, 119
Aristotle, 19, 31, 151
Augustine, St., 115
Austin, John L., 76, 153
Australia, 10
authority in Ubuntu, 51
automatons: 120; a race of, 80
autonomy: 39; and supremacy, 45; deprived us of, 92; discredit the, 142; divest people of endowed with rationality and, 99; divest people of their, 134; of other persons, 69; respects personal, 149; rationality and, 101

bankruptcy, moral, 45, 98
Beck, Lewis White, 154
benevolence: 57, 99, 108; deliberately acts of, 37; and caring, 109; infinite, 137; lack of, 107; smidgen of, 146; unforced, 30
Berkeley, George, 23
Beveridge, Henry, 154
bigots: 107; of this world; 109; religious 126; the most irrational, 133
Bitcoin, 36;
Bob, 41-42
Bourgeois, Warren, 16
boys, backroom, 33-34
Broodryk, Johann, 48
Buber, Martin, 85, 104, 154
Buffalo, 73
bullies, 35, 128

Calvin, John, 154
Canada, 77
Catholics, 104
cause, 89-91
Cave, Peter, 155
chaos effect, 70
chicken, cross the road, 78, 79
child, aboriginal, 43
China, 10
choice, 71
choice, free, 81-82
choices, rational, 95
Christians: 59, 103, 127; present day, 144; so-called, 137-138
churchmen, 126, 138-139
Cicero, Marcus, 16
circularity, 64, 65
coins, false, 113
colonialism, scourge of, 36
community in Ubuntu, 49
compassion in Ubuntu, 49
condition(s): necessary, 8, 15, 17, 18, 19, 73, 81, 86, 150; sufficient, 8, 15, 18, 19, 73, 83, 86, 150
Confucius, 105
constitution, genetic, 82, 90, 91
contracts, sign, 58
cooperation: creative products of, 131;

157

mutual tolerance and, 56; of the oppressors, 124
cosmology, Aristotelian, 18
Cotard syndrome, 84
Cram, Stephanie, 153
Cranston, Maurice, 154
creationism, baseless, 134
culpability: 8, 9, 68-71, 87; absolve us of, 92; acts for which they deny all, 100; bear moral responsibility and, 88; for his actions, 91; for their inhumane actions, 109
Curiosity, 107

Danto, Arthur, 17-18, 72-73, 151, 153
Darwin, Charles, 136
Davidson, Donald, 152, 153
Davies, William, 148, 155
deconstruction, of money, 36
Deity: 116, 123; benevolent, 132; guidance by, 137; invent a, 120; private communication with the, 118; that we have created, 130; their, 126
Delphi, 130
demeanour, children's, 51
democracy: crying lack of economic, 142; men who have subverted, 46; threats to, 34; yawping homage to, 140
Descartes, Renè: 115, 151; body-mind dichotomy, 19-20, 136; body-mind dualism, 16, 20; ghost, 84, 136; ontology, 16; theory of knowledge, 22-23; thinking thing of, 20; unity of mind and body, 17
De Spinoza, Benedict, 19, 24, 89, 116, 154
determinism, 4, 82, 88-92, 93, 94
devil: 123; someone named the, 138
devils, holy, 133
Diderot, Denis, 101, 135, 152, 153, 155
ding an sich, 116
disasters, natural, 31
dispositions: 19; morbid, 34; activation of certain propensities or, 85; evil, 98; prompting, 87; to behave automatically, 17
DNA, 5
dogma: and fantasies like miracles, 131; beliefs based solely on, 145; does not require proof, 12; dubious, 121; inflexible, 133; of their church, 122;
religion based on, 133; religious 115, 128, 137; -ridden church, 132; used to hijack, 125
Dolly, 9
Donne, John, 56, 152
Double Effect, Doctrine of, 70

education, college, 139
equality, *de jure*, 45, 140
essence: 21; existence precedes his, 48, 127; of every existent, 150; of the unchanging human property styled personhood, 151; of nature is diversity, 134; of personhood, 17-19; or gist of personhood, 16;
Eve, 10
existence: 19; achieving a moral, 92; African, 47; bare, 36, 97; dispensable elements in its, 56; disrupt their peaceful, 57; divinely revealed transcendent, 122-123; human, 7, 19, 146; of an acting entity, 64; of an immaterial soul, 115; of disembodied minds, 17, 18; of spirits, 24; of the transient "I", 84; of their Deity, 119; of transcendent forces, 111-112; precariously marginal, 13; precedes essence, 48, 127; timeless, 136; transcendent, 125, 135; violate your rights to, 52

faith: 133, 138; antithesis of evidence, 111; ardent protagonists of, 138; as knowledge, 114; blind, 113, 118, 137; divine guidance through revelation and, 113; full definition of, 112; giant leap of, 137; in the unknown, 135; irrational, 128; ninth commandment of their, 59; power of, 112; protagonists of, 136; question the, 140; teachings by, 134
fallacy, logical, 125
fatalism, 91-92
Feinberg, Joel ,152
fetuses: 12, 16, 21; innocent, 142-143; interrupt the carrying of their, 142; personhood of, 12; right to life of, 41; simple killing of, 70
Flanagan, Owen, 125, 154
Florida, 2

Forms, 14, 19, 114, 115, 117, 150, 151
(forty-seven per cent) 47%, 58
Frankenna, William, 101, 149, 153
free will, 87, 94, 152
freedom, concept of, 3
fundamentalists, religious, 142

Gaia, 1, 13
generations: despair that has plagued, 36; future, 105, 135; legal rights of all future, 12; of equally sinful humankind, 123; of false beliefs, 114; of immigrants' children, 43; of privileged oppressors, 98
generosity: 146; in Ubuntu culture, 50; is lacking, 51; material and emotional, 13; rare, 146
genes: 91; constrained his action, 82
Geometry, Euclidean, 119
ghost in the machine, 17, 84, 137
globalization: 97; and its enslaving organizations, 97; exploitation through, 147
good, common: 34, 49, 54; definition, 149; promote the, 2; promote their, 56
goods, material, 142
government, world, 143, 144
Greeks, 130
ground, stand your, 43
Group Areas Act, 77
gunpowder, 120
guns, don't kill people, 68

H_2O, 4, 15
habeas corpus, 141
Haldane, Elizabeth S., 151
Hampshire, Stuart, 74, 79, 153
happening(s): 21; actions are complexes of 98; mere, 65, 73; responsibility for the ultimate, 67-68; without verbalized intent, 66; versus actions, 21; x as a mere 71
health care: 38, 144; benefits to poor people, 139; deprive refugees of access to, 60; should be universal, 38
Hegel, Georg W., 116
heresy, 121
Hill, Gerald N., 151

Hill, Kathleen Thompson, 151
Hobbes, Thomas, 3, 127
Hobson's choice, 70, 82
Hohfeld, Wesley N., 42
holy books; 102-103, 107, 133, 143; inviolate, 102; unscientific, 142
Homo: ignārum, 25, 26, 27; sapiens, 1, 3, 25, 26, 27, 114, 130
Huahua, 9
Humanism, definition, 131
Hume, Davi; 21, 58, 83-85, 151, 153; miracles in which, 132;
hypocrisy: 126; and misanthropy, 127; scurrilous, 13; their, 147; unpalatable label of, 59

I, 84-86
I-It, 104, 133
I-You, 104, 133
immigrants: 12; undesirable, 97
immunities, 42
inequality: de facto, 45; social, 139
intention-in-action, 73-74
intentionality, 63
interdependency in Ubuntu, 56
intuition, 109-110, 151
Iqaluit, 2
island, 56

Jacob, 81
Japan, 9
Jesus, 105
Jill, 65, 73
Jim: 52; annoyed Bob, 75; Bob has a claim against, 41; Bob has a privilege against, 42; happens to be the driver, 82; is angry, 17; is mortal, 120; my wish to strike, 67; predicts, 73; the agent, 66
Johnson, Samuel, 137, 155
justice: 29, 82, 107, 149; and fairness, 35, 37, 138; bring them to, 15; clutches of, 32; courts of, 144; dispensation of, 37; freedom and, 35; principles of, 35, 37; sense of, 37, 105, 106, 152; social, 122; subvert or obstruct, 3; systems of, 82; and they call that, 100; unjust, 16, 106; will eventually prevail, 124

Kant, Immanuel: 102, 116, 117, 153; morality per, 101; stunt devised by, 33

159

Kate, 65
Kenny, Anthony, 152
Kimmerle, Heinz, 152
king: is strangled, 100; of himself, 10; self-crowned non-regal, 100
knowledge: 6, 86, 111-112, 121, 135; a posteriori, 112; a priori, 112; as justified true belief, 112; as truth, 90; bounds of, 125; common, 74; definition of, 151; Descartes' theory of, 22; faculty of, 79; fountain of, 36; gaps in their, 120; history of, 48; inadequate, 38; incomplete, 80; inhumane uses of scientific, 128; is finite, 127; is knowing that you know nothing, 134; of God's nature, 115-116; sanctified theoretical, 103; scientific, 128; self-, 20; true, 134; true objects of, 150
Kumar, Pankaj, 152
Kurtz, Paul, 155

Lamont, Corliss, 131, 155
law: 3; definition, 29; Ubuntu, 32; unjust, 30
Lawrence, David, 138, 155
laws: 29; all-encompassing deterministic, 5; expediency of statutory, 27; immoral and unjust, 30, 133; inconsiderate civic, 12; international, 34; natural, 29, 30, 32, 35, 80; of Physics, 17; secular, 11, 30; that discriminate, 3; unequal applications of, 96
Leibniz, 99
liberties: 42, 149; basic, 37; civil, 141; rights and, 29; sense of right and, 149
light spectrum, 23
Locke, John, 15-16, 22, 23, 150

Mairet, Philip, 150
Makhene, Edward R., 150, 151, 152, 153
Maritain, Jacques, 149
Mars, 107
media, 141-142
Melden, Abraham, 82, 93, 153
men, of courage and rectitude, 46
mens rea, 74, 75
mental acts, 63, 64

Miami, 73
Mike, 42, 56
Milky Way, 146
Mill, John Stuart, 43, 152
Milton, John, 138, 155
miracles: 6; believe in, 58, 132; fantasies like, 131; 132
Mohammad, 105
money: 99; alter of, 13-14; appeal of, 57; ascendency and hold of, 95; deconstruction of, 36; god of, 124; idolization of, 50; lure of, 35; lending vultures, 142, 147; power and access to, 141; power of, 96; powerful hold of, 11; spend tax payers', 60; worshipping the god of, 123
msieht, 121
mystics, 115, 136

Nabudere, Dani, 152
Nagel, Thomas, 123
NASA, 89
national security, 100, 106, 143
nature, state of, 3
Nellie, 81
Nidditch, Peter H., 150
Nietzsche, Friedrich, 128
ninety-nine per cent/99%, 3, 107, 148
Nobel Peace Prize, 34;
normality, 23-24
Norman, Richard, 128, 154
not-my-johnny syndrome, 51
NSSM 200, 143
number one, 104, 147

oblivion: death and its, 123; fear of, 123; or transcendent survival, 55; promises come to naught in the, 122; sink into, 36; temporary, 118; ultimate, 118
occupiers, 107
Ockham, William of, 72, 153
O'Hear, Anthony, 152
Ohio Northern University, 7
Olympus, 130
ontology: 21-22; Descartes', 18; Strawson's, 19
ought implies can, 71

Pacaia gracilens, 136

paranoia, 102
Parker, Theodore, 154
Pascal, Blaise, 119, 154
pawns, 35, 147
peace: and harmony, 57; citadel of, 131; lame, 34; live in, 54, 57, 103, 124; love and, 54, 124; mercy and, 139
Penfield, Wilder, 116-117
people, evil, 98-99
person: the meaning of the word, 4, 27; blind, 26; the corporate, 10-11; definition of 8-10; first, 20, 77, 85; good, 107, 109, 149, 150; legal, 11-12; moral, 14-15; social, 12-13; third, 20; virtuous, 108-109
personhood, 4-5, 8, 10, 12-13, 17, 24, 115, 150; categories of, 14; corporate, 10-11; deny certain racial groups, 32-33; essence or gist of, 16, 17-18; naïve perspective of, 9; respect the, 52-53 Thomistic approach to, 19
pets, 56, 98, 122
Physics: laws of, 17, 121; principles of, 5, 80
Pink, Thomas, 87, 152, 153
Pinto, Vivian De Sola, 155
placards, 105
Plato, 14, 19, 100, 114-115, 150, 151
politicians: 3, 10; and CEOs, 148; and their corporate friends, 122; and their rich friends, 14; corrupt 33; insincere, 139; lying, 114; rich camaraderie of executives of corporations and, 39; sacrifice the survival of the living and posterity, 13; sneaking, 102
prayer, 89, 137
predicates, M & P, 19, 20
prediction: 91; intention is not equivalent to, 73; precise and water tight, 80
Presidents, 103
principles: Humanist, 144-145; mechanistic, 80, 92; moral codes and, 101; of deontology and utilitarianism, 102; of justice and fairness, 35, 36; utilitarian, 45
Prosecutor, Mr., 105
Protestants, 103
Providence divine, 138-139
puppets, 36, 140
Purdy, Chris, 152

Putnam, Hilary, 116
qualities: primary, 22-23; secondary, 22-23
quantum: events, 89; jumps, 65, 88; mechanics, 89, 90, 93

Queen Elizabeth, 76

Rawls, John, 36-38, 152
relativism, 110
respect: 59, 97, 106, 143; animals, 26; children are taught to, 52; do not deserve any one's, 30; egotistical lack of, 99; for culture, 54; for human values, 48; governments have no regard or, 39-40; him and his life without reservation, 127; human rights, 13; lack of, 34, 52; moral agents worthy of, 32; mutual, 47, 52, 124, 134, 145; of persons in authority, 53; persons as entities that deserve, 105; the humanity of persons, 44; the lives of other persons,16; the rule of law, 23; treating others fairly and with, 27
responsibility: 6, 21, 67-70, 75; attributive, 4; for the action, 67-69; for the heinous crimes, 33; for their lives, 58; moral, 4, 11, 16, 31, 44, 88, 91-92, 100; to oneself and to all other persons, 145: ultimate, 68
Ricks, Christopher, 155
rights: 37; authority, 42; civil, 11, 35; can be asserted in singles and in combination, 43; claim, 41; conflict, 43; egregious violation of the, 3; hijacking of their, 33; human, 13, 25; immunity, 43; legal, 10, 12, 43; moral, 12, 26, 45; natural, 29; negative, 40, 44; positive, 40, 44; privilege, 42 ; universal, 30
Roberts, F. Warren, 155
Romans, 130
Ross, George R.T., 151
Rousseau, Jean-Jacques, 106, 154
rulers: 106; have triumphed, 106; God-appointed lineage of, 100; self-appointed. 97; so-called, 35
Russell, Bertrand, 126, 154
Ryle, Gilbert, 17, 113 154

sacerdotalism, 127

Santa Claus, 118, 120
Sartre, Jean Paul, 14, 19, 48, 127, 150
Schopenhauer, Arthur, 98-99, 153
Scotland, 9
Searle, John, 73, 74, 93, 152, 153
security risk, 106
self-annihilation: precipitous trend to, 147; the brink of, 54, 127; the threat of, 2
sense perceptions, 113
sharing in Ubuntu, 49
sheep, 103, 127, 141
Shiites, 103
Silvio, 42
society: African, 32; blight of their, 53; callous, 108; civilised, 50; continued improvement of, 145; "kill", 48; menace to, 96; Ubuntu, 50, 54
Socrates, 134
soul: 18-19, 114-115; -cleansing, 57; complemented by a, 9; existence of a, 136; imaginary entities called souls, 18; mysterious, 116; nebulous human entity called the, 136; theoretical, 11
squirrels, 63, 79
state, vegetative, 16, 21, 151
states, rogue, 25, 57
statesmen, 107
Stoics, 31-32
Strawson, Peter, 19, 20, 24, 47, 151
stresses: and direct lethal injuries, 13; mental disorders caused by the, 49; that characterize highly civilized societies, 54
subhuman, 44, 99, 106, 128
Sunni, 103
Swinburne, Richard, 154
syndrome, not-my-Johnny-, 51-52

taxation: brunt of, 147; unfair, 142
teleonomy, 136
theodices, 119-120
thought experiments, 40
Toronto, 73
Toronto Star, 59-60, 152
transcendence: 114-116, 118, 127; chimera of, 135; definition, 111, 114; dreams of, 127; existential self-, 125;
faith and, 112; figments of, 119; hazy concept of, 117; preachers of, 113; religious, 118; vacuous, 2
Trigg, Roger, 151

Ubuntu: concept of personhood styled, 4; culture, 51, 53; definition, 47-48; is a philosophy of love and peace, 54; law, 32; 61, 152; philosophy, 52, 59, 60; the wholeness of, 24;
United Nations, 144, 145
universal and particular, 114
Urmson, James O, 153
Utilitarianism, 102, 104, 152, 153
utterance, performative, 75-76

value, face, 125-126
Venus, 76
verb "to be", 22
veterans, 55, 60
virtue, 108
volition, 82-83, 86
Voltaire, 98

wannabes, 98, 106, 107
warmongers: self-absorbed, 99; reckless, 55
Warnock, Geoffrey, 153
war, of all against all, 3
wars: 100, 102; and destroying the habitations, 102; atrocities of unnecessary, 54; churchmen who wage, 126; costly, 140; endless, 25; of domination, 54; proxy, 35; ravages and destruction of self-serving, 96-97; sophisticated weapons of, 48; unjust, 134
White, Alan, 152, 153
Whittington, Les, 59
will: 63, 64, 71-72, 83-87; free, 87, 94, 152; mysterious entity called the, 85; mysterious instrument named the, 81-82
Williams, Bernard, 105
will-o'-the-wisps, 124
Wittgenstein, Ludwig, 131, 153; asks the pivotal question of agent action, 83
wolf, 101
Wolf, Abram, 154
World Parliament, 144

Zeno, 116
Zeus, 130

Zhongzhong, 9
Zoology, 50

www.ingramcontent.com/pod-product-compliance
Lightning Source LLC
Chambersburg PA
CBHW031631160426
43196CB00006B/362